"*The Future of Work* is a refreshingly clear-eyed take on the challenges and opportunities for Australia from new technologies. Any policy maker grappling with questions of the social and economic changes wrought from technological change would do well to keep a copy handy."
—**Danielle Wood**, *CEO, Grattan Institute*

"This book delivers clear opinion pieces on how our world, and in particular our work is changing and will continue to change as AI matures and penetrates all aspect of human activity. The book is highly recommended for anyone who wants to understand better how technology and society are, or should be co-evolving."
—**Iven Mareels**, *Executive Dean, Institute of Innovation, Science and Sustainability, Federation University Australia*

T0383612

The Future of Work and Technology

This book examines how global technological advances shape the way we work and allocate work today, and how we might do so in the future, exploring advances in robotics, artificial intelligence, green technology and implications for workforce skills and future welfare. It uses Australia as a case study, contrasting the country's experience to those elsewhere.

The book is a cross-disciplinary collaboration that brings together the expertise of engineers, data scientists, economists and sociologists. The reader is offered an overview of the current uses of advanced digital technologies and what it means for today's workforce, society and economy. The book also looks to the future. Current uses of advanced technologies lag its already existing capability. The contributions note potential future applications of technology and the economic, social and workplace implications of technological change.

This book should be of interest to anyone studying and wishing to better understand what work might look like in the future and how we might prepare for likely changes.

The Future of Work and Technology

Global Trends, Challenges and Policies with an Australian Perspective

Edited by
Andreas Cebulla

CRC Press
Taylor & Francis Group
Boca Raton London New York

CRC Press is an imprint of the
Taylor & Francis Group, an **informa** business

A CHAPMAN & HALL BOOK

First edition published 2024
by CRC Press
2385 NW Executive Center Drive, Suite 320, Boca Raton FL 33431

and by CRC Press
4 Park Square, Milton Park, Abingdon, Oxon, OX14 4RN

CRC Press is an imprint of Taylor & Francis Group, LLC

British Library Cataloguing-in-Publication Data
A catalogue record for this book is available from the British Library

ISBN: 978-1-032-49428-9 (hbk)
ISBN: 978-1-032-49425-8 (pbk)
ISBN: 978-1-003-39375-7 (ebk)

DOI: 10.1201/9781003393757

Typeset in Minion
by SPi Technologies India Pvt Ltd (Straive)

Contents

Editor

Andreas Cebulla is Associate Professor in the Future of Work in the Digital Age at the Australian Industrial Transformation Institute, Flinders University, and Research Associate of the South Australian Centre for Economic Studies, University of Adelaide.

Contributors

Gemma Beale is Researcher at the Australian Industrial Transformation Institute, Flinders University. Her PhD explored the impact of precarious employment on the closure of the South Australian automotive manufacturing industry.

Hugh S. Bradlow is Chair of the Board of ASX-listed company RocketBoots. He is past President of the Australian Academy of Technology and Engineering and an Emeritus Professor at the University of Wollongong.

Andreas Cebulla is Associate Professor in the *Future of Work in the Digital Age* at the Australian Industrial Transformation Institute, Flinders University, and a Research Associate of the South Australian Centre for Economic Studies, University of Adelaide.

Mark Dean is National Research and Planning Officer at the Australian Manufacturing Workers Union and Adjunct Principal Research Fellow of the Royal Melbourne Institute of Technology (RMIT) University's Graduate School of Business and Law.

Hamish Gamble is Senior Economic Analyst at the Australian Industrial Transformation Institute, Flinders University. His research focuses on the intersection between reindustrialisation, climate change and the circular economy.

Sara Howard is Senior Research Fellow and Registered Psychologist with more than 15 years of applied research experience and stakeholder liaison across education, defence, government, health, agriculture and manufacturing settings.

Navinda Kottege is the Research Director of the Cyber-Physical Systems Research Program at the Commonwealth Scientific and Industrial Research Organisation's (CSIRO) Data61. Navinda is Senior Member of the IEEE and Adjunct Associate Professor at both Queensland University of Technology and the University of Queensland.

Valerie O'Keeffe is Senior Research Fellow in Human Factors at the Australian Industrial Transformation Institute, Flinders University, and Certified Professional in both human factors and ergonomics and work health and safety.

John Quiggin is Professor of Economics at the University of Queensland. He is Fellow of the Econometric Society and the Academy of the Social Sciences in Australia and a prominent commentator on Australian and international economic policy.

Zygmunt Szpak is Co-founder and Director of Insight Via Artificial Intelligence (IVAI) Pty Ltd, an Australian AI/ML technology company, and Adjunct Senior Lecturer at the Australian Institute for Machine Learning, University of Adelaide.

Toby Walsh is Laureate Fellow and Scientia Professor of Artificial Intelligence at the University of New South Wales (UNSW) and Chief Scientist at UNSW.AI, UNSW's new AI Institute. He is Fellow of the Australia Academy of Science.

CHAPTER 1

Introduction

Perspectives of Technology-Driven Economic and Social Change

Andreas Cebulla

MUCH HAS ALREADY BEEN written about the future of work in an age when advances in digital technology ("digitalisation") appear to challenge conventional approaches to production, service delivery and consumption. The literature has explored the potential for the automation of work tasks, jobs and entire workplaces, and the implications this may have for skills and labour markets (Brynjolfsson et al., 2018; OECD, 2021). It has shown interest in smart factories (OECD, 2017; Osterrieder et al., 2020) and smart specialisation (Morisson & Pattinson, 2020; Di Cataldo et al., 2022) and has explored digitalisation's contribution to employment and productivity (Anderton et al., 2023; Arsić, 2020; Petropoulos, 2023; Brynjolfsson et al., 2019). This book adds to that literature with a cross-disciplinary perspective on Australia.

This book evolved from presentations given during 2022 as part of an online seminar series at the Australian Industrial Transformation Institute (AITI) of the Flinders University of South Australia. The seminars had been designed – and speakers invited – to approach the topic of the future of work from diverse thematic and disciplinary angles: covering engineering, computer science, economics and sociology.

The global economy, and industries and businesses within it, has undergone marked changes since the beginning of the Fourth Industrial Revolution or Industry 4.0 (Schwab, 2017; Yin et al., 2018). The proliferation of personal computers and their networking in workplaces and most apparent during the COVID-19 pandemic, networking between workplaces and the home, is changing how, where and when we work. Technology

DOI: 10.1201/9781003393757-1

creates new commercial and competitive opportunities but also creates pressures on business as they compete for markets on cost and efficiency as well as scale – and for employees who are looking for better, more accommodating workplaces. Recent leaps in the production and productivity of automating tools, such as Generative Pre-Trained Transformers (ChatGPT/GPT-4) in their many versions, are challenging preconceptions of work and labour, determining who has the appropriate skills to remain working and in work in the future (Eloundou et al., 2023).

The chapters in this book explore various aspects of new technologies challenging and re-shaping labour markets, workplaces and workplace relations. Whilst the focus is on Australia, this is applied with a comparative perspective in mind. The authors explore not just the technical and technological aspects of recent developments but also their broader economic and social implications, including for those most directly affected: workers in the factories and offices that use these new technologies.

1.1 GLOBAL TREND: NEW TECHNOLOGY, INVESTMENT AND AI

At the turn of the millennium, the dot-com crisis (Kindleberger & Aliber, 2005; Cassidy, 2009) saw the demise or collapse in value of many of the early, venture-capital-backed technology companies (lastminute.com, pets.com, but also Amazon and CISCO) built around the then emerging internet for online service delivery. In part, businesses failed because they lacked customers – the internet had not yet reached the large number of potential buyers that were needed to sustain the business (McCullough, 2018). They also failed because, beyond selling online, their business models by and large merely replicated that of the typical "offline" business. This changed with the growth in internet up- and download capacity and speed, its growing global reach (UNCTAD, 2019, 2021), more capable IT hardware and software, the emergence of novel or improved (and increasingly affordable) digital technologies (blockchain, 3D printing and mobile applications) and the need for investment capital to find new outlets.

Digitalisation that was initially measured in terms of internet broadband availability and speed, and the use of enterprise resource planning (ERP) and customer relationship management (CRM) software, became quantified in relation to the utilisation of cloud computing and big data analytics (OECD, 2019). Soon the focus shifted again with more ambitious digital tools in sight, such as blockchain technology (Nascimento et al., 2019) and quickly advancing artificial intelligence (AI).

The radical nature of the technological change that the world has experienced in the last decade or two is demonstrated by the rate at which these new technologies have been adopted by consumers. Since the dot-com crisis, the world has witnessed a steep rise in the use of social media platforms, growing exponentially from virtually no presence in 2004 to some 7.7 billion users in 2019 (Ortiz-Ospina, 2019). Originally operating as a DVD mail service before turning to online movie streaming, it took Netflix, launched in 1999, 3.5 years to reach 1,000,000 users; Twitter (2006) took 2 years to record the same achievement; Facebook (2004) 10 months, Spotify (2008) 8 months – and ChatGPT (2022) 5 days.[1]

The dot-com bust of the earlier 2000s had been followed by a steep, but brief, decline in investment in Information and Communication Technology (ICT), soon returning to growth but without ever reaching prior levels. Measured in terms of gross fixed capital formation (GFCF), investment as a percentage of GDP fluctuated around the 25 percent mark in Australia and somewhat closer to the 20 percent mark across all OECD countries; in both instances, on a generally downward slope (Figure 1.1 – top two lines and trendlines; World Bank, 2023). Annual GFCF growth rates fluctuated yet more strongly and were again on a generally downward slope, most notably in Australia (Figure 1.1. – bottom two lines and trend lines, OECD, 2023a). Noticeable are the trend interruptions during the dot-com crisis and, later, the Global Financial Crisis (GFC), albeit with different outcomes in Australia and the collection of OECD countries. In contrast, movements were more aligned, albeit somewhat time-delayed, during the recent COVID-19 pandemic.

Since 2001, spending on Research and Development (R&D) has increased by 81 percent across OECD countries to total USD 1.6 trillion in 2021 (OECD, 2023b). More remarkable than the generic R&D increase was the growth in publicly funded R&D in AI, which saw a 17-fold increase between 2001 (USD 207 million) and 2019 (USD 3.6 billion) in just six of the major OECD economies, including Australia, the UK, the US, France, Spain, Japan and European Commission programme funding (Galindo-Rueda & Cairns, 2021). The total R&D spending in those six countries grew by a below-OECD average of 57 percent (2019: USD 1,014 billion), accentuating the shift towards AI as the new key ingredient to technological development.

As Galindo-Rueda and Cairns (2021) point out, public AI R&D funding, although growing, was very likely dwarfed by private investment in AI. Perrault et al. (2019) estimated the contribution to have amounted to USD 70 billion in 2019, including start-up funding, mergers and acquisitions

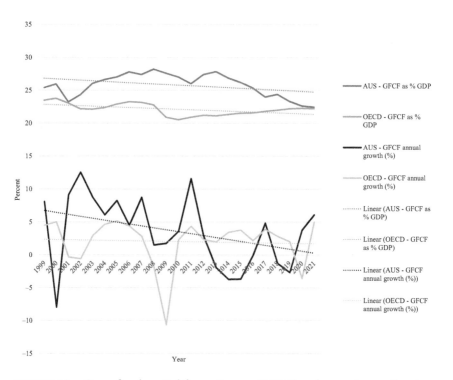

FIGURE 1.1   Gross fixed capital formation, as % GDP and annual growth rates, Australia and OECD.

Source: Author's calculation using data from World Bank, 2023 (GFCF as % GDP) and OECD, 2023a (GFCF growth rates).

(M&A) and Initial Public Offerings (IPOs). By 2021, this had increased to USD 93.5 billion (Zhang et al., 2022). The expansion in private AI R&D was firmly rooted in big data and AI development, which saw patents increase seven-fold between 2016 and 2020 (WIPO, 2022a, p. 8).

1.1.1 Global Private Concentration

The majority of AI R&D is today undertaken by the world's major firms (Dernis et al., 2019; Gestrin and Staudt, 2018), often geographically concentrated in a few technology hubs across the globe (cp. Holicka & Vinodrai, 2022, for an illustration of the global concentration of blockchain businesses). Academia, which had traditionally been at the forefront of scientific discovery, acquisition and, importantly, dissemination of technological knowledge, plays a diminishing role whilst industry-led R&D asserts its supremacy. In their 2022 State of AI Report, Benaich and Hogarth (2022) find that, a decade ago, academia still contributed 60 percent of large-scale

AI experiments; today this has shrunk to "almost 0%" (Benaich and Hogarth, 2022, slide 7). A similar trend has been observed in Australia (Hajkowicz et al., 2022). Benaich and Hogarth (2022, slide 82) note their concern that, if this trend were to continue, the world economy would end up with a "chasm of "have" and "have nots" creating "significant challenges for AI safety, pursuing diverse ideas, talent concentration, and more".

1.1.2 Reducing Costs: A Silver Lining?

As investment in R&D in advanced technologies grew, the technology itself became cheaper. This has especially been the case for AI and, more specifically, the training of AI tools (Thompson et al., 2021). Robots have followed a similar trend. The Stanford AI index survey suggests that "the median price of robotic arms has decreased by 46.2% in the past five years—from $42,000 per arm in 2017 to $22,600 in 2021" (Zhang et al., 2022, p. 3). Perhaps unsurprisingly, the number of robots has gone up as prices went down: between 2020 and 2021, an extra 517,000 robots were deployed in industry worldwide, increasing the total stock by 15 percent to 3.5 million (IFR, 2022).

But cost reductions can be deceptive and, in fact, elusive, especially in AI, where the increasing complexity of AI systems absorbs apparent per-unit cost reductions, ultimately leading to de facto rising cost (Thompson et al., 2021). Here again, we witness the cumulative advantage that large, global businesses have over their smaller revivals – and also nation states whose revenue is often dwarfed by that of the world's frontier companies.

1.2 NEW ECONOMIES, CHANGING LABOUR MARKETS AND AUTOMATING WORKFORCES

Whilst the ICT revolution of the late 1990s into the early 2000s and its subsequently conceptual integration into the production process as Industry 4.0 were expected to rebalance economies towards renewed and more equitable growth and development, this expectation has been left largely disappointed. Nor has this new technology enhanced productivity (de Vries & Wunsch-Vincent, 2022), which may be attributable at least in part to decreasing research productivity (Bloom et al., 2020), sluggish consumer and producer demand prolonged by the GFC and, until the lifting of restrictions, the COVID-19 pandemic and a waning of restructuring and offshoring across tech manufacturing subsectors (MGI, 2018).

The global and industry-specific concentration of investment and innovation produced its own winners and losers (Financial Times, 2020;

Bloomberg, 2021), segregating technological and commercial frontier (leading) from zombie (lagging) firms (Autor et al., 2020) and their workforces (Song et al., 2019). National public policy and inter-governmental bodies have taken notice of the risks of economic and social inequality to economic development and societal cohesion (Cerdeiro et al., 2022; Aiyar et al., 2023), preparing statements and strategies, launching initiatives to drive technological change and developing regulatory frameworks and concepts for the ethical application of the new technologies.

1.2.1 National AI Strategies

The international space of technology announcements is presently dominated by strategies concerned with AI – and there are many. Dutton (2018) identified 25 such national strategies, plus one prepared by the European Union for its 27 members. The OECD entertains a National AI policies and strategies repository (https://oecd.ai/en/dashboards/overview), which as on March 2023 holds data for 69 countries and supra-national organisations, identifying 269 national strategies, agendas and plans and 201 initiatives concerned with "Emerging AI-related regulation" (OECD.AI, 2021). National strategies and plans typically take a sectoral focus, including the initial AI strategy documents prepared by the Australian government and its main research facility (Australian Government 2021a; Hajkowicz et al., 2019), which include specific references to agriculture and food, health care and smart cities/construction (as well as more broadly the environment).

Investing in AI R&D, building national AI infrastructures (including in public sector), facilitating and regulating data access and sharing, developing funding streams and networking and collaboration supports are key objectives (Gallindo et al., 2021). Only a few agendas specifically – and across sectors – concern themselves with productivity (namely in Finland, Japan, Poland and Turkey) (Galindo et al., 2021, p. 10). This may be changing though, as making better economic use of advanced technology edges more firmly onto the policy agenda, perhaps heeding the Organisation for Economic Co-operation and Development's "Blueprint for building national compute capacity for artificial intelligence" (OECD, 2023c).

1.2.2 AI Ethics

Like any technology AI is not without its risks and hazards. In fact, AI may arguably have more than its fair share of risks and hazards, opening doors to manipulation, remote and stealth control and monitoring, automating bias (and inequality), intensifying and displacing labour and even undermining political systems (MDI, 2020) – to name but a few. A plethora of AI ethics statements and policy documents and directions have sought to address these risks (in Australia: Dawson et al., 2019; DISR, 2023).

Research on fairness and transparency in AI presented at conferences has increased fivefold since 2014 according to one estimate (Zhang et al., 2022, p. 3); the presentations focussing specifically on algorithmic fairness and bias, offering to correct AI bias and model opacity models with more technical or technological solutions. As with AI R&D and R&D funding, conference contributions also increasingly come from researchers with industry affiliation rather than academia. Whilst this may indicate an awareness amongst the producers of AI of the risk their products pose to human rights and well-being, it also reflects the concentration of research amongst industry affiliates. That concentration carries its own technocratic bias in that it leads to dominant presentation of AI risks as merely computationally solvable matter, that is, AI calling for more AI. As Ahmed et al. (2023, p. 885) argue, this risks leading to a "socially suboptimal trajectory" that ignores the social, behavioural and organisational context and purpose in and for which AI is deployed.

1.2.3 Regulation and Standards

Public policy hems in this technocratic bias with bespoke legislation. Examining the national legislative records in 25 OECD countries, Zhang et al. (2022) noted an increase in the number of bills containing the term "artificial intelligence" and passed into law from just 1 in 2016 to 18 in 2021, totalling 55 over the period. The focus of those bills has so far been largely domain-specific rather than addressing AI generically, preferencing risk mitigation via extant consumer and social protection legislation, monitoring human safety (mainly physical and mental harm impacts of technology), reaffirming data protection and data rights to privacy and requiring fair and non-discriminatory application. Moreover, risk mitigation is sought to be achieved via the formulation of codes of conduct, guidelines and standards (in Australia: Standards Australia, 2020), typically relying on (voluntary) industry self-regulation. A closer examination of legislation passed reveals a primary concern with regulating the narrow field of autonomous driving and autonomous vehicles, the core theme of 15 of the 63 listed policies.[2]

Spain, the UK, the USA, Japan and Australia topped the list of AI mentions in legislative proceedings, but those mentions did not necessarily equate with legislation passed. Thus, Australia in fact did not legislate on

AI during that period and has no dedicated legislation concerning AI, machine learning or big data (Cox et al., 2022), instead relying on conventional data privacy, telecommunication, health and safety, and anti-discrimination legislation to regulate the technology and its application. Accumulating evidence of the vulnerability of AI tools to misuse, a plethora of breaches and leaks of "big data" and the launch in March 2022 of the Federal Government's consultation on artificial intelligence and automated decision-making regulations may change that in the future (cp. Commonwealth of Australia, 2022).

1.3 POSITIONING AUSTRALIA INNOVATION ECONOMY

Although Australia finds itself amongst the top tiers of countries in terms of capital investment and AI R&D spend, according to the analysis undertaken by the World Intellectual Property Organization (WIPO, 2022b), the country struggles to convert its R&D inputs into matching outputs. Internationally, the country lags other nations in generating patents, growth in labour productivity, high-tech manufacturing and export complexity. Australia, however, is not alone in that respect; in fact, it is in good company, sharing this fate with several other developed economies, including Singapore, Canada, Hong Kong and Norway (WIPO, 2022b, p. 53), but outperformed by China, the Republic of Korea, Germany and the Netherlands – all with similar innovation input scores.

Arguably contrary to popular perception, Australians work a lot and more of them do so than in many other developed countries. This combination of high levels of labour market participation and long hours worked has been used to explain the country's living standards that are high by international comparison, despite sluggish and, over time, decreasing labour productivity (Productivity Commission, 2023), dragged down especially by the service sector which makes up some 90 percent of employment in Australia (Campbell & Withers, 2017).

Australia's aggregate economic output (GDP) has been sustained by population growth, itself fuelled by international migration, masking more moderate and occasionally negative growth in per capita GDP over time. During the last century since Australia's foundation in 1901, national GDP growth averaged 3.4 percent, compared with per capita GDP growth of 1.7 percent (Australian Treasury, 2001). This trend has continued into the current century, albeit at lower growth levels (O'Brien, 2019).

There is an expectation – and indeed some tentative evidence from the recent past – that technology may offer a route out of this apparent cul-de-sac of sluggish economic growth, which has come with equally sluggish wage growth (Treasury, 2017; Stewart et al., 2022) and sustained income and wealth inequalities (Productivity Commission, 2018). In the 1990s, capital deepening following the greater use of, and investment in, information technology contributed to a greater output growth of up to a quarter of the annual total (Simon & Wardrop, 2002) and almost half (45 percent) of the labour productivity growth recorded in that decade (Parham et al., 2001, p. 79), most evidently in the service-oriented sectors of telecommunications and finance and insurance. More recent data has confirmed greater engagement with and adoption of digital technology in the Australian economy, especially through e-commerce (ABS, 2019, 2022). The national value added of total digital activity, which includes the production of digital enabling technology, digital media and ecommerce, is estimated to have increased by 8 percent in 2020–2021 (compared to 2019–2020), exceeding the total national value added by three percentage points. Accounting for 6 percent of total economy value added, the digital economy thus became one of the largest sectors in Australia behind mining (11.5 percent), health (8.1 percent), finance (8.1 percent), professional, scientific and technical services (7.7 percent) and construction (7.5 percent).

Against a background of international competition over technological advancement and, indeed, dominance, it is perhaps unsurprising that there continues to be unabated enthusiasm for technological change in Australia (e.g., CEDA, 2018), mixed with concern about Australia losing ground and a call to arms (e.g., NCICS, 2019). When the (then Liberal-Conservative) Federal Government launched its digital economy strategy in 2021 (Australian Government, 2021b), updated in 2022, it came with a promise of substantive investment into AI infrastructure, capacity building (including increasing the digitally capable workforce) and application. Since then, and following a change in Federal Government, the strategy has remained under review, alongside a list of "critical technologies" (DISR, 2022) to be targeted and supported by policy. The latest list includes advanced manufacturing and material technologies; AI technologies; advanced information and communication technologies; quantum technologies; autonomous systems, robotics, positioning, timing and sensing; biotechnologies and clean energy generation and storage technologies (Husic, 2023).

1.4 THIS BOOK

Almost out of necessity, given the multi-layered nature of industrial policy, this introductory chapter has above all focussed on one aspect of industrial policy, namely AI. The following chapters in this book branch out to discuss the potential for, and risks associated with, this and other advanced technologies from both technological and human perspectives. AI, digitisation and robotics are their main themes, exploring the scope for and current limits to technological capabilities; machine–human co-working, and wider social, economic and environmental agendas.

In Chapter 2, Navinda Kottege examines current applications of robotics in industry and the technology's potential for developing the Australian economy, where it has particular utility in mining and agriculture. Globally, robotics has witnessed significant growth in sales of robots and their use in business. Kottege points out opportunities for the use of robots in Australia, including examples of successful and unsuccessful commercialisation of robotics researched and developed in the country. He discusses the challenges that the sector needs to overcome to have a greater impact on the Australian economy and ecology

In Chapter 3, Hugh Bradlow takes a deep look at how automation and digitisation, that is, the conversion of information into a digital format, are likely to develop in the years to come. Drawing on his background in electrical engineering and nuclear physics, Bradlow discusses the core elements that enable digitisation and their combination and integration in today's Internet of Things (IoT). He explains the building stones of the IoT, their current potential but also technological boundaries that limit the scope and scale of IoT utilisation. Recent acceleration in machine learning capabilities may nonetheless push those boundaries, which Bradlow illustrates with examples from Australian mining and agriculture.

Mark Dean presents a case study of the technological and economic opportunity for injecting new capacity in Australia's manufacturing sector by stepping into the emerging electric vehicle (EV) market in Chapter 4. Extracting lessons from economies elsewhere, which have already gained a foothold in EV manufacturing, Dean looks at the intersections of manufacturing, natural resource extraction and the potential for developing a greener economy. His is a plea for a strategic approach to injecting new life into Australia's manufacturing industry by building on the country's rich natural resource base, connecting advanced technological expertise and accessing emerging markets to build an ultimately greener national economy.

In Chapter 5, Hamish Gamble further develops the theme of developing Australia's economy capability by applying economic complexity to illustrate Australia's current strengths and weakness in the global supply chain. Economic complexity theory has seen few strategic applications in Australia and, indeed, globally, where it has been used more as an analytical tool than as an instrument for policy design. Gamble places Australian innovation policy in a national and international comparative context before detailing opportunities for strengthening Australian industry based on analysis that applies economic complexity to Australian trade data.

Gemma Beale's contribution in Chapter 6 takes a social and sociological perspective, asking how technology and technological change can be reconciled with the need for social justice. Basing her contribution on her longitudinal qualitative study of unemployed workers following the closure of Australia's last car manufacturing plant, General Motors Holden, in 2017, Beale links the experience of retrenched factory workers to the broader challenge on ensuring a "just transition" for workers likely affected by economic and environmental decarbonisation strategies to halt global warming. Beale argues that, in light of much larger structural challenges, conventional job search and placement services will be insufficient to ensure dislocated workers are successfully directed and integrated into a new, greener labour market.

Chapter 7 is the first of two chapters explicitly concerned with technologies impact on workplaces. Valerie O'Keeffe and Sara Howard delve into the automating and automated world of working with robots, in particular collaborative robots – or cobots – where humans not just undertake their tasks alongside, but physically and purposely interact with machines. Here the boundaries between human decision-making and machine-operated execution are blurred, if not merged, and the presence becomes humanoid. The authors document the global uptake of increasingly capable, versatile robots and review current uses of robotics in private, public and business, examining the conditions for safe and beneficial adoption.

In Chapter 8, Andreas Cebulla and Zygmunt Szpak look at the workplace health and safety implications of introducing the AI into the workplace. Their previous empirical work on the topic in Australia had concluded the need for involving operational and technological roles and expertise at all levels of the organisation in preparing for the safe, ethical and responsible use of AI, protecting human rights and well-being. The authors argue for active workforce engagement from the start – facilitated by a democratic approach to collective decision-making, something that union representations at workplaces and industry (or indeed national) levels have begun to address.

Toby Walsh casts a critical eye on the social and economic impact of artificial intelligence in Chapter 9. Walking us through a brief history of economists' (erroneous) predictions of "technological unemployment", Walsh critically reviews recent apocalyptic automation impact projections. Walsh highlights differences in opinions between experts in AI and robotics, and non-experts, and cautions against simplistic and simplifying assumptions of the relationship between technology and (the volume of) work. Walsh concludes with a view on future skills, proposing a "triangle of opportunity": being/becoming a technologically literate geek, an emotional and social "intelligentsia" or a creative or artisan as a world dominated by machine craves for things "made by hand".

In Chapter 10, John Quiggin invites readers to think outside the box and rediscover radical, utopian thinking. Mapping the failures of hegemonic neoliberal policy since the Golden Age of the post–World War II era, and the abandoning of progressive, utopian aspirations in favour of dystopian realities, Quiggin provokes readers to consider a new possible reality. This new reality de-centres labour from human activity. Quiggin argues for a Jobs Guarantee alongside a Liveable Income Guarantee to make paid work a "genuine choice" and to return the decisions on, and the design of, how we live and what we do to each and all of us.

The final chapter (Chapter 11) looks at policy-making, exploring the current and potentially extended use of mission orientation framework, advanced by Mariana Mazzucato and her colleagues, for progressing industrial policy and innovation in Australia. As authors in this volume point out, a more strategic, concerted and collaborative approach to industry policymaking may help to overcome the lagging nature of industry innovation and innovation investment in Australia. The data to date suggest that Australia is beginning to adopt the language of "missions", without necessarily following up with substantive investment. The chapter identifies a lack of policy experimentation, policy expertise, governance structures and corporate capture as impediments to accelerated innovation in innovation policy.

NOTES

1 https://www.statista.com/chart/29174/time-to-one-million-users/
2 https://oecd.ai/en/dashboards/policy-instruments/Emerging_technology_regulation, accessed 22 March 2023.

REFERENCES

Ahmed, N., Wahed, M., & Thompson, N.C. (2023). The growing influence of industry in AI research. Industry is gaining control over the technology's future. Science, 379(6635), 884–886.

Aiyar, S., Chen, J., Ebeke, C., Garcia-Saltos, R., Gudmundsson, T., Ilyina, A., Kangur, A., Kunaratskul, T., Rodriguez, S., Ruta, M., Schulze, T., Soderberg, G., & Trevino, J. P. —with contributions from Atashbar, T., & Ghosh, R. (2023). Geoeconomic fragmentation and the future of multilateralism. IMF Staff Discussion Notes SDN/2023/001. International Monetary Fund, Washington.

ABS. (2019). Digital activity in the Australian economy. 2019, October 15. Australian Bureau of Statistics. https://www.abs.gov.au/articles/digital-activity-australian-economy

ABS. (2022). Digital activity in the Australian economy, 2020–21. 2022, October 28. Australian Bureau of Statistics. https://www.abs.gov.au/articles/digital-activity-australian-economy-2020-21

Anderton, R., Reimers, P., & Botelho, V. (2023). Digitalisation and productivity: Gamechanger or sideshow?. ECB Working Paper No. 2023/2794. http://dx.doi.org/10.2139/ssrn.4382563

Arsić, M. (2020). Impact of digitalisation on economic growth, productivity and employment. Economic Themes, 58(4), 431–457. https://doi.org/10.2478/ethemes-2020-0025

Australian Government. (2021a). Australia's AI action plan. Commonwealth of Australia. https://www.industry.gov.au/publications/australias-artificial-intelligence-action-plan

Australian Government. (2021b). Digital economy strategy. A leading digital economy and society by 2030. Commonwealth of Australia. https://apo.org.au/sites/default/files/resource-files/2021-05/apo-nid312247.pdf

Australian Treasury. (2001). Australia's century since Federation at a glance. Economic Roundup, 1, 53–63. The Treasury, Australian Government.

Autor, D., Dorn, D., Katz, L. F., Patterson, C., & Van Reenen, J. (2020). The fall of the labor share and the rise of superstar firms. The Quarterly Journal of Economics, 135(2), 645–709. https://doi.org/10.1093/qje/qjaa004

Benaich, B., & Hogarth, I. (2022). State of AI report. 2022, October 11. https://docs.google.com/presentation/d/1WrkeJ9-CjuotTXoa4ZZlB3UPBXpxe4B3FMs9R9tn34I/edit#slide=id.g164b1bac824_0_2748

Bloom, Nicholas, Jones, Charles I. Van Reenen, John, & Webb, Michael (2020). Are Ideas Getting Harder to Find? American Economic Review, 110(4): 1104–1144.

Bloomberg. (2021). World-dominating superstar firms get bigger, techier, and more Chinese. 2021, 21 May. https://www.bloomberg.com/graphics/2021-biggest-global-companies-growth-trends/#xj4y7vzkg. Accessed 4 April 2023.

Brynjolfsson, E., Mitchell, T., & Rock, D. (2018). What can machines learn, and what does it mean for occupations and the economy? AEA Papers and Proceedings, 108, 43–47.

Brynjolfsson, E., Rock, D., & Syverson, C. (2019). Artificial intelligence and the modern productivity paradox: A clash of expectations and statistics. In A. Agrawal, J. Gans, & A. Goldfarb (Eds.), The economics of artificial intelligence: An agenda. https://www.nber.org/books-and-chapters/economics-artificial-intelligence-agenda

Campbell, S., & Withers, H. (2017). Australian productivity trends and the effect of structural change. https://treasury.gov.au/sites/default/files/2019-03/p2017-t213722-Roundup_Productivity_trends_and_structural_change.pdf

Cassidy, J. (2009). Dot.con: How America lost its mind and its money in the internet era. HarperCollins.

CEDA. (2018). Connecting people with progress: securing future economic development. Committee for Economic Development of Australia. https://www.ceda.com.au/ResearchAndPolicies/Research/Institutions/Connecting-people-with-progress-securing-future-ec

Cox, J., & Siu, B. (2022). AI, machine learning and big data laws and regulation 2022, Australia. Global Legal Insights. https://www.globallegalinsights.com/practice-areas/ai-machine-learning-and-big-data-laws-and-regulations/australia

Commonwealth of Australia. (2022). Positioning Australia as a leader in digital economy regulation – Automated decision making and AI regulation. Issues Paper. Department of the Prime Minister and Cabinet. https://consult.industry.gov.au/automated-decision-making-ai-regulation-issues-paper

Dawson, D., Schleiger, E., Horton, J., McLaughlin, J., Robinson, C., Quezada, G., Scowcroft, J., & Hajkowicz, S. (2019). Artificial intelligence: Australia's ethics framework. Data61 CSIRO, Australia.

Dernis, H., Gkotsis, P., Grassano, N., Nakazato, S., Squicciarini, M., van Beuzekom, B., & Vezzani, A. (2019). World corporate top R&D investors: Shaping the future of technologies and of AI. A joint JRC and OECD report. EUR 29831 EN, Publications Office of the European Union, Luxembourg. https://doi.org//10.2760/16575, JRC117068

de Vries, K., & Wunsch-Vincent, S. (2022). What is the future of innovation-driven growth: Productivity stagnation or revival? Global Innovation Index 2022. World Intellectual Property Organization (WIPO).

DISR. (2022). List of Critical Technologies in the National Interest. Consultation Paper. Department of Industry, Science and Resources. https://consult.industry.gov.au/critical-technologies-2022

DISR. (2023). Safe and responsible AI in Australia. Discussion Paper. Department of Industry, Science and Resources. https://consult.industry.gov.au/supporting-responsible-ai

Cerdeiro, D.A., Eugster, J., Mano, R.C., Muir, D., & Peiris, S.J. (2022). Sizing Up the Effects of Technological Decoupling. IMF Working Paper WP21/69. International Monetary Fund.

Di Cataldo, M., Monastiriotis, V., & Rodríguez-Pose, A. (2022). How 'Smart' Are Smart Specialization Strategies?. JCMS: Journal of Common Market Studies, 60, 1272–1298. https://doi.org/10.1111/jcms.13156

Dutton, T. (2018). An overview of national AI strategies. 29 June. https://medium.com/politics-ai/an-overview-of-national-ai-strategies-2a70ec6edfd

Eloundou, T., Manning, S., Mishkin, P., & Rock, D. (2023). GPTs are GPTs: An early look at the labor market impact potential of large language models. arXiv:2303.10130 [econ.GN], https://doi.org/10.48550/arXiv.2303.10130

Financial Times. (2020). Prospering in the pandemic: The top 100 companies. 2020, June 19. https://www.ft.com/content/844ed28c-8074-4856-bde0-20f3bf4cd8f0

Galindo, L., Perset, K., & Sheeka, F. (2021). An overview of national AI strategies and policies. OECD Going Digital Toolkit Notes, No. 14, OECD Publishing, Paris, https://doi.org/10.1787/c05140d9-en

Galindo-Rueda, F., & Cairns, S. (2021). A new approach to measuring government investment in AI-related R&D. 2021, July 5. OECD.ai policy observatory. https://oecd.ai/en/wonk/government-investment-ai-related-r-and-d

Gestrin, M. V., & Staudt, J. (2018). The digital economy, multinational enterprises and International investment policy. OECD, Paris. www.oecd.org/investment/the-digital-economy-mnes-and-international-investment-policy.htm

Hajkowicz, S.A., Karimi, S., Wark, T., Chen, C., Evans, M., Rens, N., Dawson, D., Charlton, A., Brennan, T., Moffatt, C., Srikumar, S., & Tong, K.J. (2019). Artificial intelligence: Solving problems, growing the economy and improving our quality of life. CSIRO Data61, Australia. https://apo.org.au/node/268341

Hajkowicz, S., Naughtin, C., Sanderson, C., Schleiger, E., Karimi, S., Bratanova, A., & Bednarz, T. (2022). Artificial intelligence for science – Adoption trends and future development pathways. CSIRO Data61, Brisbane, Australia. https://www.csiro.au/-/media/d61/ai4science-report/ai-for-science-report-2022.pdf

Holicka, M., & Vinodrai, T. (2022). The global geography of investment in emerging technologies: The case of blockchain firms. Regional Studies, Regional Science, 9(1), 177–179, https://doi.org/10.1080/21681376.2022.2047769

Husic, E. (2023). Critical technologies securing Australia's future. Media Release. 19 May. https://www.minister.industry.gov.au/ministers/husic/media-releases/critical-technologies-securing-australias-future

IFR. (2022). World robotics 2022. Presentation by the International Federation of Robotics.https://ifr.org/downloads/press2018/2022_WR_extended_version.pdf

Kindleberger, C.P., & Aliber, R.Z. (2005). Manias, panics, and crashes: A history of financial crises. Palgrave Macmillan London. https://doi.org/10.1057/9780230628045

McCullough, B. (2018). How the internet happened – From netscape to the iPhone. Liveright.

MDI. (2020) Artificial intelligence and democratic values. The AI social contract index 2020. Center for AI and Digital Policy, Michael Dukakis Institute (MDI) for Leadership and Innovation, Boston, MA. https://caidp.dukakis.org/aisci-2020/

MGI. (2018). Solving the productivity puzzle: the role of demand and the promise of digitization. McKinsey Global Institute. www.mckinsey.com/mgi

Morisson, A., & Pattinson, M. (2020). Smart specialisation strategy (S3). Interreg Europe Policy Learning Platform, Lille. https://www.interregeurope.eu/sites/default/files/inline/Smart_Specialisation_Strategy__S3__-_Policy_Brief.pdf

Nascimento, S., Pólvora, A., Anderberg, A., Andonova, E., Bellia, M., Calès, L., Inamorato dos Santos, A., Kounelis, I., Nai Fovino, I., Petracco Giudici, M., Papanagiotou, E., Sobolewski, M., Rossetti, F., & Spirito, L. (2019). Blockchain now and tomorrow: Assessing multidimensional impacts of distributed ledger technologies. Publications Office of the European Union, Luxembourg. https://doi.org/10.2760/901029

NCICS. (2019). Preparing for Australia's digital future: A strategic plan for information and communications science, engineering and technology. National Committee for Information and Communication Sciences, Australian Academy of Science and Australian Academy of Technology and Engineering. https://www.science.org.au/support/analysis/decadal-plans/ics/preparing-australias-digital-future

O'Brien, G. (2019). 27 years and counting since Australia's last recession. Parliament of Australia, briefing book – Key issues for the 46th Parliament. Commonwealth of Australia, pp. 60–67. https://www.aph.gov.au/About_Parliament/Parliamentary_Departments/Parliamentary_Library/pubs/BriefingBook46p/LastRecession

OECD. (2017). The next production revolution: Implications for governments and business. OECD Publishing, Paris. http://dx.doi.org/10.1787/9789264271036-en

OECD. (2019). Measuring the digital transformation: A roadmap for the future. Sections 4.2 and 6.1. OECD Publishing, Paris. https://dx.doi.org/10.1787/9789264311992-en

OECD. (2021). AI and the future of skills. Volume 1: Capabilities and assessments, educational research and innovation. OECD Publishing, Paris. https://doi.org/10.1787/5ee71f34-en

OECD. (2023a) Investment (GFCF) (indicator). https://doi.org/10.1787/b6793677-en. https://data.oecd.org/gdp/investment-gfcf.htm

OECD. (2023b). Gross domestic spending on R&D (indicator). https://doi.org/10.1787/d8b068b4-en. https://data.oecd.org/rd/gross-domestic-spending-on-r-d.htm

OECD. (2023c). A blueprint for building national compute capacity for artificial intelligence. OECD Digital Economy Papers No. 350. https://www.oecd-ilibrary.org/science-and-technology/a-blueprint-for-building-national-compute-capacity-for-artificial-intelligence_876367e3-en

OECD.AI. (2021). National AI policies & strategies. Database of national AI policies. Powered by EC/OECD (2021). https://oecd.ai/en/dashboards/overview

Ortiz-Ospina, E. (2019). The rise of social media. OurWorldInData.org. https://ourworldindata.org/rise-of-social-media

Osterrieder, P., Budde, L., & Friedli, T. (2020). The smart factory as a key construct of industry 4.0: A systematic literature review. International Journal of Production Economics, 221, 107476. https://doi.org/10.1016/j.ijpe.2019.08.011

Parham, D., Roberts, P., & Sun, H. (2001). Information technology and Australia's productivity surge. Productivity Commission Staff Research Paper, AusInfo, Canberra. https://www.pc.gov.au/research/supporting/it-surge/itaaps.pdf

Perrault, R., Shoham, Y., Brynjolfsson, E., Clark, J., Etchemendy, J., Grosz, B., Lyons, T., Manyika, J., Mishra, S., & Niebles, J.C. (2019). The AI Index 2019 Annual Report. AI Index Steering Committee, Human-Centered AI Institute, Stanford University, Stanford, CA.

Petropoulos, G. (2023). Artificial intelligence: How to get the most from the labour-productivity boost. Analysis 02/2023, Bruegel. https://www.bruegel.org/analysis/artificial-intelligence-how-get-most-labour-productivity-boost

Productivity Commission. (2018). Rising inequality? A stocktake of the evidence. Canberra, Australia. https://www.pc.gov.au/research/completed/rising-inequality

Productivity Commission. (2023). 5-year productivity inquiry: Keys to growth. Inquiry report – Volume 2. Canberra, Australia. https://www.pc.gov.au/inquiries/completed/productivity/report/productivity-volume2-keys-to-growth.pdf

Schwab, K. (2017). The fourth industrial revolution. Crown Business, New York.

Simon, J., & Wardrop, S. (2002). Australian use of information technology and its contribution to growth. Research Discussion Paper 2002–02. Economic Research Department, Reserve Bank of Australia. https://www.rba.gov.au/publications/rdp/2002/pdf/rdp2002-02.pdf

Song, J., Price, D. J., Guvenen, F., Bloom, N., & von Wachter, T. (2019). Firming up inequality. The Quarterly Journal of Economics, 134(1), 1–50. https://doi.org/10.1093/qje/qjy025

Standards Australia. (2020). An artificial intelligence standards roadmap: Making Australia's voice heard. https://www.standards.org.au/news/standards-australia-sets-priorities-for-artificial-intelligence

Stewart, A., Stanford, J., & Hardy, T. (2022). The wages crisis revisited. The Australia Institute. https://australiainstitute.org.au/wp-content/uploads/2022/05/Wages-Crisis-Revisited-WEB

Thompson, N.C., Greenewald, K., Lee, K., & Manso, G.F. (2021). Deep learning's diminishing returns. The cost of improvement is becoming unsustainable. https://spectrum.ieee.org/deep-learning-computational-cost

Treasury. (2017). Analysis of wage growth. November 2017. The Australian Government, The Treasury. https://treasury.gov.au/sites/default/files/2019-03/p2017-t237966.pdf

UNCTAD. (2019). Digital economy report 2019: Value creation and capture: Implications for developing countries. United Nations publication. New York and Geneva. https://digitallibrary.un.org/record/3833647?ln=en

UNCTAD. (2021). Cross-border data flows and development: For whom the data flow. United Nations, Geneva. https://www.unilibrary.org/content/books/9789210058254

WIPO. (2022a). World intellectual property report 2022: The direction of innovation. World Intellectual Property Organization, Geneva.

WIPO. (2022b). Global innovation index 2022: What is the future of innovation-driven growth? World Intellectual Property Organization, Geneva. https://doi.org/10.34667/tind.46596

World Bank. (2023). World Bank national accounts data, and OECD national accounts data files. https://data.worldbank.org/indicator/NE.GDI.FTOT.ZS?end=2021&locations=OE-AU&start=1971&view=chart&year=2021

Yin, Y., Stecke, K. E., & Li, D. (2018). The evolution of production systems from Industry 2.0 through Industry 4.0. International Journal of Production Research, 56(1–2), 848–861. https://doi.org/10.1080/00207543.2017.1403664

Zhang, D., Maslej, N., Brynjolfsson, E., Etchemendy, J., Lyons, T., Manyika, J., Ngo, H., Niebles, J. C., Sellitto, M., Sakhaee, E., Shoham, Y., Clark, J., & Perrault, R. (2022). The AI index 2022 annual report. AI Index Steering Committee, Stanford Institute for Human-Centered AI, Stanford University.

CHAPTER 2

Robotics in Australia

Uses, Opportunities, and Challenges

Navinda Kottege

A UTOMATION HAS BEEN A topic of discussion for many years, with arguments for and against its potential positive and negative impacts on the global economy (McKay et al., 2019). While automation can boost economic growth, create jobs, and improve living standards, it can also present serious challenges for workers and communities, including job displacement, disruptions to local economies, changing skill needs, and rising inequality.

According to PwC analysis, AI, robotics, and other forms of smart automation have the potential to contribute up to USD15 trillion to the global GDP by 2030, bringing great economic benefits but also potentially displacing existing jobs (PWC, 2018). The impact of potential job losses due to automation was considered to disproportionately affect unskilled workers, especially in developing economies (The World Bank, 2016). However, more recent and rapid advancements in AI, mainly related to large language models (LLMs) have demonstrated their ability to accelerate automation of tasks that are done by skilled workers, such as programming, designing, and teaching (Dodd, 2023; Eloundou et al., 2023). Therefore, it is important to monitor the impact of automation on the global economy and work towards solutions that benefit everyone.

Australia has long been a leader in technological development, and the field of robotics is no exception. However, despite significant advancements in research and innovation, the country's robotics ecosystem remains fragmented, with the commercial application of new technologies lagging behind other nations (Robotics Australia Group, 2022). This chapter examines actual

DOI: 10.1201/9781003393757-2

and potential uses of robotics and Australia's position in the global robotics landscape, delving into the challenges of adopting and commercialising cutting-edge technology, and exploring the implications for the future of automation in the workplace, as well as the broader economic and ecological consequences.

2.1 ACTUAL AND POTENTIAL USES OF ROBOTICS

Many technology developments in robotics are motivated by challenges faced by humans doing dull, dirty, and dangerous work, often referred to as the 3 'D's for robotic applications. Examples range from working in factory assembly lines doing repetitive tasks to sorting rubbish or working at heights to do maintenance work on high tension power lines. In the 'dull' category, applications in factory assembly line automation are quite mature and broadly adopted across the manufacturing industry sector, from automotive assembly to consumer electronic device manufacture. Most items we use as commodities these days would not be affordable if not for the robotics and automation technologies used in their production process. The ability to scale up manufacturing and to have continuously running production lines has driven up productivity while improving safety in these sectors. For the 'dirty' category, rubbish sorting, sewer inspections, and even underground mining are example applications seeing adoption of robotic technology at various levels. The 'dangerous' category of work has examples in mining where humans have to load explosives for blasting, emergency response workers doing search and rescue operations. A fourth 'd' has been proposed by McAfee and Brynjolfsson as 'dear' – as in tasks that are too expensive to be performed by humans (McAfee & Brynjolfsson, 2017; Marr, 2017). This category is sometimes intertwined with the previous categories as scaling up volume of a process, while improving safety, can directly lead to boosting efficiencies and reducing cost. There are many applications that include more than one 'd' as well. Cargo handling and warehouse logistics can be both dull and dangerous where human workers often suffer injuries (Zorpette, 2023).

While these 4 'D's are commonly referred to, a fifth 'D' had been suggested by some – 'devilishly impossible' tasks. Examples of these are entering and operating in environments not only dangerous for humans but in most cases impossible for humans. Most space exploration missions qualify for this category and are currently carried out by robotic technology. The Parker Solar Probe,[1] which collects invaluable information about the Sun while flying in extreme temperature and radiation conditions, is an example. Searches for human habitable subterranean environments on the Moon and Mars as well as building habitats for future human colonists in these extra-terrestrial environments are examples where applying robotic technology would offer the only viable solution.

The recent COVID-19 pandemic also helped accelerate adoption of robotic technology and somewhat shifted public perception towards application of these technologies. The value of using robots for remote inspection and remote operations was highlighted in many application domains due to inability and unavailability of humans to perform these tasks.

Furthermore, in Australia the agriculture sector was severely impacted by the unavailability of seasonal farm workers due to border closures during the pandemic. Large quantities of produce went to waste, limiting supply and driving up prices. This is a strong driver for potential use of robots in agriculture. To meet the demands of the growing global population, food production will need to increase. Reduction in arable land and effects of climate change would make traditional farming techniques infeasible to meet these requirements in the long term. Use of precision agriculture, novel methods of farming, and a massive scale-up of robotics and automation in farming would be imperative to meet these challenges.

The development of effective vaccines in response to the COVID-19 pandemic was done at an unprecedented speed. Laboratory-based development and testing to trials to mass production happened within months rather than years. Such scale-up in vaccine production within months to have many millions of vaccine doses manufactured simply would not have been possible without robotic technology.

Therefore, robotics has many uses – to perform dull, dirty, dangerous, dear, and devilishly impossible tasks while not only keeping humans out of harm's way but also keeping humans well fed and healthy.

2.2 AUSTRALIA'S POSITION IN THE FIELD OF ROBOTIC DEVELOPMENTS AND ADOPTION

Australia's prowess in robotics research and development (R&D) is evident in the numerous academic institutions, research organisations, and private companies working on diverse applications such as mining, agriculture, healthcare, and defence. Some examples of globally renowned robotics research labs include the Commonwealth Scientific and Industrial Research Organisation's (CSIRO) Robotics and Autonomous Systems Group, University of Sydney's Australian Centre for Field Robotics (ACFR), University of Technology Sydney's Robotics Institute, Monash University's

Robotics Centre, and Queensland University of Technology (QUT) Centre for Robotics (QCR). QUT's team winning the global Amazon Picking Challenge in 2017[2] and the team led by CSIRO winning second place in the US Defense Advanced Research Projects Agency (DARPA) Subterranean Challenge in 2021[3] had cemented Australia's international standing as a significant player in this domain (Montgomery, 2021; Devis, 2021).

The Australian mining industry has been one of the early adopters in deploying fleets of fully autonomous mining trucks in production environments (GlobalData, 2020; Cossins-Smith, 2023). Australia has also been a pioneer in port automation with autonomous straddle carriers in operation at ports in Brisbane, Sydney, and Melbourne, starting as early as 2014 (Wiggins, 2014; Dunn, 2020; Vrakas et al., 2021). There are also Australian examples of agriculture automation and advanced precision agriculture systems (DAWR, 2018; see also Bradlow, in this volume). Australia's first 'hands-free farm' will be created at Wagga Wagga, New South Wales, using robots and artificial intelligence. The farm is planned to be built at Charles Sturt's AgriPark at the University's Wagga Wagga campus (Claughton, 2021).

Despite these advancements, the adoption and commercialisation of these technologies are not as widespread as one might expect.

2.3 CHALLENGES OF ADOPTING AND COMMERCIALISING CUTTING-EDGE TECHNOLOGY IN AUSTRALIA

The fragmented nature and the smaller size of Australia's robotics ecosystem present several challenges for the adoption and commercialisation of new technologies. While there had been two well-received robotics roadmaps for Australia published in the recent past (Robotics Australia Group, 2022), a cohesive national strategy for robotics is still being developed (DISR, 2023).

When compared to other nations leading in robotics, such as the US, Japan, South Korea, and Germany, Australia lags in terms of investment, infrastructure, and industry collaboration. Inadequate incentives for collaboration between researchers and industry and lack of late-stage funding for translating research into industry have exacerbated the technological 'valley of death' in commercialisation of cutting-edge robotics technology in Australia. Given the nature and scale of these issues, it would require a coordinated national approach to adequately address. The establishment of a National Robotics Strategy Advisory committee by the Australian government in late 2022 with the mandate for developing a National Robotics Strategy has been a step in this direction.[4]

Further unpacking the challenges in adopting and commercialising robotics, limited investment is one of the biggest hurdles faced by Australia's robotics industry. Investment in robotics R&D has been limited in Australia, which has made it difficult for the country to compete with larger international players. This lack of investment can be due to a range of factors, such as a lack of government support, limited access to venture capital, and a risk-averse business culture.

Australia's robotics ecosystem is also fragmented, with research being conducted across multiple institutions and organisations. This fragmentation makes it difficult to coordinate efforts and develop a cohesive strategy for robotics development and commercialisation. Limited funding and a lack of incentives for collaboration can contribute to this fragmentation. Furthermore, this fragmentation leads to low visibility of Australian robotics capability for industry-seeking solutions. As a consequence, Australian industry would often seek robotic technology solutions from overseas entities instead of directing funding towards local R&D and technology translation.

Two of Australia's largest export industry sectors are mining and agriculture. Both are rife with opportunities for applying robotics and automation to improve safety and scale up productivity. However, despite the existence of a handful of small and medium-sized businesses, there aren't any major mining robotics industries or agriculture robotics industries based in Australia. The mining and agriculture automation technology deployed in Australia are often imported from large multi-national corporations based outside of Australia. In some cases, the R&D of these core technologies has taken place in Australia, but the commercialisation has taken place elsewhere, often funded by large multi-national corporations, such as the underground load haul dump (LHD) truck automation work originating in Australia, which was commercialised through Caterpillar (Evans, 2007).

Another challenging aspect of the Australian economy is that it lacks diversity in comparison to other OECD countries and offers a much smaller market for specialised robotic solutions. Therefore, Australian robotics companies would need to seek global markets to scale up. Australia's geographic location can also be a disadvantage when it comes to accessing global markets. The country is located far from major markets in Asia, Europe, and North America, which can make it difficult for Australian robotics companies to access these markets and compete with established players. High transport costs and a lack of local networks and partnerships can further contribute to this disadvantage. These factors combined with the lack of commercialisation funding can lead to technological developments funded through Australian R&D to move overseas to be set up as companies.

Robotics is a highly specialised field that requires a skilled workforce with expertise in areas such as engineering, computer science, and artificial intelligence. Australia currently faces a shortage of workers with these skills, which can make it difficult to develop and commercialise cutting-edge robotics technologies. Limited investment in Science, Technology, Engineering and Mathematics (STEM) education and a lack of incentives for skilled workers to remain in Australia can contribute to this shortage. However, Australia offers a relatively high living standard and has socio-political stability. This can be leveraged to attract skilled migrant workers into the country to bridge skill gaps in robotics technology development.

Developing and deploying robotics technologies can be subject to regulatory barriers, particularly in areas such as safety and privacy. Australia's regulatory environment can be complex and can slow down the commercialisation process for new robotic technologies. The lack of regulatory harmonisation across jurisdictions and a lack of clarity around regulatory requirements can contribute to these barriers.

Despite these challenges, some Australian companies have successfully adopted and commercialised robotics technology. Sydney-based Marathon Targets, a company formed by the alumni of University of Sydney's Australian Centre for Field Robotics, supplying their key technology to the US Department of Defence and Brisbane-based Emesent that spun out of CSIRO's Robotics and Autonomous Systems Group, servicing over 400 clients globally, are successful examples of Australian companies commercialising robotics technology and performing well in overseas markets. FBR (formerly Fastbrick Robotics) has developed a robotic bricklaying system called Hadrian X, which has the potential to revolutionise the construction industry. The system has been piloted on construction sites around the world (Quirke, 2021). As examples of Australian companies adopting technology, Cochlear has successfully integrated robotics into their manufacturing process, improving efficiency and precision in the production of their implantable hearing devices. There is also a significant increase in the adoption of medical robotic technology in Australia with a 10-fold increase in the number of robot-assisted surgical procedures in the past decade, with nearly 10,000 procedures performed in 2020 alone (Kirk et al., 2022).

However, there have also been unsuccessful attempts by Australian companies to adopt and commercialise robotics technology. Titan Medical had a R&D partnership with the Australian company Mulpha Australia Limited aimed at developing a new robotic surgical system, but the project was ultimately unsuccessful due to challenges in funding. Carbon Revolution attempted to adopt robotics technology in their manufacturing process but ultimately faced challenges in finding a cost-effective way to integrate the technology into their production line. Despite a heavily subscribed early adopter programme setup to provide industry with access to CSIRO's Wildcat SLAM technology used in the DARPA Subterranean, plans for spinning out this technology had to be scaled back due to limited investor interest despite USD 9.8 billion invested across robotics companies globally in 2022.[5]

In conclusion, the challenges faced by Australia in adopting and commercialising cutting-edge technologies in robotics can be attributed to limited investment, smaller local market size and distance from major markets, a fragmented ecosystem, a shortage of skilled workers, and regulatory barriers. Addressing these challenges will be critical to strengthening Australia's robotics ecosystem and enhancing the country's competitiveness in this important area.

2.4 IMPLICATIONS FOR THE FUTURE OF AUTOMATION IN WORKPLACES

The future of automation in workplaces is a complex and multifaceted issue that has many implications. According to McKinsey & Company, automation and artificial intelligence are transforming businesses and will contribute to economic growth via contributions to productivity. They will also help address societal challenges in areas from health to climate change. However, automation will displace some workers, especially those doing basic data entry and processing. It is predicted that around 15 percent of the global workforce, or about 400 million workers, could be displaced by automation in the 2016–2030 period (Manyika & Sneader, 2018).

In Australia, it is predicted that many organisations will continue to struggle to attract talent to fill critical skills gaps. Major international technology companies, especially those based in the US laying off large numbers of workers recently, may have an effect on talent availability for Australian companies, especially in robotics and AI-related domains (PWC, 2023). As the automation technology continues to evolve, it is becoming an integral part of many modern business processes. While some fear automation is an existential threat to livelihoods, jobs, and the economy, among other benefits, it can also foster the advancement of society and may assist companies in keeping workers safe on-site.

The future of automation in workplaces is likely to continue to grow and change rapidly, with significant implications for industries and workers alike. As technology continues to advance, more jobs will become automated, leading to both job losses and job creation in different industries. Some of the key implications for the future of automation in workplaces include:

1. **Job displacement**: One of the most significant impacts of automation on the workforce is job displacement. As machines and robots become more capable, they are increasingly able to perform tasks that were once done by humans. This will lead to job losses in some industries, particularly those that rely on repetitive, manual labour.

2. **Skills gap**: Automation will also lead to a growing skills gap in the workforce. As machines take over more jobs, workers will need to develop new skills and competencies to remain relevant in the job market (see also O'Keeffe and Howard, in this volume). This will require significant investment in education and training programs to ensure workers have the necessary skills to succeed in the digital age.

3. **Increased productivity**: Automation can also lead to significant increases in productivity in many industries. By automating repetitive tasks, machines can work faster and more efficiently than humans, allowing companies to produce more goods and services at a lower cost.

4. **Improved safety**: Robots and machines can also be used to perform dangerous tasks that would be too hazardous for humans to undertake. This includes tasks such as working in hazardous environments, handling dangerous materials, and performing tasks that require a high degree of precision.

5. **New job creation**: While automation will lead to job losses in some industries, it will also create new jobs in others. As new technologies emerge, new industries will be created, requiring workers with new skills and expertise. For example, the development of autonomous vehicles will create new jobs in fields such as software development, data analysis, and robotics engineering.

As automation continues to reshape the workforce, the adoption of robotics technologies has significant implications for Australia's economy and labour market, especially the demand for high-skilled workers in the robotics sector. In Australia, McKinsey & Company estimates that 25 percent to 46 percent of current work activities could be automated by 2030, which could help drive a renaissance in productivity, personal income, and economic growth (Taylor et al., 2019). However, automation also presents challenges related to job displacement, skills shortages, and related need for reskilling and upskilling as well as ethical concerns related to income inequality and lack of social cohesion. Therefore, the impact of automation on the future of workplaces in Australia is a complex issue that requires consideration of multiple factors. While automation presents opportunities for increased productivity and economic growth, it is important to mitigate the potential negative impacts on workers and ensure that automation is implemented in an ethical and responsible manner[6] (see also Cebulla and Spzak, in this volume).

2.5 IMPLICATIONS FOR AUSTRALIA'S ECONOMY AND ECOLOGY

The potential impact of increased automation on the Australian economy and ecology is significant. On one hand, automation has the potential to increase productivity, reduce costs, and create new industries and job opportunities. On the other hand, there are concerns that increased automation could result in job losses, exacerbate income inequality, and have negative environmental consequences. To maximise the benefits of automation and minimise the risks, the government has a crucial role to play. This includes investing in R&D, promoting the adoption of automation in key industries, providing incentives for the development of new technologies, and developing policies to support workers affected by automation.

An analysis of the potential benefits and risks of automation on Australia's economy and ecology indicates that the adoption of robotics and automation technologies has the potential to bring several benefits, including increased productivity, reduced labour costs, improved efficiency, and the potential for new job creation. The potential may be greatest in agriculture and mining, where the application of robotics technologies could significantly reduce the environmental impact of these industries by improving resource efficiency, reducing waste and pollution, and promoting more sustainable land management practices. However, there are also risks associated with increased automation, such as the potential for job displacement, increased inequality, and ecological impacts.

To improve its capabilities in robotics and leverage the benefits of automation, Australia should take several steps. First, it should encourage collaboration between research institutions and industry to foster innovation and the development of new technologies. Second, the government should increase funding for R&D in robotics, automation, and related fields. Third, Australia needs to develop a national strategy for robotics and automation that includes policies and initiatives to support the growth of the industry and ensure that the benefits of automation are maximised while minimising the risks. Fourth, the government should encourage the adoption of robotics and automation in industries by providing incentives and support for companies that invest in these technologies. Fifth, the education system should be improved to develop the necessary skills, including STEM education and vocational training in robotics and automation. Finally, ethical and social concerns should be addressed by developing ethical guidelines and frameworks for the development and use of these technologies.

2.6 CONCLUSIONS

Australia's robotics landscape presents a complex mix of challenges and opportunities. By addressing the issues hindering the adoption and commercialisation of new technologies, the country can unlock the full potential of its robotics capabilities and secure a leading position in the global robotics market. The future of Australia's economy and ecology hinges on its ability to adapt to the changing landscape of automation, and the nation's success in navigating these challenges will determine its role in shaping the future of work and the environment.

NOTES

1 https://solarsystem.nasa.gov/resources/2848/parker-solar-probe/?category=heat
2 https://research.qut.edu.au/qcr/Projects/amazon-picking-challenge-2017/
3 https://www.subtchallenge.com/
4 https://www.minister.industry.gov.au/ministers/husic/media-releases/committee-appointed-help-guide-robotics-strategy
5 Crunchbase news: Here Are The Robot Startups Getting Funded, Even As Investors Pull Back: https://news.crunchbase.com/ai-robotics/funded-startups-locus-amp-exits-spac-ipo/
6 National AI Centre's Responsible AI Network: https://www.csiro.au/en/work-with-us/industries/technology/national-ai-centre/responsible-ai-network

REFERENCES

Claughton, D. (2021, May 27). Robots and artificial intelligence to guide Australia's first fully automated farm. Retrieved from: Australian Broadcasting Corporation: https://www.abc.net.au/news/rural/2021-05-27/automated-farm-to-use-robots-and-artificial-intelligence/100169302

Cossins-Smith, A. (2023, April). Automation in Australia: How the future of mining could change. Mine Australia. Retrieved from: https://mine.nridigital.com/mine_australia_apr23/automation_mining_future

DAWR. (2018). Agricultural innovation—A national approach to grow Australia's future. The Australian Government department of agriculture and water resources.

Devis, D. (2021, September 27). Robot 'Olympians' bring home the silver and $1.3million prize. Retrieved from: https://cosmosmagazine.com/technology/robotics/robot-olympians-bring-home-silver-from-darpa/

DISR. (2023). National robotics strategy discussion paper.

Dodd, E. (2023, April 20). AI like ChatGPT could change the day-to-day of white-collar jobs the most and reverse decades of tech-driven inequality — If we use it the right way. Retrieved from: https://www.businessinsider.com/jobs-pay-changed-most-college-workers-ai-chatgpt-inequality-skills-2023-4

Dunn, J. (2020, September 18). The Australian. Retrieved from: https://www.theaustralian.com.au/special-reports/ports-australia/automation-creates-safer-more-efficient-workplace/news-story/9be78eacc7072c611eaf924a5360029a

Eloundou, T., Manning, S., Mishkin, P., & Rock, D. (2023). GPTs are GPTs: An early look at the labor market impact potential of large language models. arXiv:2303.10130v5. https://doi.org/10.48550/arXiv.2303.10130

Evans, G. (2007, August 29). Look – No hands! Retrieved from: https://www.mining-technology.com/features/feature1209/

GlobalData. (2020, March 17). Australia dominates global autonomous haul truck use with numbers set to triple. Retrieved from: https://www.mining-technology.com/comment/australia-autonomous-haul-trucks-use/

Kirk, A., Halifax, A., Orr, W., & Robertson, D. (2022, April). Robots in health-care. Retrieved from Australian Unity: https://www.australianunity.com.au/wealth/-/media/RebrandWealth/Documents/Funds/AustralianUnity/Future-of-Healthcare-Fund/Announcements/042022Spotlight-Series-Robotics.pdf

Manyika, J., & Sneader, K. (2018, June 1). AI, automation, and the future of work: Ten things to solve for. Retrieved from McKinsey & Company: https://www.mckinsey.com/featured-insights/future-of-work/ai-automation-and-the-future-of-work-ten-things-to-solve-for

Marr, B. (2017). The 4 Ds of robotisation: Dull, dirty, dangerous and dear. Retrieved from: https://bernardmarr.com/the-4-ds-of-robotisation-dull-dirty-dangerous-and-dear/

McAfee, A., & Brynjolfsson, E. (2017). Machine, platform, crowd: Harnessing our digital future. New York: W. W. Norton & Company.

McKay, C., Pollack, E., & Fitzpayne, A. (2019). Automation and a changing economy: The case for action. Washington DC: Aspen Institute.

Montgomery, D. (2021, November 10). The Pentagon's $82 Million Super Bowl of Robots. Retrieved from: https://www.washingtonpost.com/magazine/2021/11/10/darpa-robot-competition/

PWC. (2018). Will robots really steal our jobs? An international analysis of the potential long term impact of automation. PWC. https://www.pwc.co.uk/services/economics/insights/the-impact-of-automation-on-jobs.html

PWC. (2023). 2023 future of work outlook. PWC. https://www.pwc.com.au/future-of-work-design-for-the-future/2023-future-of-work-outlook.html

Quirke, J. (2021, October). Hadrian the construction robot to build eight houses in Western Australia. Retrieved from: https://www.globalconstructionreview.com/hadrian-the-construction-robot-to-build-eight-houses-in-western-australia/

Robotics Australia Group. (2022). A robotics roadmap for Australia 2022. Retrieved from: https://roboausnet.com.au/wp-content/uploads/2021/11/Robotics-Roadmap-for-Australia-2022_compressed-1.pdf

Taylor, C., Carrigan, J., Noura, H., Ungur, S., van Halder, J., & Dandona, G. S. (2019, March 3). Australia's automation opportunity: Reigniting productivity and inclusive income growth. Retrieved from: https://www.mckinsey.com/featured-insights/future-of-work/australias-automation-opportunity-reigniting-productivity-and-inclusive-income-growth

The World Bank. (2016). World development report: Digital dividends. Washington Dc: The World Bank. https://www.worldbank.org/en/publication/wdr2016

Vrakas, G., Chan, C., & Thai, V. V. (2021). The effects of evolving port technology and process optimisation on operational performance: The case study of an Australian container terminal operator. The Asian Journal of Shipping and Logistics, 37(4), 281–290

Wiggins, J. (2014, May 19). Automation 'inevitable' at Port Botany. Retrieved from: https://www.afr.com/companies/automation-inevitable-at-port-botany-20140519-iuc4h

Zorpette, G. (2023, May 17). Just calm down about GPT-4 already. IEEE Spectrum. Retrieved from: https://spectrum.ieee.org/gpt-4-calm-down

CHAPTER 3

The Promise of Digitalisation and Automation

Hugh S. Bradlow

MUCH HAS BEEN WRITTEN in recent years about automation and the replacement of human labour in vast swathes of the economy. Perhaps best known is the seminal 2013 paper from Oxford University by Frey and Osborne (2013) which concluded that 47 percent of jobs could potentially be automated. The Frey and Osborne paper was based on expert advice about which job categories could be replaced by artificial intelligence. A subsequent more nuanced approach by McKinsey (Manyika et al., 2017) looked at the actual jobs performed by workers and considered which components of a worker's role could be automated. This came to a very different conclusion. First of all, it concluded that there was a very high level of uncertainty and that the actual number of roles that might be replaced would be between 0 percent and 30 percent. As for all significant industrial transitions, new jobs will also emerge, and the McKinsey paper estimated that 0–14 percent of workers would need to change their job category.

These studies have created widespread speculation about the future of our economy and employment in particular. The more pessimistic studies (e.g., Frey & Osborne, 2013) cause concern over rampant unemployment, inequity and massive social dislocation. Even a more realistic view (Manyika et al., 2017) will require governments to prepare for an economy that is very different from today's. For example, clearly there will be a need to facilitate worker transitions (e.g., training, economic support) into new roles.

DOI: 10.1201/9781003393757-3

In this chapter, instead of speculating about the economic impact of automation, which is subject to significant uncertainty, we take the approach of first trying to understand the technologies behind digitalisation and automation and then apply this understanding to what capabilities are actually likely to appear in the economy.

3.1 THE TECHNOLOGIES OF DIGITALISATION: THE SEVEN SISTERS

In relation to digital technologies, the first and obvious question is 'why is this happening now?' To answer this, we need a historical view of how digital technologies have evolved up to the point where we are today and what is likely to happen in the future. For a technology to be disruptive it needs to become a 'platform'. Platforms allow multiple applications on the same technology which thus achieves economies of scope and scale. Without this platform capability, technologies remain niche. Today's digital disruption is based on seven sets of 'mainstream' platforms. We call these 'mainstream' because they are in general used by most people and/ or businesses.

The **first platform** was the Personal Computer (PC) which became widely available in the late 1970s and early 1980s. Prior to the introduction of the PC, computers were only affordable to governments, large enterprises and academic institutions. However, the advent of the solid-state transistor and integrated circuits in the 1940s and 1950s led to the relentless march of miniaturisation which became known as 'Moore's Law' (an observation by Gordon Moore, one of the co-founders of the Intel Corporation, that the number of transistors that could be put into a silicon chip doubled approximately every two years[1]). This enabled the key ingredients of the von Neumann computer architecture (the computer architecture that is the basis of all modern computers and divides a computer into four basic constituents – a processor, memory, storage and input/output mechanisms[2]) to be produced with ever-increasing scale and everdeclining cost.

As soon as personal computers were in the hands of users, they realised how much more could be achieved if the machines could communicate with each other. This led to the **second platform** – The Internet. The foundational technologies for the Internet (the TCP/IP protocols) were laid in the 1970s, but in the 1980s they became a *lingua franca* which was widely adopted and hence became the mechanism for allowing computers to talk to each other.

As an aside, there has recently been much commentary about blockchain being the 'second coming of the Internet'. Blockchain is a distributed ledger shared by many users, who may or may not be known to each other, where no individual user controls the data that is stored in it and once entered, the data cannot be changed.[3] While blockchain does promise a shared control of data, it lacks a single technical standard to allow open and widespread interaction. Whether one will emerge is a moot question. During the 1980s, there were many different protocols for performing inter-computer communication, some industry specific (e.g., X.25 from the telecommunications industry) and some proprietary (e.g., IBM's SNA, Digital Equipment Corporation's DECNET, Novell's IPX and Microsoft's NetBIOS). However, the attractiveness of a single standard overcame all these solutions and led to the Internet technology becoming *the* platform for computer communications. It is still not clear, however, whether blockchain can go beyond the 'Tower of Babel' phase and achieve a common 'lingua franca' adopted by all users.

The **third platform**, the World Wide Web (WWW), arose because, while computers could exchange *data*, humans needed to exchange *information*. Accordingly, the standards (HTML and HTTPS) developed at CERN (the European nuclear research organisation) laboratories by Sir Tim Berners-Lee (a scientist working there) were again widely adopted because they allowed the widespread sharing of information. Over the past three decades, the WWW and its extensions have effectively led to the digitisation of all human knowledge. This is a profound step. When seminal science fiction writer Isaac Asimov wrote his Foundation Trilogy,[4] in the 1950s, he did not envisage that the *Encyclopedia Galactica* would not be produced by a foundation of elite scholars but, rather, crowd-sourced from millions of people.

Because use of knowledge requires cycling through many different possibilities, there was a need to speed up the network technology for accessing the WWW. The method available at the end of the last century (dial-up over the telephone network) could not meet this need, which led to very rapid rise at the end of that century of the **fourth platform**, namely Broadband Access. Innovative repurposing of existing access communication technologies (particularly copper telephone lines which connected almost all houses and businesses in developed economies, or Hybrid Fibre Coax – HFC – which was used for pay TV) enabled rapid introduction of broadband to businesses and homes. Coupled with the development of Wi-Fi, this satisfied the human desire for instant gratification and provided high-speed and convenient access to the WWW.

The rapid scaling of the WWW and broadband access created a new set of challenges, particularly the ability to swiftly scale up/down computing capability, the management of vast swathes of data (both public and personal) as well as cyber security challenges. The logical solution was the **fifth platform**, namely Cloud Computing, which can be considered as having been initiated in March 2006 with the launch of Amazon Web Services (AWS). The sharing of data centre technology offloaded many of the computing burdens from individual organisations or persons and, most importantly, provided access to essentially infinite computing capability, scalable in very small increments. This led to a Cambrian explosion of start-up companies that could try out new ideas at low cost but keep pace with growth if they were successful (Uber being an excellent example).

Parallel to the computing developments in the 1990s, mobile telephony was becoming affordable to the average person. Even in developing economies, the utility brought by mobile phones justified their use. For example, the famous story of the Kerala fisherman (Jensen, 2007) illustrates how transformational mobile telephony was. Fishermen returning to port in the Gulf of Arabia were price takers because they did not have time to sail to the next port for a better offer, as the fish would rot in the heat. With mobile phones, fishermen were able to text several ports within range to see who would give them the best offer and, by doing so, saw an immediate increase in their incomes.

The obvious result of the side-by-side development of broadband access and mobile telephony was the **sixth platform**, namely Mobile Broadband. The third generation of cellular mobile technology was extended at the beginning of the 21st century to allow handheld devices to connect to the Internet with sufficiently increased speed and reduced latency to make the experience worthwhile.

The **seventh platform**, a direct consequence of mobile broadband and handheld phones, is possibly the most profound change in technology in human history. As of May 2019, there were 5.3 billion people over the age of 15. Five billion had a phone and four billion of these had a smartphone.[5] The combination of mobile broadband and the smartphone has made information and computing available on a scale that affects almost every human family. They have changed the way we navigate, how we shop, how we interact with our government, how we obtain services, how we work (gig economy) and virtually every aspect of our daily lives.

3.2 THE INTERNET OF THINGS

Why is all this history relevant? The answer lies in the fact that today's 'seven sister' technology platforms (the seven technology platforms described in Section 3.1) have succeeded, as stated above, in digitising human knowledge. The 'Encyclopedia Galactica' as envisioned by Asimov in the 1940s, now exists (although, as stated above, Asimov did not foresee crowd-sourced knowledge – he assumed the *Encyclopedia Galactica* would need to be written by experts).

So where do we go now? The answer, in short, is digitising the physical world we live in using new technology platforms which are collectively called the 'Internet of Things' (henceforth to be referred to herein as the 'IoT').

In reality, the IoT is multiple sets of platforms: sensors and actuators; communications networks; cloud service and middleware platforms. This sits alongside new analytic capabilities offered by artificial intelligence (discussed in Section 3.3). It is worthwhile considering the platforms' capabilities in more detail because they make yet another massive transitional leap possible.

3.2.1 Sensors and Actuators

Beyond the impact on our daily lives, smartphones have had another overwhelming effect. Because they are produced on a massive scale – billions of devices, they have created unprecedented economies of scale for the manufacture of sensor and communications technologies. Smartphones include audio sensors (microphones), imaging sensors (cameras), motion sensors, light sensors, location sensors (GPS), environmental sensors (pressure, temperature) and radio sensors (cellular, Bluetooth, Wi-Fi, NFC, etc.).

Because of the production scale, these items can now be manufactured at such low cost that they become affordable in previously unthinkable applications (some of which will be discussed below), but ultimately this all comes down to the ability to measure our physical world in real time.

3.2.2 Communication Networks

The stream of measurement data coming out of the myriad of physical sensors is only useful if it can be analysed. To do this, we invariably must move the data from the location of the sensor to computing facilities ('in the cloud'). Fortunately, the production scale of smartphones has enabled communication technologies cheap enough to be incorporated into distributed sensors.

However, there are still big challenges in creating communications systems that will make IoT effective. A network design must (ideally) address the following 10 challenges:

1. **High-speed broadband**: Communication networks dedicated to IoT will miss out on the economies of scale and scope achieved by networks that can serve human needs as well. The main human need is high-speed broadband networking (to access the Internet) so the peak speed achievable on such networks must be adequate – 10s, if not 100s, of megabits per second (mpbs) or even gigabits per second (gbps) – to satisfy that requirement (for reference, most connections of Australia's National Broadband Network would be 50 or 100 mbps. In any event, many IoT devices (e.g., surveillance cameras) also require broadband networking (but mainly in the upstream as opposed to downstream direction because video is the main driver of the need for network speed and a video camera produces rather than consumes video).

2. **Capacity and scalability**: While networks may have high peak speeds, they still need to carry the traffic from millions or billions of devices. Thus, they need to have sufficient capacity (throughput) to allow thousands of devices to transmit simultaneously on the same network segment. This capacity needs to be available in both the upstream and downstream directions, unlike human-oriented networks. The latter mainly need capacity in the downstream direction because humans are consumers of video which is the dominant traffic source. On the other hand, as already pointed out, devices such as surveillance cameras send video upstream.

   In addition, there is a second dimension to capacity, namely the ability of the network control systems to handle the signalling traffic of millions or billions of devices. While many devices do not generate much traffic, they are nevertheless 'chatty' in that they need to signal back and forth to the network. There is a limit to such load that the network can tolerate unless it is designed with this requirement in mind.

3. **Spectrum**: Spectrum is the 'land' on which the wireless communications industry is built. However, not all spectrum is created equal. At lower frequencies, the propagation characteristics are better. Nonetheless, the lower the frequency the larger the antenna required

to achieve antenna 'gain' (the amplification of the transmitted or received signal). At higher frequencies, the signal transmission can be interrupted by obstacles such as foliage and buildings. The ideal frequency range for mobile networks from a transmission perspective is between 300 MHz and 3 GHz. However, because every network wishes to occupy this range, the available spectral bandwidth is highly contested. As you go beyond 3 GHz, more bandwidth becomes available.

Another critical aspect of spectrum is ownership. Spectrum, like land, is treated as property. Wireless carriers purchase licenses to operate exclusively in given bands in various geographic regions. The successful operation of cellular mobile networks relies on such exclusive ownership because it enables the wireless network operator to control the use of the network and prevent interference from other users.

However, because such spectrum is expensive (billions of dollars) it is considered an inhibitor to innovation. As a result, spectrum regulation authorities have made certain bands available based on a 'public license'. This is often erroneously referred to as 'unlicensed' spectrum. While the spectrum is subject to license conditions, the license is not exclusive to any organisation or person. A public license allows anyone to use the spectral band without seeking authorisation, providing they fulfil the license conditions which are designed to avoid the 'tragedy of the commons'.

These public licensed spectral bands have been critical in the development of important technologies such as Wi-Fi and Bluetooth and will also be very important for the IoT. Nevertheless, because there is no control of who uses such spectrum, reliability is often an issue. For example, smarthome devices often run on Wi-Fi in the 2.4 GHz public license band. Most users will have experienced the phenomenon whereby a network that is seemingly operating well suddenly becomes unreliable due to a neighbour switching on a new device which uses the same frequency.

4. **Power and battery life**: The power consumption of wireless networks is a critical issue, not only to avoid the emissions of greenhouse gases but also to ensure that the network does not drain the batteries of the devices connected to it. For the IoT this will be particularly important as most devices will be battery powered and will need to operate for years between battery changes (e.g., think of a sensor implanted in the road to determine if a car parking space is occupied).

The battery life is significantly affected by the signal processing required to connect to the wireless network. The more sophisticated the signal processing, the greater likelihood of CPU intensity and hence battery consumption. In addition, functions such as encryption can be processor-intensive and often will not be possible in battery-powered sensors.

5. **Latency**: Latency is the time between action and response. In a network it is the delay – in each direction – of sending a signal and receiving a response. For many applications (e.g., think of a pilot controlling a drone via a video signal from a camera on the drone), the latency needs to be well below the scale of human perception.

   On the other hand, achieving low latency requires the transmitted signals to be sent in very short bursts (known as 'packets'). A long packet takes time to be transmitted onto the network which adds to the latency. While short packets reduce latency, some applications (such as high-speed broadband) must be sent in larger packets to maximise the network efficiency. Meeting the challenges of both types of applications is a complicated network design problem.

6. **Quality of service (QoS)**: Not all applications are of equal importance. A surgeon performing remote surgery cannot tolerate a network that may or may not get the signals through. On the other hand, if the reading of an electricity meter is delayed by a few seconds it does not matter. To enable some applications to have priority, it is possible for networks to incorporate a concept called 'Quality of Service' whereby applications that need it are given preferential access to the network to ensure the predictability of their communications. This is a complicated issue because in wireless networks it comes at the expense of overall network capacity, so must be limited to as little traffic as possible.

7. **Mobility**: Many IoT applications will require the network to be able to cope with signals coming from very fast-moving objects (e.g., a supersonic fighter plane). This imposes challenges to what are often tight signalling timing constraints in mobile cellular networks.

8. **Coverage**: Obviously network coverage is a key consideration. This (as explained above) is partially related to the spectral band in which the network operates, but it is mainly dependent on the investment

in network infrastructure. Terrestrial networks are limited by the diminishing returns of adding more coverage in increasingly sparsely populated areas. For example, Telstra's network in Australia is one of the largest in the world, and it covers more than 99 percent[6] of Australia's population, but only about one-third of Australia's land mass (2.5 m sq km[7] out of 7.69 m sq km).

Satellite networks can increase coverage dramatically but geo-stationary satellites, at an altitude of 35,786 km, have a significant latency due to the propagation delay for the signal to travel to and from the satellite (approximately, a round trip of ¼ of a second). A new generation of so-called LEO (Low Earth Orbit) satellites is coming on stream with the first services offered in the early 2020s. LEOs have performance in terms of latency and bandwidth comparable to terrestrial cellular networks, can potentially provide 100 percent pole-to-pole global coverage, but require constellations of thousands of satellites.

Even with LEOs and extended terrestrial coverage, for the IoT you also need to plan for the fact that sometimes there will be no network or the delay in signals going back and forth to network towers (or satellites) would be too long. In such cases, it is desirable for the network design to include point-to-point (without a network) communications capability, or to 'mesh' (where nodes in the network act as relays for other users). As an example of an application for which this is critical, consider two Connected Autonomous Vehicles (CAVs) driving in the Australian outback where there is no network. The cars can communicate their position, speed and direction directly with each other to avoid a collision using a 'network-less' transmission capability.

9. **Reliability**: Wireless networks, no matter how well designed, are subject to random variations. The path a signal may take can randomly vary due to atmospheric fluctuations, buildings, foliage, etc. This leads to a phenomenon known as 'Rayleigh Fading'[8], whereby a received wireless signal varies in strength for no obvious reason.

The only way to avoid this fading affecting the reliability of the network is to design and control the signal with sufficient margin of error. As mentioned under the spectrum above, this is very difficult to do in public spectrum and is a significant challenge for IoT devices. Consider a door sensor which detects whether a door is open or closed. The sensor does not send out much data, but when it does, it is critical that it gets through. If someone breaks into a house and the door sensor 'falls off the network' due to interference or fading, this could cause an important event to be missed.

Modern signal processing techniques such as beam steering and MIMO (Multiple Input Multiple Output[9]) can mitigate fading and interference but are costly to implement and consume processing power (and hence battery power).

10. **Privacy and security**: Ideally, IoT networks and devices will encrypt their traffic. However, as mentioned above, under battery consumption, this can come with a significant performance penalty for battery life.

    Even if signals are encrypted, there can still be security risks. For example, burglars have been able to listen to the signal traffic from smart electricity meters and, even though it was encrypted, determine from the level of activity on the network that no one was at home.

    IoT devices by their nature often (usually?) do not present a software user interface to the user (e.g., a camera presents a video image to the user, not details such as the software version). Thus, it is difficult to prompt the user to upgrade their software (which is absolutely necessary for security), thereby exposing these devices to hacking. For example, the Mirai botnet[10] was able to commandeer vulnerable, unpatched security cameras and use them to perform distributed denial of service (DDOS) attacks on corporations.

The above 10 challenges make it almost impossible to design an ideal IoT communications network. As a result, a plethora of different network designs have emerged. However, they can be broadly divided into two streams:

1. **Cellular mobile networks**: The rise of the IoT coincided with the growth in 4G networks. Carriers saw the opportunity to extend their services to IoT devices and hence extended the 4G standards with special capabilities to serve such devices (NB-IoT and Cat-M). Because these networks are controlled by the carrier, they achieve high levels of reliability.

By the time 5G was designed, the need to serve IoT devices was well understood and 5G is intended *ab initio* to support millions of IoT users as well as human users.

In theory, the economies of scale of carrier networks should also make the modems cheap. However, carriers have a business model which involves charging per network device and their tariffs are not particularly friendly to IoT devices. As a result, adoption has been limited and has encouraged the design of alternative network solutions.

2. **Public spectrum networks**: The ability to avoid being beholden to wireless carriers was a strong attraction for IoT users to adopt public spectrum solutions. Wi-Fi, the most prolific technology using public spectrum, lends itself to the connection of IoT devices in the local network and was soon adopted for the IoT.

   However, Wi-Fi can also be a battery drain, and for many applications (e.g., the parking sensors referred to above) is an overkill. Consequently, a number of low power local network solutions have emerged for IoT, the most well-known being Zigbee and Z-wave. Besides the low power consumption, the modems for these networks are very cheap. Obviously, like Wi-Fi, these networks require a gateway to connect the traffic to the cloud.

   Because of the limitations of local coverage (e.g., your house is covered but your dog leaves the grounds), there have been attempts to create wide area public spectrum solutions such as LoRa. Other solutions have ingeniously attempted to crowd-source network infrastructure (e.g., the Helium network where users allow random devices (e.g., your dog's collar) to connect to their private network in exchange for network credits).

Overall, each of the above solutions has limitations in terms of the set of 10 requirements outlined above and as a result, IoT networking technology is in a state of flux. While this is good for innovation, it is also frustrating for users due to the competing standards and compatibility issues. In the smarthome field, where network limitations are a considerable inhibitor, the Matter alliance[11] is attempting to create standards which will result in a high degree of compatibility between the devices of different manufacturers.

3.2.3 Cloud Services and Middleware

The IoT is capable of generating vast amounts of data. For example, it is estimated that a self-driving car would produce almost four terabytes of raw data an hour.[12] Clearly, this data needs to be organised and made available for analysis which is invariably done using cloud services like Amazon, Azure and Google. A variety of technologies exist to store, retrieve and process vast quantities of data. For the purposes of this discussion, we accept that these capabilities exist and do not delve into the capability further.

3.3 NEW ANALYTIC CAPABILITIES – ARTIFICIAL INTELLIGENCE

The technologies of the IoT described above have created the ability to collect data from the physical world, in vast quantities, and to transfer that data to scalable cloud computing systems where it can be analysed. Until 2010, data was mostly analysed using rule-based systems and parameterised models. While this works well in many situations, it works very poorly for certain tasks which humans are very good at, specifically pattern recognition. However, in the 21st century, computing capability and data availability made it possible to train artificial neural networks (Grosan & Abraham, 2011) to perform pattern recognition with human-like ability.

To illustrate this, consider machine speech recognition. For decades, scientists had been using parametric models to try and interpret human speech. The results as illustrated in Figure 3.1 below were not particularly promising. Over a four-decade period, the accuracy only improved from 50 percent to 70 percent. Even with limited vocabularies, a recognition

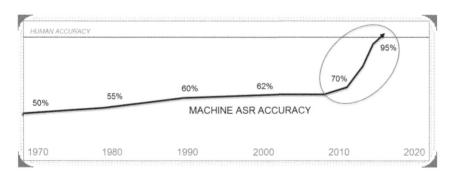

FIGURE 3.1   Speech recognition accuracy over time.

Source: Sharma, 2016.

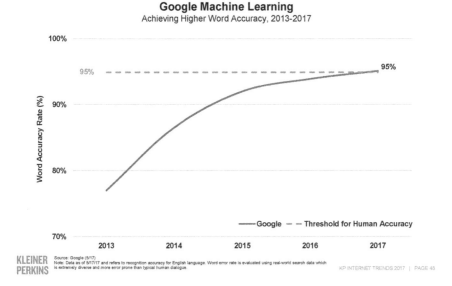

FIGURE 3.2 Speech recognition accuracy in the 2010s since the advent of artificial neural networks and other machine learning (ML) algorithms.

Source: Meeker, 2017.

accuracy of 70 percent is not particularly useful. Then in about 2010, Google (and others) applied artificial neural networks (ANNs and variants such as deep learning) to the problem and, as the graph illustrates, an inflection point was reached. By the end of the decade, speech recognition was close to human levels as shown in Figure 3.2.

In domains such as speech and image recognition, these machine learning (ML) algorithms have been extraordinarily successful. However, it must be emphasised that this does not make ML a substitute for human intelligence except in limited ways.

3.3.1 Limitations of Machine Learning Algorithms

In essence, machine learning is just pattern recognition. You train an algorithm with copious amounts of data, and it will recognise a pattern by finding the closest statistical match to the type of object you wish to recognise, using the objects it has been trained on. Human intelligence goes far beyond pattern recognition and includes many forms of logic and inference in addition to pattern recognition. To fully emulate human capabilities, you would need Generalised Artificial Intelligence which is nowhere near being available.

Even in terms of pattern recognition, ML has some fundamental limitations.

1. **One-shot learning**: Machine learning algorithms need to be trained on hundreds or thousands of examples of the pattern you are trying to recognise. By contrast, the human brain is remarkably adaptable and can learn from a very limited set of examples. You do not need to show a small child many examples of a dog before that child knows what a dog is, despite the variety of breeds, sizes and colours.

   The training of ML algorithms requires a large number of example patterns and so is computationally expensive, time-consuming and power-hungry. In addition, if you need to update the training examples, you need to completely retrain the algorithm.

2. **Data bias**: The data on which a ML algorithm is trained will significantly influence the results produced by the algorithm. For example, a face recognition algorithm trained on white male faces recognised a white male with less than 1 percent error. By contrast, the error rate of that same algorithm in recognising black females was 35 percent.[13]

   Unless you have a fully representative training set, the output of machine learning algorithms can be extremely misleading. However, it must also be born in mind that humans display bias in their recognition algorithms, no doubt due to cultural background.

3. **Explainability**: ML algorithms will produce the most statistically likely object (or pattern) for which the input is a match. Why a particular object is chosen is not indicated by the algorithm. As explained above, data bias can influence the algorithm's result but how you correct the problem can be very obscure (if possible at all). This is known as the 'explainability problem'.

   Again, it needs to be noted that often humans have a similar explainability problem because on many occasions they are incapable of justifying the choices they have made.

4. **Replicability**: Machine learning relies on the statistics of the pattern you are trying to recognise being the same as the patterns on which the algorithms were trained. If the statistics change over time, the applicability of the algorithm will decline commensurately. As an example, consider the weather or the stock market, neither

of which have stationary statistics (e.g., in the financial markets COVID-19 was a 'never-seen-before' pattern). This limits the ability of machine learning to predict the weather or the stock market or similar systems.

5. **Classification nuance**: Algorithms will often throw up answers which are basically the same as many other choices. Consider, for example, navigation algorithms which will often advise you to take some really obscure route to save 30 seconds in a three-hour journey. ML algorithms yield a single answer and thus obscure other answers which may be better for extraneous reasons.

6. **Scalability**: The more ambitious the recognition problem, the larger the algorithm that needs to be trained and the more data required to train it. Consider the current algorithm *du jour* (December 2022), GPT-3, which is used in the much-vaunted ChatGPT chatbot. GPT-3 is trained to recognise phrases as opposed to isolated words. This enables it to locate material on the web that relates to a concept as opposed to a string of words. However, to achieve this feat the GPT-3 algorithm has 175 billion parameters which need to be trained.[14] This requires about 45 terabytes of text data.[15] The energy consumption for the training of the algorithm (which can take days or even weeks) is almost a GWhr.[16]

To put the scalability problem into context, the human brain consumes about 20 watts of power. By contrast, the Summit supercomputer, one of the largest in the world, consumes about 13 megawatts of power and by some estimates has 20-fold less computational power than the human brain.[17]

Given the above limitations of today's artificial intelligence (AI), we cannot expect algorithms to perform with human capability (even if some of the AI limitations are shared by humans). Which then begs the obvious question, what can we expect from AI in the short to medium term?

3.4 AUTOMATION AND ARTIFICIAL INTELLIGENCE

As already discussed, it is unlikely that AI will replace vast swathes of whole job categories in the short/medium term. However, it clearly has the ability to augment human capability and the combination of the Internet of Things and machine learning will enable automating certain types of tasks. Such automation will be particularly desirable for:

1. Chores where humans are prone to error and/or where it is danger-ous for humans to perform such tasks.

2. Chores where it is not effective use of human time to do such tasks and/or where a machine will augment human work and make the human more productive.

We illustrate these uses of automation through examples below.

3.4.1 Connected Autonomous Vehicles

One of the most obvious tasks in the first category is driving. Human error is the sole cause of 57 percent of road accidents and a contributory cause in 90 percent of accidents.[18] In the middle of the last decade there was a great deal of optimism about the ability to automate the driving process, triggered by the technologies of the IoT and artificial intelligence. Machine learning enables the creation of perceptual systems out of cam-eras, lidars, radars and ultrasound. Perceptual systems enable a vehicle to accurately measure the location, velocity and acceleration of objects in its vicinity. Furthermore, simultaneous localisation and mapping technolo-gies will enable the vehicle to know exactly where it is (potentially to the nearest centimetre) and its relation to fixed objects (such as the edge of the road). Finally, the communication technologies created for the Internet of Things, as discussed above, will allow vehicles to communicate with each other and the road infrastructure.

Such 'Connected Autonomous Vehicles' (CAVs) have the potential to be fully self-driving. In the 2010s there was a significant amount of optimism about – and investment in – Connected Autonomous Vehicles, and even though progress towards fully self-driving vehicles has been slower than anticipated,[19] it has nevertheless been steady.[20] More importantly, the per-ceptual technologies have been used to create Advanced Driver Assist Systems (ADAS) which have a significant beneficial effect on vehicle safety due to their ability to compensate for a certain amount of driver error. For example, ADAS technology has reduced rear-end collision rates by up to 80 percent and pedestrian collision rates up to 50 percent when compared to similar vehicles without the technology.[21]

The ultimate goal of CAVs is to achieve 'Level 5 Automation'[22] which are vehicles that can self-drive on all roads, in all traffic conditions and in all weather conditions. When achieved, this will result in a considerable reduction in road congestion, a much more flexible and environmentally friendly transport system and improved mobility for disadvantaged groups (e.g., the elderly). Ultimately there is no technological reason why this goal cannot be achieved but it will take time to overcome numerous challenges. For example, the perceptual systems will need to use a combination of technologies to meet the required level of reliability. In addition, the highly complex and flexible logic used by human beings will be a challenge (but not impossible) to emulate.

3.4.2 Productivity

In the second category above, there are tasks which a human being can perform but are simply too tedious and expensive to ask a human to do. Consider the example of 'time and motion' studies where a person observes and records the activities of people performing their jobs. The most obvious example of such a situation is in the retail branch context. Despite the massive adoption of online interaction, physical branches for retail organisations such as banks and shops are not disappearing. Humans still crave face-to-face contact, and retail organisations use branch networks as a source of competitive differentiation.

However, the challenge with branch networks is to determine the optimum number of servers to achieve a desired level of service. For example, a bank may wish to ensure that four out of five customers wait less than five minutes for service. Of course, an expensive way of achieving this is to over-staff the branch, but the preferable method is to observe the arrival rate of customers and how long it takes to serve each of them and use this data to estimate the number of servers required. Often the organisation will use people to observe and record the arrivals of customers, the queue lengths and the service time. This is done on a sampled basis and is often inaccurate due to fluctuations with time of day, day of week, month of year.

Technology developed in Australia,[23] offers a much more satisfactory solution. They use machine vision to continuously measure, in real-time, the arrival of customers, their wait time in the queue, the time to serve them and hence predict the necessary staff load at any time of day to achieve the desired service level. The machine vision takes the feeds from cameras in the branches and applies machine learning techniques to recognise 'people objects' and track their progress through the branch. It is important to note that it recognises 'people objects', not individuals, so there is no violation of either customer or staff privacy. A 'people object' is no different from a 'cat object' other than cats do not usually go shopping or go into bank branches.

Such technology improves human–human customer service as it allows organisations to meet their service targets at the optimum cost, thus improving customer satisfaction and staff satisfaction (the latter do not have to deal with frustrated customers).

Another intriguing example of this second category, that gained prominence during 2022, is the ChatGPT chatbot developed by OpenAI.[24] As stated above, ChatGPT is based on the GPT-3 algorithm which is still a machine learning algorithm and does not constitute Generalised AI. Because of its ability to recognise phrases as opposed to keywords, ChatGPT is effectively a 'question and answer system'. When you give it a query, instead of providing you a series of possible answers, ChatGPT constructs the most relevant answer based on the context it can achieve due to the phrase recognition. It is not totally clear how much of these answers are 'generated' as opposed to 'constructed' from material it has access to on the web or in its own databases.

ChatGPT is generating a great deal of excitement, not only because of its ability to write software programs, but also because of its ability to create written materials in different styles. Educational institutions are expressing great concern that it will be used by students to cheat. For example, I asked ChatGPT to answer a Year 12 English exam question and it was able to write an essay that experienced Year 12 English teachers say would have achieved a passing grade. While the essay itself would have satisfied the examiners, it was formulaic and 'wooden'. More importantly, there is an explainability problem as ChatGPT simply provides an answer without indicating its sources, thereby regularly leading to factual errors.[25]

Some educational establishments have responded to the ChatGPT issue by banning students from using it, which is a facile response. It is much more important to allow students to improve their productivity using ChatGPT and then focus on the limitations and aspects of the problem that are uniquely human. More to the point, by denying students access to ChatGPT they are actually denying students the ability to learn to use these new tools. It is not clear whether ChatGPT will replace human jobs (e.g., copywriters) or enhance them (e.g., by improving grammar, clarity and structure), but either way it is pointless training students in tasks which are better done using the tool.

3.5 DIGITAL TWINS

The second potentially enormous impact of the Internet of Things and machine learning is what are called 'Digital Twins'. Digital Twins are accurate simulations of real-world situations that can be updated in real time using measurements from the real objects.

The importance of Digital Twins is that they allow testing of situations that are not possible in the real world. For example, it would be difficult to safely test a huge wind turbine to destruction, but that could be done using a digital twin. Digital Twins also allow experiments to be run much more rapidly than is often possible in the real world, thereby allowing many more options to be tested in much shorter time.

Like cloud services, Digital Twins are expected to enable another 'Cambrian Explosion' of innovation, because of their ability to allow innovators to create and test many possible solutions to real-world problems.

3.6 AUTOMATION AND THE INTERNET OF THINGS IN AUSTRALIA

Australia has a long history of using technology to enhance primary industries, particularly agriculture and mining. The IoT is another step up in technology capability that can be applied to enhancing these industries, so like all developed countries, Australia is rapidly adopting the Internet of Things. However, what distinguishes Australia is its vast size and low population density which present unique challenges. In particular, the economics of deploying terrestrial wireless networks present considerable hurdles to viable business cases.

The new generation of LEO satellite networks referred to above have the potential to overcome the coverage challenges in that they ultimately promise to offer nationwide (indeed, global) coverage. However, the ground terminals and cost of service will in the short- to medium-term be somewhat expensive for most IoT applications. Consider an example of a farmer in the outback who wishes to monitor the water levels in all their remote boreholes. Some of these farms can cover millions of acres, so each borehole would probably require its own satellite terminal and service. At today's prices that represents an upfront cost of approximately A$500 and another approximately $1700 per annum for service.[26] This is a high price for a service which uses a few bytes of data per day.

An alternative would be for the farmer to purchase one (or a few) satellite terminals and then set up their own antenna to cover their farm using Wi-Fi or LoRA radio technologies. However, that has the disadvantage of the farmer needing to install and maintain their own farm-wide network which can also be problematic as wireless networks are subject to the vagaries described above and can be difficult to keep up.

3.6.1 Examples of Adoption

Despite these challenges, IoT is gaining adoption in Australia as the following examples illustrate.

3.6.1.1 Mining

The mining industry in Australia often operates in remote areas where finding workers is challenging and has thus been an early adopter of automation and the tele-operation of equipment. Because of the challenges of distance and the rewards from mining, the business cases for the adoption of automation and the IoT in mining are much easier to justify.

For example, recruitment challenges can be addressed by using autonomous and tele-operated trucks to move ore out of mines and load it onto autonomous trains.[27] Sensors on trucks can determine device wear and thus enable proactive maintenance. Underground operations can also be enhanced through autonomous or remotely controlled systems.[28]

3.6.1.2 Agriculture

Automation and IoT technologies can offer considerable advantages to farmers. Besides enabling the remote monitoring of distant infrastructure or livestock (as in the borehole example described above), new opportunities are emerging such as precision farming which allow farmers to minimise the use of scarce resources such as water and fertiliser. Drones or satellites are used to monitor crop health and identify areas needing additional attention. Robots can be used to inject just the right amount of water or fertiliser at each spot in the paddock. Australian farmers have been adopting such techniques for decades[29] and the wider adoption of IoT can be expected to make such methodologies more widespread.[30]

The use of 'robot cowboys' to facilitate the management of livestock is also being tested.[31]

While these are often early examples, the propensity of Australian farmers to adopt new technology means that these solutions will continue to grow and spread, thereby continuing Australia's leadership in effective and efficient agriculture.

3.7 CONCLUSION

Horatio
O day and night, but this is wondrous strange.

Hamlet
> And therefore as a stranger give it welcome.
> There are more things in heaven and earth, Horatio,
> Than are dreamt of in your philosophy.[32]

The digitisation of the physical world is going to create many issues, just as the digitisation of information has. Humans will inevitably find ways of abusing the power of the technology and creating unintended consequences, most of which we cannot foresee.

As an example, facial recognition technology, which is a consequence of machine learning and machine vision, can be used for many positive purposes such as allowing automatic correlation of a passport with the person standing at passport control, thereby improving the efficiency of airports. However, there are equally many ways of abusing the technology particularly if it is applied in a crass manner. US police, for example, are well known for taking the results of facial recognition systems and making arrests without checking the results. There have been cases of police arresting a perfectly innocent person in front of their family because they were incorrectly identified from surveillance camera footage using facial recognition technology.[33]

Despite the negative unintended consequences of the technology, we need to 'surf the wave' rather than trying Canute-like to stop it. As I have argued, the technology has enormous power to change human lives for the better. Banning the use of ChatGPT by students is a futile approach. It is far more preferable to transform the education system by incorporating the latest technology tools, allowing students to reach further and faster.

We also need to be realistic about the technology capabilities. Assuming that artificial intelligence is capable of achieving more than is realistically possible will lead to frustration and disappointment. For example, IBM pitched their 'Watson' AI software as being able to lead to a 'revolution in healthcare'. The results were underwhelming to say the least.[34] The point being that AI can make a difference in healthcare but only by incrementally complementing human physicians, not by replacing them in some revolutionary manner.

In conclusion, technology has the potential to slay the four horsemen of the modern apocalypse (climate change, healthcare, food and water supply, urbanisation), but we must understand its capabilities, apply it judicially and ensure laws and regulations are sufficiently up to date to steer it in the right direction.

NOTES

1 https://en.wikipedia.org/wiki/Moore's_law
2 https://en.wikipedia.org/wiki/Von_Neumann_architecture
3 https://www.ibm.com/au-en/topics/what-is-blockchain
4 https://en.wikipedia.org/wiki/Foundation_series
5 https://www.ben-evans.com/benedictevans/2019/5/28/the-end-of-mobile
6 https://www.whistleout.com.au/MobilePhones/Guides/who-has-the-best-mobile-coverage
7 https://www.telstra.com.au/content/dam/shared-component-assets/tecom/iot/capabilities/iot-global-connect/pdf/iot-global-connect-brochure.pdf
8 https://en.wikipedia.org/wiki/Rayleigh_fading#:~:text=Rayleighpercent20fadingpercent20modelspercent20assumepercent20that,twopercent20uncorrelatedpercent20Gaussianpercent20randompercent20variables
9 https://www.youtube.com/watch?v=tTdIM2HtA00&ab_channel=TechTrained
10 https://www.csoonline.com/article/3258748/the-mirai-botnet-explained-how-teen-scammers-and-cctv-cameras-almost-brought-down-the-internet.html
11 https://csa-iot.org/
12 https://www.wsj.com/articles/verizon-invests-in-self-driving-car-startup-renovo-1493298001
13 https://www.nytimes.com/2018/02/09/technology/facial-recognition-race-artificial-intelligence.html
14 https://www.analyticsinsight.net/what-are-gpt-3-parameters/#:~:text=Aboutpercent20175percent20billionpercent20MLpercent20parameters,createdpercent20aspercent20ofpercent20earlypercent202021
15 https://www.springboard.com/blog/data-science/machine-learning-gpt-3-open-ai/
16 https://www.numenta.com/blog/2022/05/24/ai-is-harming-our-planet/#:~:text=Onepercent20popularpercent20modelpercent2Cpercent20GPTpercent2D3,GPTpercent2D3percent20consumedpercent20936percent20MWh
17 A human brain has been estimated to process at 4 exaflops (https://newsroom.ucla.edu/releases/ucla-research-upend-long-held-belief-about-how-neurons-communicate) compared to the 200 petaflops of the Summit supercomputer.
18 https://www.nrspp.org.au/resources/human-error-in-road-accidents/
19 https://futurism.com/video-elon-musk-promising-self-driving-cars
20 http://www.bikewalknc.org/2018/02/autonomous-driving-and-collision-avoidance-technology/
21 http://www.bikewalknc.org/2018/02/autonomous-driving-and-collision-avoidance-technology/
22 https://www.nhtsa.gov/sites/nhtsa.gov/files/2022-05/Level-of-Automation-052522-tag.pdf
23 https://www.rocketboots.com/
24 https://openai.com/
25 https://www.cnbc.com/2023/02/10/steve-wozniak-warns-about-ai-chatgpt-can-make-horrible-mistakes.html#:~:text=Whenpercent20CNBCpercent20

Makepercent20Itpercent20asked,mathpercent20equationspercent20orperce
nt20logicpercent20problems

26 https://www.starlink.com/
27 https://www.okc-sk.com/integrating-automated-mining-equipment/#:~:text=
   Examplespercent20ofpercent20automatedpercent20miningpercent20technol
   ogy,controlledpercent20trainspercent20andpercent20otherpercent20vehicles
28 https://www.austrade.gov.au/ArticleDocuments/2814/Mining-Automation-
   Technologies-flyer.pdf.aspx
29 https://ag.purdue.edu/ssmc/newsletters/march03_glimpseofprecisionagri
   cultureaustralia_gregedit1.htm
30 https://www.youtube.com/watch?v=LTNdQk_u-gI&ab_channel=Facultyof
   Engineeringpercent2CUniversityofSydney
31 https://www.youtube.com/watch?v=cZVUYJhXXzo&ab_channel=
   NewScientist
32 Hamlet, Act 1, Scene 5. https://myshakespeare.com/hamlet/act-1-scene-5
33 https://www.wired.com/story/wrongful-arrests-ai-derailed-3-mens-lives
   /#:~:text=Robertpercent20Williamspercent2Cpercent20Michaelpercent
   20Oliverpercent2Cpercent20and,impactpercent20castpercent20apercent
   20longpercent20shadow.&text=Robertpercent20Williamspercent20wasperc
   ent20doingpercent20yard,neededpercent20apercent20familypercent20meet
   ingpercent20immediately
34 https://www.statnews.com/2017/09/05/watson-ibm-cancer/

REFERENCES

Frey, C. B., & Osborne, M. A. (2013). The Future of Employment: How Susceptible
   Are Jobs to Computerization? Oxford Martin School Working Paper.
   https://www.oxfordmartin.ox.ac.uk/downloads/academic/The_Future_of_
   Employment.pdf

Grosan, C., & Abraham, A. (2011). Artificial Neural Networks. In: Intelligent
   Systems. Intelligent Systems Reference Library, vol. 17. Springer, Berlin,
   Heidelberg. https://doi.org/10.1007/978-3-642-21004-4_12

Jensen, R. (2007). The Digital Provide: Information (Technology), Market
   Performance, and Welfare in the South Indian Fisheries Sector. The Quarterly
   Journal of Economics, 122(3), 879–924. http://www.jstor.org/stable/25098864

Manyika, J., Lund, S., Chui, M., Bughin, J., Woetzel, J., Batra, P., Ko, R., & Sanghvi,
   S. (2017).5 Jobs Lost, Jobs Gained: Workforce Transitions in a Time of
   Automation.McKinseyGlobalInstitute.https://www.mckinsey.com/featured-
   insights/future-of-work/jobs-lost-jobs-gained-what-the-future-of-work-
   will-mean-for-jobs-skills-and-wages

Meeker, M. (2017). Internet Trends 2017 – Code Conference. https://www.
   kleinerperkins.com/perspectives/internet-trends-report-2017/

Sharma, G. (2016). The Future of Search, Commerce, and Payments: Why VOICE
   Is the New Platform You Need to Pay Attention To. https://medium.com/@
   gaurav.sharma/voice-is-the-new-o-s-and-the-future-of-search-commerce-
   and-payments-64fc8cc848f6

CHAPTER 4

Charging Ahead

Electric Vehicles as Advanced Industrial Opportunity

Mark Dean

G LOBAL ECONOMIC ACTORS ARE rapidly mobilising to capture competitive shares of new technologies, industries, supply chains and
markets relating to the renewable energy transition. This presents significant opportunities for the development of new skills and occupations for
the future of work in the global manufacturing sector. Within the renewable energy transition, manufacturing industries will be a major driver of
decarbonisation in the global economy and thus define, to a significant
extent, how the world responds to threats posed by climate change and
ecological collapse. A future of work that is shaped by "reindustrialisation
as decarbonisation" (Worrall et al., 2022) will be coloured by major technological innovations emanating, as before, from global manufacturing
industries with automotive production at their core.

Many advanced industrial nations possess highly innovative automotive industries, and most of the major global automotive OEMs (Original
Equipment Manufacturers) are quickly moving towards global production platforms with increasing shares of electric vehicles (EVs). According
to data from the International Energy Agency, shares of EV sales in Asia,
Europe and North America increased modestly between 2017 and 2020,
but exponentially between 2020 and 2021 (IEA, 2022). By 2030, many
OEMs will produce only EVs, most of which will contain a lithium-ion
battery as a "substitution is unlikely to emerge over the medium term"
(DISER, 2019, p. 12). By the 2040s, it is possible that the global market for
new light passenger vehicles will comprise entirely EVs.

DOI: 10.1201/9781003393757-4

The global supply chain implications of a shift from internal combustion engine (ICE) vehicles to battery electric vehicles (BEV) are immense. There is an essential difference between an EV-powered industrial transformation and its ICE predecessor: the energy source for EVs is the most complex and valuable component of the vehicle itself, rather than just an external energy source produced for use as an input (i.e., fossil fuel–based sources like diesel and petroleum). Hence, the future of work and industry in EV manufacturing depends intrinsically on global value chains for critical and rare earth metals. On a scale like nothing before, the demand for global critical minerals and rare earths will integrate the resources sectors of nations like Australia with its resurging manufacturing sector and supply chains. This chapter will explore the possibilities of such economic sectoral integration in the EV-powered industrial transformation and focus on the Australian case of a nation that has much to gain from an EV-charged future if it can develop the production and policy environment to both address challenges, and capture opportunities.

4.1 IS AUSTRALIA PREPARED FOR THE FUTURE OF WORK?

An EV-driven future of work presents one of the best opportunities for Australia to restore its industrial base. Manufacturing underpins innovation and transformation in all advanced industrial nations. It is a knowledge- and technology-intensive activity central to the process of economic development; its activities form the foundations of more economically complex and competitive economies. This is evidenced throughout modern history and is detailed in studies that highlight the central role of manufacturing in all stages of the development of industrial nations (see Kaldor, 1967; McCausland & Theodossiou, 2012; Porter, 1990; Wang, 2009). According to Stanford (2020a), manufacturing is not just another sector; rather, it carries strategic importance. It is the most innovation-intensive sector of the economy and anchors hundreds of thousands of other jobs throughout the economy through its dependence on long and complex supply chains. It offers relatively high-quality jobs and is more likely to provide full-time hours and above-average incomes. In the international context, manufactured goods account for most of international trade, and hence an undersized manufacturing sector will contribute to trade deficits and balance-of-payments problems. Such external economic problems are driven by major internal economic issues and these problems, though brought to the surface by the COVID-19 pandemic, are ultimately the products of a long and serious failure of Australian policy-makers to prepare for the future of work.

Despite the importance of manufacturing to a nation's economy, a significant amount of Australia's manufacturing capabilities has been off-shored since the 1990s. Such offshoring had occurred under government policy responses common throughout advanced industrial nations, typically defined by free trade agreements with "newly" industrialising nations that would thereafter supply far cheaper imports of manufactured goods. In the decades since, this has left Australia ill-prepared to capture emerging industrial opportunities. The consequences of a "resource curse" – massive economic growth that is not accompanied by proportionate economic (and social) development – have become embedded in Australia's industrial strategy, as made evident in Figure 4.1.

This comparison of Australia's resource commodity exports to manufacturing exports illustrates the clear industrial policy failures of Australian governments' support for resource extraction and commodities export, which has been given at the expense of manufacturing. In the

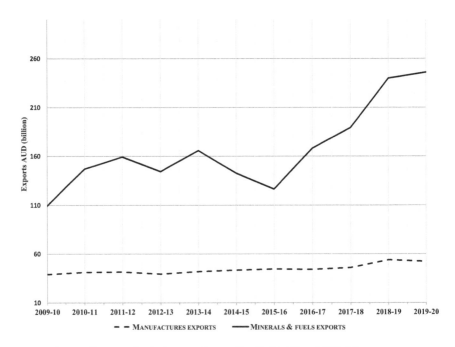

FIGURE 4.1   Exports by industry: Australia, 2009–10 to 2019–20.

Source: author's analysis based on data in DFAT, 2021.

years after the Global Financial Crisis, the Coalition government had rein-
forced the default setting of Australian industrial policy – that of an
approach to economic growth which has favoured resource commodity
extraction for more than 30 years. The extraction and export of unpro-
cessed, non-renewable resources does not produce the same developmen-
tal opportunities for a nation's economy and, therefore, minimises
opportunities for social development in terms of jobs, skills, and communities (see Fernandes, 2021).

4.2 THE CONSEQUENCES OF NOT PREPARING FOR THE FUTURE OF WORK AND A RETURN TO STRATEGY

In the 1960s, the manufacturing sector accounted for approximately 30
percent of Australia's GDP and total employment. But since the disman-
tling of tariff protection from the 1970s and subsequent decline in industry assistance, Australia's manufacturing sector has struggled (Weller and
O'Neill, 2014). The share of both GDP and employment has undergone a
significant decline, accounting for just 10 percent of GDP and less than 6
percent of employment in 2020 (Productivity Commission, 2021a). This
decline reflects changes brought about by the forces of economic globalisation, whereby manufacturers relocated much of their production to
cheaper, industrialising nations and work in more developed nations like
Australia shifted rapidly to services sector employment (i.e., health, ICT,
finance). But the rate at which this decline in manufacturing employment
took effect results from a lack of industrial strategy, as tariffs on imports
were gradually rolled back after the post-war boom period and replaced
with only a market-oriented treatment of industrial development. The
2017 closure of the Australian automotive industry illustrated for many
how precarious the country's manufacturing sector had become under
these policies (Clibborn et al., 2016).

Like Australia, many other industrial nations offshored segments of
their manufacturing capabilities. However, these other nations also
retained whole industries they considered key to guaranteeing an ongoing
sovereign capability with which to develop competitive strengths and, via
exports, service growing overseas markets where sustainable domestic
demand cannot alone sustain domestic production. Arguably no developed nation relinquished as much of their manufacturing capability as
Australia has over the past 30 years. This has made Australia the least self-
sufficient country for manufacturing in the OECD, producing the lowest

proportion of its own domestic requirements for consumption of manufactures of any OECD country (AITI, 2021). Much of the vulnerability this reflects was entrenched with the decision of the Federal conservative Liberal–National Party Coalition government to remove fiscal support to the automotive industry, leading to the closure of General Motors-Holden in 2017, the last OEM building light passenger vehicles in Australia. The government at the time provided no coordinated response to the industry's closure, narrowing the path by which automotive supply chains could transition to other high value-adding industries and retain the complexity of Australia's industrial base.

Through strong lead customer relationships in automotive industries had come the transmission of requirements along the value chain, and the development of common high competences and standards. Today, Australian manufacturing SMEs (small- and medium-sized enterprises) are less likely to be part of such a complex, articulated vertically integrated value chain, or substantial positive ecosystem. Before the COVID-19 pandemic, voices within the manufacturing sector were already warning that Australia's antipathy to value-adding activities, like manufacturing, in favour of industries that require little more than digging up and exporting raw commodity resources with no added value, had left the nation dangerously dependent on "quarrying" (Roberts, 2019, blogging in *Australian Manufacturing Forum*). These voices were proved correct when, as Australia came to grips with the economic effects of the pandemic, it was left critically vulnerable in terms of sovereign manufacturing capability. The lack of Australian manufacturing self-sufficiency was brought to the fore when, as reviewed in *The Lancet*, the nation was soon unable to provide its own supply of personal protective equipment (PPE) to frontline health workers, requiring extensive over-reliance on offshore supply chains (Basseal et al., 2023). By 2021, Australian manufacturing employed around 908,000 people; less than 7 percent of the total workforce (ABS, 2023), and representing a weak position from which to rebuild the nation's industrial capabilities.

Australia's "extractivist" industry policy focus means the nation's economy ranks poorly in terms of economic complexity – a measure of how well a nation can assemble diverse elements of knowledge and technology to create high-value, innovative products for export (see Gamble, this volume, for an in-depth analysis). This is an industrial failure – one evident in the global analysis of economic complexity carried out by The Growth Lab at Harvard University (2022), which ranks Australia 86th out of 133 countries surveyed. This is a surprisingly weak position for an advanced industrial economy.[1] Other major industrial nations rank mostly within the top 20 for economic complexity.

Despite poor economic complexity rankings, Australia's performance on key indicators of innovative capability has improved in recent years. In 2022, Australia ranked 19th out of 63 countries in the Institute for Management Development's World Competitiveness Ranking, moving up three places since 2021 (IMD 2022; 2021). The Committee for Economic Development Australia (CEDA) considered Australia's pandemic recovery and strong terms of trade as primary factors in this jump in position; but noted that, compared with top-performing nations, a weak policy environment and lack of investment in technology, energy, skills and training, entrepreneurship, tax and productivity would continue to hold Australia back from creating a sustainable economic environment for emerging global industrial opportunities (CEDA, 2022). Previous studies of these indicators within Australia determined that the nation was poorly connected into Global Value Chains (GVC) (apart from the resources sector) and that even Australian small businesses did not have a great record of innovation (Cunningham et al., 2016). Hence, CEDA further noted that "Australia's export concentration remains an area of vulnerability. Australia must lift its game on trade – diversifying its trading partners and continuing to build new markets for the goods and services in which we compete" (CEDA, 2022). Reinforcing this position, the OECD (2023, p. 5) recommended that the best policies to strengthen the resilience of GVCs following the COVID-19 pandemic would be to mobilise government fiscal support for technological innovations and worker skills developments that reduce foreign dependencies.

Essentially, the peak global institution for economic policy prescriptions for the advanced industrial nations of the world has recommended government investment in the future of work and workers as the pathway to build more resilient, productive and innovative economies. Thus, Australia must seek an industrial policy aimed at developing its workforce and preparing them for work with the technologies of the future to lift its level of economic complexity. As evidenced by its burgeoning rankings on the measures for competitiveness, this is something Australia can achieve with the right strategic policy and institutional settings. This will need to exhibit a radical departure from the orthodox policy prescription of market-based industry "policy", supported by a political philosophy of neoliberalism.

4.3 A NEW APPROACH TO THE FUTURE OF WORK IN AUSTRALIA

Despite many fundamental advantages, Australia has gone backwards in terms of advanced manufacturing in recent decades. This is evidenced by Australia's declining economic complexity and diminishing investment in industrial machinery and equipment discussed above. In these respects, we are an international outlier, as other developed countries and emerging economies have generally been investing in advanced manufacturing capabilities. The pandemic revealed the shortcomings of deliberately deindustrialising advanced economies and drew widespread attention to a relative "reversal" of neoliberalism amongst industrialised and industrialising countries alike – a phenomenon noted by Worrall et al. (2022, p. 1):

> Although it is far from universal or uniform, many advanced nations are retreating from the former orthodoxy of "the best government is the least government". The idea that government should confine its economic roles to macroeconomic stabilisation and correcting occasional "failures" in a generally "perfect" market, has gone under.

These authors continue that that there is growing evidence of "ambitious and expansive ideas of active industrial policy" (ibid.), characterised by the *opposite* of neoliberal, market-based prescriptions. Industrial policies that target specific sectoral development for strategic advantages are again a major undertaking of nations that seek new sources of inclusive growth to address systemic challenges like climate change and social and economic inequality.

What explains Australia's comparative decline? Several observers – from unions, industry and academia – have argued that Australia has failed to develop a co-ordinated industry policy (see Wood, 2022; AMWU, 2021). The outcome of the situation that Australia currently faces presents its economy and institutions with major challenges as it attempts to shape the future of work. Where this will be one defined to a significant extent by industrial opportunities in manufacturing industries, taking the right approach to production and policy responses becomes crucial. Therefore, the new Australian government's ambitious industrial policy aims in its AUD15 billion *National Reconstruction Fund* (DISR, 2023) have been a welcome sign of leadership following ten years of relative neglect by the conservative Coalition government it replaced at the 2021 federal election.

The failures of a neoliberal, "small-government" mean it is now incumbent upon the federal government to enact strategic industrial policy measures that can restore the sovereign capabilities Australia requires to create and sustain a future of work in high-value manufacturing industries.

As this chapter will show, a reindustrialisation of Australia's economy through strategic industrial policy begins with EV industries but continues in the form of far wider-ranging sustainable technology industries that integrate and coordinate multiple sectors of the economy. This will create a significant industrial base for Australia's acquisition of the skills and capabilities necessary for a range of advanced forms of manufacturing, including for defence materiel and renewable energy infrastructure. Although the focus of this chapter is on the case for rebuilding Australia's skills and industrial base, the same industrial transformation processes are applicable for all nations that seek to advance their economies or reindustrialise their manufacturing sector in a decarbonising global economy.

4.4 FRAMING THE FUTURE OF WORK: PRODUCTION AND POLICY

Australia's future of work must be one enabled by advanced industry; and in turn, advanced industry will only be enabled by a strategic focus on the development of "sovereign capability". A framework in which to explore the key technologies that will be part of achieving sovereign capability is offered by Worrall (2023) in a recent contribution in the *Australian Manufacturing Forum* blog, which explains that for the Australian economy "to produce goods and services that are of strategic value to the national interest" "production" and "policy" are both essential. In the same piece, Worrall (ibid.) elaborates on "production", arguing that

> Direct onshore production and manufacture are almost always the necessary condition (if not always a sufficient one) for capture of dynamic broader capacities relating to design, systems integration, technological innovation, through-life support and maintenance, and overall operational capability, that are also critical to sovereign capability.

The purpose of government is to set national directions for industrial policy within which to establish and develop onshore production that meets strategic economic and societal aims. Such policy, Worrall contends, must hold strategic intent to develop:

the economic, technological, organisational, logistic and operational capacities of the nation [without which] sovereign capability is just a hope. Political leadership, authoritative, expert and accountable institutions, and explicit targets are critical.

(WORRALL, IBID.)

These principles are the logical distillation of strategic industrial policy concepts iterated throughout the work of Mariana Mazzucato and colleagues (Mazzucato 2022; Mazzucato & Perez, 2022; Mazzucato et al., 2022) and indicate the importance of redirecting economic growth away from speculative, short-term and finance-based incentives and towards inclusive, sustainable and innovation-led transformations – in other words, massive reinvestment in the "real" economy (i.e., that based in trade of goods and services, rather than company shares and digital currencies). In the wake of a global health crisis exacerbated by neoliberalism, the only legitimate way to achieve sustainable, innovation-led growth – and accompanying economic development rather than just economic growth (as measured by GDP) – is to mobilise the institutional and policy instruments of government to develop productive capacity. In the following section, these principles of production and policy are applied to an overview of the key enabling technologies and opportunities that can (a) emerge from the economic integration of strategic economic sectors of Australia's economy; (b) help to underwrite further economic opportunities in sustainable industries and (c) contribute towards the augmented development of Australia's sovereign capabilities. The analysis below demonstrates that a future of work that focuses on complex, advanced manufacturing opportunities that begin with an EV manufacturing industry, results in a diverse range of innovative, inclusive forms of industrialisation.

4.5 THE PATH TO REBUILDING ADVANCED INDUSTRY

The first step towards an advanced industrial future of work in Australia is realising the importance of developing productive capabilities that significantly reduce the nation's dependence on the export of raw commodities. The export of raw materials may yield high returns over temporary periods of strong commodity prices, but as a long-term economic strategy, extraction hollows out higher-value manufacturing industrial capabilities. In the case of Australia, this places it on a pathway to eventual economic stagnation. Ultimately a successful nation in the globalised economy must export complex, elaborately transformed manufactured goods to develop and retain high standards of living, skilled workforces and productive economies. In Australia's case, this means shifting its resources sector towards more elaborately transformed manufactured goods which have undergone value-adding processes at higher stages of the critical minerals value chain.

Australian exports of commodities including lithium, cobalt, bauxite, zinc, silicon and rare earth elements (i.e., vanadium and graphite) have significant relevance to EV industries. Lithium, cobalt and nickel are the primary minerals critical to the electrification of road transport, given that they are the primary metals forming the base of lithium-ion battery technologies (IEA, 2021). Geoscience Australia has reported that the refining opportunities for all these minerals are significant, and especially so in the case of spodumene[2] processing. Whilst the export value of spodumene increased in 2021–22 to AUD4.9 billion with export figures at 335,000 tonnes, this was projected to increase to 399,000 tonnes in 2022–23 (an export revenue value of AUD16.1 billion) and 470,000 tonnes in 2023–24 (AUD17 billion in export revenue) (DISER, 2022). But without manufacturing production further along the value chain, Australia will continue to yield revenues far short of the expected returns from downstream value-adding especially as demand for inputs to manufacturing batteries for EVs increases exponentially. This is confirmed by analysis of lithium opportunities from the Future Battery Industries Cooperative Research Centre (FBICRC), which showed that production of spodumene yielded AUD1.1 billion in 2017, whereas "the major value-adding steps, including precursor production that was worth $22.1 billion" was carried out overseas instead of in Australia's downstream processing industries (FBICRC, 2020, p. 7).

A strategy to participate in the higher value-adding phases of battery and component production could be a boon for Australia. The Global Battery Alliance (2019) has suggested that there are far greater value-adding and employment opportunities to be gained from stages beyond extraction, particularly in production phases focused on refining battery materials like lithium, developing battery cells and packs, and eventually processing these materials for reuse and recycling. Aiming for such higher levels of participation in global renewables manufacturing could see more advanced forms of manufacturing and more jobs in value-adding industries in Australia – particularly in regions transitioning from fossil fuel–based energy production – if policy is strategically shaped to maximise emerging opportunities.

Other major employment opportunities in the resources sector can be gained by Australia through attention to a long-term plan for local battery recycling, as recommended by researchers at Australia's Commonwealth Scientific and Industrial Research Organisation (CSIRO) (King & Boxall, 2019). Several Australian companies are already exploring commercial battery lifecycle opportunities, demonstrating how manufacturing supply chains can participate in the recycling of batteries at their end-of-life, breaking them down for reconstitution into batteries or repurposing them as storage for home solar energy or commercial energy storage applications. In these and other ways, EV battery manufacturing can put domestically mined minerals into Australian-made batteries. An EV industry could become the centrepiece of a complex web of supply and value chains connected to the circular economy, spurning collaborative R&D initiatives, diverse market demand and reduced costs to consumers.

The connection of EV industries in the manufacturing sector to critical mineral industries in the resources sector is further elucidated with reference to the future of work Australia can develop in relation to secure supplies of critical elements for energy generation, such as silicon which is needed for photovoltaic technologies (as well as computer chips and other electronics). Although Australia has a high level of both domestic and commercial solar cell application, as of 2023 there is only one Australian-owned manufacturer based in the country and that firm assembles units imported from China. The solar panel supply chain is at present dominated by China, which holds more than 70 percent of all downstream activity, including 85–97 percent of all ingot, wafers and solar cell manufacturing (How, 2022a, 2022b). Miller (2021) notes that nations in East Asia produce a total of 90 percent of memory chips globally, 75 percent of all processor (logic) chips and 80 percent of all silicon wafers.

Within this geopolitical context, Australia's national science agency in 2022 published the *Australian Silicon Action Plan* (CSIRO, 2022) exploring opportunities for the future of work in advanced manufacturing industries. It argued that the country needed to develop its own fully integrated domestic solar supply chain to not remain vulnerable to overseas suppliers for solar cell technology. Thus, silicon has been identified by the government as a critical element for the purpose of becoming more self-sufficient in domestic supply chains for solar cell, semi-conductor, optical alloy and battery storage. This was necessary for not only being a critical step towards energy security but, furthermore, to support economic growth and jobs across Australia's regions and cities (Ibid.).

4.6 SKILLS FOR EV SUPPLY CHAINS AND CAPABILITIES

Before Australia can manufacture advanced components that contain domestically mined, processed and refined critical minerals, it must guarantee supply chains for these inputs. An EV industry makes such downstream developments feasible. Australia will require skilled labour to grow and develop sophisticated EV industry supply chains. This presents significant challenges, but Australia already possesses an industrial workforce of skilled and experienced workers, capable of building the foundational industrial base of what can become a growing EV industry.

New models of advanced manufacturing naturally require large numbers of highly trained workers in all occupations: production workers, skilled trades people, technicians and engineers. Despite having skills shortages in many of these areas, Australia nonetheless maintains a base of highly skilled manufacturing workers which forms a base upon which an advanced manufacturing sector can be built (Stanford, 2020a). Vehicle components manufacturing has retained a significant footprint in Australia despite ICE assembly plant shutdowns in the past decade entailing a significant loss of jobs. In recent years, the vehicle components manufacturing sub-sector has even shown indications of expansion, as shown in Table 4.1 (ABS, 2023). Thousands of workers continue to build automotive parts, meaning Australian products are still supplied to heavy vehicle (i.e., bus, truck and trailer) manufacturing firms throughout the country, and to global automotive manufacturing industries.

To support the expansion of EV components production and final assembly work, Australia must also invest urgently in the relevant skills that underpin greater domestic involvement in global EV supply chains. Developing and delivering new training programs for EV industry apprentices will be essential to preparing skilled labour for the future of

TABLE 4.1 Motor Vehicle and Motor Vehicle Part Manufacturing (ANZSCO sub-sector 231) Australia – 2019–20 – 2020–21 (AUD millions)

Indicator	2019–20	2020–21	2021–22
Employment (at end June)	34,258	33,494	36,953
Wages and salaries	2,274	2,285	2,428
Sales and service income	14,753	15,069	16,951
Industry value-added	3,956	4,500	5,498

Note: ANZSCO = Australian and New Zealand Standard Industrial Classification.

EV manufacturing work. Australia's Vocational Education and Training (VET) system will need to deliver whole new units of competency and there are currently acute skills and training barriers to expanding EV production in Australia. In 2020, the Industry Reference Committee representing the automotive industry, along with the Australian Industry and Skills Committee, proposed changes to the "Automotive Retail, Service and Repair" Vocational Education Training Package to create new qualifications and units of competency that support skills for the EV industry (PwC & DESE, 2020). But the proposed changes, being the implementation of Certificate II (non-trade traineeship) qualifications, do not support the creation of pathways for workers into higher-paid and higher-skilled jobs, which would involve at least a Certificate III-level qualification (trade-based apprenticeship). This results in a backwards step from the base-level trade qualification required for work in EV industries. But the advanced technological nature of EVs means associated occupations will be characterised by higher-level jobs requiring Certificate III or higher qualifications. A narrow scope of skills reform for EV industries will continue to limit Australia's opportunities to capture a valuable share of production work in global value chains.

A root-and-branch industry profiling exercise is required to fully account for the future workforce needs of an advanced EV industry in Australia. The Australian Manufacturing Workers' Union (AMWU) has for several years been proposing the establishment of "Occupational Profiles". Based on several components, these would include an occupational standard and a collaboratively developed national industry framework curriculum or training standard. Occupational Profiles would ideally contain two types of industry-level categorisation of jobs and occupations. The first categorisation would cover occupations where there is a high level of consistency and mobility in the skills and capabilities required and where there is industry consensus that a full nationally recognised Occupational Profile is warranted. The second categorisation is of occupations that may require consistent underpinning foundation and core skills, but the inherent diversity of work associated with the occupation would make an Occupational Profile inappropriate.

For a successful future of work driven by appropriate industrial skills transformation, the development of the labour market must be industry driven and prescribed to delivery by the relevant government agencies. Union involvement in the identification, design and development of Occupational Profiles is critical where, even as increased digitalisation and automation shapes manufacturing, the role of workers remains pivotal to highly skilled and complex manufacturing processes. Subsequently, EV industry policy must be developed in a way that recognises workers possess not only qualifications, but also skills informed by experience. Studies of some of the world's most sophisticated automotive supply chains have determined that even in highly automated workplaces, the experiential knowledge and skills of workers is an essential ingredient in highly advanced, digitalised and automated industrial systems (see Pfeiffer & Suphan, 2015). Human skills become critical inputs in firms that acknowledge workers' first-hand knowledge of production processes is more than just "routine", and therefore is not straightforwardly replaced by labour-saving technologies. The ramifications of this recognition of the value of workers' all-round knowledge for transforming VET-based skills provision are enormous. Industry policy that places skills at its centre will manage the transition to an EV industry by ensuring competent workers are active in shaping advanced manufacturing workplaces.

4.7 FROM EV INDUSTRIES TO RENEWABLE TECHNOLOGIES

As mentioned previously in this chapter, the renewable transformation of Australia's economy can be made sustainable by grounding it in advanced manufacturing innovation shaped by EV industries. However, the role of vehicle manufacture is itself limited if we are to address our climate change obligations (discussed later in this chapter). Ford Chief Executive Jim Farley has even pointed out that electric vehicles need 40 percent fewer workers to assemble than cars and trucks powered by petrol, largely because battery electric vehicles have fewer parts and are easier to assemble (Bushey, 2022). Reaching the maximum figure by 2040 requires significant investment in the enabling industries now – EVs and the related supply chains that can build the skills base for a future of work shaped significantly by renewable energy industries.

Australia has unrivalled access to natural resources in terms of sun (solar), wind and waves, among other resources, of any developed nation (Garnaut, 2019). The aim of an EV industry would be to develop industrial capacity to develop a future of work that broadens extensively into a range of renewable industries in which Australia's natural endowments are a prerequisite from which it can develop competitive advantages in global value chains. Rutovitz et al. (2022) have estimated that renewably transforming Australia's energy grid will require at least 15,000 workers by

2025 just to get the power grid to 82 percent renewables by 2030. Other estimates of employment growth in renewable energy industries from 2020 to 2035 vary from 21,000 to 34,400 (Clean Energy Council, 2022). Yet a report prepared by Accenture (2021) for the FBICRC claimed that clean export industry opportunities have the potential to generate AUD89 billion of gross value-add to the Australian economy and 395,000 jobs in 2040, let alone created across the next two decades.

But as with EVs, whatever figure for renewable jobs becomes reality, elaborate policy is required for production. In reports produced for the Centre for Future Work, Nahum (2020, p. 51) has argued that the future of work in Australia's renewable industries requires coordinating a national response, underwriting state-level policies and partnering with renewable energy firms and manufacturers. Jim Stanford (2020b, pp. 54–55) has shown how conventional statistics on renewable energy job-creation opportunities in Australia typically understate the total employment in renewables: most projections do not count indirect renewables jobs across the economy, such as in electricity supply, construction, and, of course, manufacturing. The combination of production with policy will grow and sustain a labour market that builds off the EV industrial base for generations to come.

4.8 THE FUTURE OF WORK BEYOND CARS

With reference to such possibilities and developments already underway, an EV industry in Australia is not a magic bullet for ending our social, political, and environmental woes – and nor should it be. An Australian EV strategy based simply on a 1:1 replacement of ICEs with EVs would "lock in" systems of production and transportation, and an over-reliance on private vehicles, that are ecologically unsustainable. Not just Australia, but the global community too, must rethink our relationship to cars and consider more socially and environmentally sustainable modes of transport (i.e., public transport, cycling, walking) to meaningfully address climate change (Mattioli et al., 2020; Morgan, 2021). Therefore, an Australian EV manufacturing industry should be seen as one major component of a far more wide-reaching approach to addressing climate change and creating a sustainable future.

Australia is thus in an enviable position of being able to rethink what an EV industry could look like. For example, by utilising its existing industrial base and mobilising it for a renewable future, Australia can develop its industrial capabilities around a competitive advantage in what could be broadly described as "applied renewable energy solutions". The Australian EV manufacturing industry would then produce not just cars for private use and for government and private business fleets, but also Australian-made electric-powered trains, trams, buses, ferries, motorcycles, bicycles, scooters and more. The domestic refining of lithium would supply industries that develop batteries for these forms of transport, as well as for energy infrastructure networks. As Australia's energy system increasingly draws on renewable sources, the capacity to utilise abundant renewable energy resources to support high-value product and service exports will grow as well.

Governments in Australia can mobilise and advertise this global competitive advantage and its related products and services as a nation-building strategy, and as a global export opportunity. The goal should be to provide sustainable solutions to problems that emerge from dependence on ICEs and other carbon-intensive forms of transport, and ways of living and doing business. This would focus Australian technological innovations on decarbonising transport systems and demonstrating an economy-wide store of renewable energy knowledge, skills and capabilities, expressed in the form of increased economic complexity.

4.9 THE DEFENCE INDUSTRIAL COMPLEX AND ALTERNATIVES FOR THE REINDUSTRIALISATION OF AUSTRALIA

Much comment has been made regarding the 15 March 2023 AUKUS (Australia–United Kingdom–United States) announcement that the governments of Australia, the US and the UK will work in partnership to build a future generation of nuclear-powered submarines. AUKUS commits the partners to the full-scale construction of "SSN-AUKUS"-class nuclear-powered (but not nuclear-armed) submarines in Adelaide, Australia, for the Australian Navy from the mid-2030s. The enormous scale of AUKUS prompted the Australian Prime Minister Albanese in his remarks at the announcement to note the project's significance:

> just as the vision of my predecessors, Curtin and Chifley [wartime and post-war Labor Government leaders, respectively], in creating our automotive industry, lifted up our entire manufacturing sector, this investment will be a catalyst for innovation and research breakthroughs that will reverberate right throughout the Australian economy and across every state and territory. Not just

in one design element, not just in one field, but right across our advanced manufacturing and technology sectors, creating jobs and growing businesses, right around Australia, inspiring and rewarding innovation, and educating young Australians today for the opportunities of tomorrow.

(PRIME MINISTER OF AUSTRALIA, 2023)

Albanese's conjecture regarding the project's innovation and economic growth potential may be correct; and indeed, the AUKUS project drew immediate and widespread support in mainstream Australian media (Lewis, 2023). Even with the attached AUD368 billion price tag that Australian taxpayers will foot over the next several decades, some commentators lauded the government's "missiles and people" approach of AUKUS in conjoining foreign policy and economic policy (Crowe, 2023). But others have hinted at the likely cuts to social, health and education spending that the government will justify in paying for it (Hurst & Borger, 2023).

This presents a tricky political position for the current government, and any decisions it makes regarding public expenditure in the years to come will attract major scrutiny. The Australian Shipbuilding Federation of Unions (ASFU) has been warning for several years that Australia still faces questions of workforce development and industrial capability (ASFU, 2022). Without addressing these factors in the very near term, the AUKUS project risks failing to overcome the dreaded "valley of death" that results when major defence projects end and workforces are not rapidly retrained and redeployed to begin work, relatively seamlessly, on a new project which amounts to a "continuous build" and the sustainment of industrial capabilities. The ASFU (2022, p. 10) has explicitly warned of a capability gap of approximately ten years between the end of the "Collins"-class submarine sustainment program and the commencement of the AUKUS submarine project. This gap could be a death knell for the shipbuilding industry, and rather than AUKUS be the catalyst for Australia's reindustrialisation, it would entrench its deindustrialisation and hollow out the manufacturing workforce further. Thus, the threat of a valley of death being realised could mean also the Australian Government making the wrong bet on AUKUS as the driver of sovereign capability.

Australia must build something to reindustrialise its economy. Although the major focus from the government in this regard is on manufacturing naval vessels for defence, the reality of AUKUS is that there is no way to know with any certainty that this policy stance secures Australia's advanced industrial future. From a future of work perspective, a far less risk-laden option – and one that, despite some risk, already holds growing global market opportunity and proven demand – is the EV manufacturing sector and the lucrative role that Australia can play within its global value chain. An Australian EV industry connected upstream to critical minerals industries in the resource sector and downstream to renewable energy industries more broadly could increase the economic complexity of Australia through the creation of knowledge-intensive decarbonised industries with significant export value. In this process, the EV industry would develop the scale of highly skilled and deeply knowledgeable blue- and white-collar workforces that create depth and breadth in terms of workforce, apprenticeships and traineeships, and inevitably feed into a future, ongoing shipbuilding industry.

After decades of neoliberal neglect, Australian industrial policy must prepare the manufacturing sector to walk before it can run. Thus, when considering the future of work in Australia, the most immediate task is to rebuild its sovereign capabilities in manufacturing, which can centre on an EV industry that meets local demand for zero-emissions transport, renewable energy sources for our built environment and innovative solutions to build principles of reuse, recycle and refurbishment into the industrial system. An industrial policy for EV industries can also service public procurement policies that help develop supply chains, build economies of scale and hence provide thousands of high-skill, high-quality jobs to the next generation of Australians. The opportunities intrinsic to such a task are extensive. And, ultimately, an EV industry can facilitate the growth of the broader ecosystem from which shipbuilding draws talent, innovation and complex forms of knowledge fuelled by ongoing research and development.

4.10 CONCLUSION

As a strategic approach to the future of work, an EV industry policy presents a major active opportunity to gear economies and societies towards meeting the mutually reinforcing goals of environmental sustainability, economic prosperity and social participation. The opportunities for a future of work shaped and driven by an EV manufacturing industry are massive, and Australia retains competitive strengths and advantages in advanced manufacturing that can help it achieve a future of work shaped by advanced industrial transformations.

With coordinated industrial policy implemented strategically at the federal level, an EV manufacturing industry can become the foundation from which Australia grows competitive advantages in the renewable energy transition occurring globally. Despite systematic policy neglect and the hollowing out of Australia's vocational education and training system over several decades, Australia maintains a highly skilled manufacturing workforce. Australia possesses a superabundance of renewable energy resources, and the international transition to renewable energy represents an unprecedented opportunity to revive Australia's battered, but resilient, manufacturing industry. Through investments in future skills and industries required to process the critical minerals that will be in high demand in the coming decades, including lithium, which is essential to produce batteries for electric vehicles and other high-demand applications, Australia can build its massive advantage and create a future of work that shapes and determines the innovation pathways that help global industry to decarbonise. Harnessing Australia's immense renewable energy resources would generate an abundance of cheap power which can be used to revitalise existing industries and build new ones. This includes building the renewable energy infrastructure like wind towers and solar panels. If Australia were to commit to adding value to critical minerals prior to exporting them, it has the potential to generate thousands of good manufacturing jobs and help insulate its economy from volatile global markets.

Australia's secure domestic supply of critical minerals required for EV technologies can be deeply integrated into downstream supply chains comprising thousands of Australian SMEs that employ highly skilled manufacturing workers to produce high value-added products for renewable industries, which sustain a skill base for the growth of a sovereign shipbuilding industry that could even expand into civilian vessel construction. Beginning from a foundation of EV industries, Australia can charge ahead as a global leader in the reindustrialisation and decarbonisation of the global economy, and a future of work focused on the social and environmental values that all can benefit from.

NOTES

1 This was Australia's ranking in Harvard's 2019 data, the most recent release of economic complexity world rankings. According to Harvard's Economic Complexity Index, Australia's highest recorded position was 55th in 1995, still far behind most advanced industrial nations.
2 Spodumene is the primary ore comprising lithium carbonate, the precursor necessary for lithium-ion batteries.

REFERENCES

ABS. (2023). Labour Force – Manufacturing Industry. 81550DO003_202122 Australian Industry, 2021-22. Canberra: Australian Bureau of Statistics.

AITI. (2021). Manufacturing Transformation: High Value Manufacturing for the 21st Century. Adelaide: Australian Industrial Transformation Institute, Flinders University of South Australia.

AMWU. (2021). Submission to the senate economics references committee inquiry into the Australian manufacturing industry. https://www.amwu.org.au/submission_manufacturing2021

ASFU. (2022). Building Australia's Future: The Enduring Workforce and Industry Development of an Australian Marine Engineering Build. Melbourne: Australian Shipbuilding Federation of Unions.

Basseal, J.M., Bennett, C.M., Collignon, P., Currie, B.J., Durrheim, D.N., Leask, J., McBryde, E.S., McIntyre, P., Russell, F.M., Smith, D.W., Sorrell, T.C. & Marais, B.J. (2023). Key lessons from the COVID-19 public health response in Australia. The Lancet, 30, 1–8.

Bushey, C. (2022). Ford chief warns electric vehicles require 40% less labour, Financial Times, 16 November.

CEDA. (2022). IMD World Competitiveness Yearbook 2022. Melbourne: The Committee for Economic Development of Australia. https://www.ceda.com.au/ResearchAndPolicies/Research/Economy/World-Competitiveness-Yearbook-2022

Clean Energy Council (2022). Skilling the Energy Transition. Melbourne: Clean Energy Council.

Clibborn, S., Lansbury, R.D. & Wright, C.F. (2016). Who killed the Australian automotive industry: The employers, government or trade unions? Economic Papers: A Journal of Applied Economics and Policy, 35(1), 2–15.

Crowe, D. (2023). Missiles and people: Why Australia is scaling up AUKUS pact. The Age, 13 March.

CSIRO. (2022). Australian Silicon Action Plan. Canberra: Commonwealth Scientific and Industrial Research Organisation.

Cunningham, S., Theilacker, M., Gahan, P., Callan, V., & Rainnie, A. (2016). Skills and capabilities for Australian enterprise innovation. Report for the Australian Council of Learned Academies, Melbourne: Australia.

DFAT. (2021). Trade and Investment at a Glance. Canberra: Department of Foreign Affairs and Trade, Commonwealth of Australia.

DISER. (2019). Australia's Critical Minerals Strategy. Canberra: Australian Trade and Investment Commission, Department of Industry, Science, Energy and Resources, Commonwealth of Australia.

DISER. (2022). Resource and Energy Quarterly – December 2022. Canberra: Department of Industry, Science, Energy and Resources, Commonwealth of Australia.

DISR. (2023). National reconstruction fund: Diversifying and transforming australia's industry and economy. https://www.industry.gov.au/news/national-reconstruction-fund-diversifying-and-transforming-australias-industry-and-economy

FBICRC. (2020). Li-ion battery cathode manufacture in Australia: A scene setting project. Future Battery Industries Cooperative Research Centre, Perth: Australia.

Fernandes, C. (2021). The Rules Based Order. Arena Quarterly, No. 7. https://arena.org.au/the-rules-based-order/

Garnaut, R. (2019). Superpower: Australia's Low-Carbon Opportunity. Carlton: La Trobe University Press.

Global Battery Alliance (2019). A Vision for a Sustainable Battery Value Chain in 2030: Unlocking the Full Potential to Power Sustainable Development and Climate Change Mitigation. Geneva: World Economic Forum.

How, B. (2022a). Pilbara lithium pant. InnovationAus, 11 November. https://www.innovationaus.com/250m-loan-for-pilbara-lithium-plant/

How, B. (2022b). CSIRO calls for domestic silicon, solar cell manufacturing boost. InnovationAus, 9 December. https://www.innovationaus.com/csiro-calls-for-domestic-silicon-solar-cell-manufacturing-boost/

Hurst, D. & Borger, J. (2023). Aukus: Nuclear submarines deal will cost Australia up to $368bn. The Guardian, 14 March, https://www.theguardian.com/world/2023/mar/14/aukus-nuclear-submarines-australia-commits-substantial-funds-into-expanding-us-shipbuilding-capacity

IEA. (2021). The Role of Critical Minerals in Clean Energy Transitions. Paris: International Energy Agency. https://www.iea.org/reports/the-role-of-critical-minerals-in-clean-energy-transitions

IEA. (2022). Electric Vehicles – Technology Deep Dive. Paris: International Energy Agency: https://www.iea.org/reports/electric-vehicles

IMD. (2021). World Competitiveness Ranking 2021 – Country Profile: Australia. Lausanne: Institute for Management Development.

IMD. (2022). World Competitiveness Ranking 2022 – Country Profile: Australia. Lausanne: Institute for Management Development.

Kaldor, N. (1967). Strategic Factors in Economic Development. Frank W. Pierce memorial lecture series, October 1966. New York: New York State School of Industrial and Labor Relations, Cornell University.

King, S. & Boxall, N. (2019). Lithium battery recycling in Australia: Defining the status and identifying opportunities for the development of a new industry. Journal of Cleaner Production, 215, 1279–1287.

Lewis, C. (2023). Whatever floats your boats. Crikey Worm, 15 March. https://www.crikey.com.au/2023/03/15/aukus-368b-spend-positive-reaction/

Mattioli, G., Roberts, C., Steinberger, J.K., & Brown, A. (2020). The political economy of car dependence: A systems of provision approach. Energy Research & Social Science, 66. https://doi.org/10.1016/j.erss.2020.101486

Mazzucato, M. (2022). Mission Economy: A Moonshot Guide to Changing Capitalism. London: Penguin.

Mazzucato, M., Kattel, R., & Ryan-Collins, J. (2022). Challenge-driven innovation policy: Towards a new policy toolkit. Journal of Industry, Trade and Competition, 20, 421–437.

Mazzucato, M., & Perez, C. (2022). Redirecting Growth: Inclusive, Sustainable and Innovation-Led. London: University College London Institute for Innovation and Public Purpose.

McCausland, W.D., & Theodossiou, I. (2012). Is manufacturing still the engine of growth? Journal of Post Keynesian Economics, 35(1), 79–92.

Miller, J. (2021). Volkswagen boosts electric investment by €17bn after clash with union. Financial Times, 9 December.

Morgan, J. (2021). Electric vehicles: The future we made and the problem of unmaking it. Cambridge Journal of Economics, 44, 953–977.

Nahum, D. (2020). Powering Onwards: Australia's Opportunity to Reinvigorate Manufacturing through Renewable Energy. Canberra: Centre for Future Work at the Australia Institute.

OECD. (2023). Policies to strengthen the resilience of global value chains: Empirical evidence from the COVID-19 shock. OECD Science, Technology and Industry Policy Papers, No. 141, Paris: Organisation for Economic Co-operation and Development.

Pfeiffer, S., & Suphan, A. (2015). The labouring capacity index: Living labouring capacity and experience as resources on the road to industry 4.0. Working Paper #2, Hohenheim: Chair of Sociology, University of Hohenheim.

Pitron, G. (2020). The Rare Metals War: The Dark Side of Clean Energy and Digital Technologies. Brunswick, Victoria, Australia: Scribe Publications.

Prime Minister of Australia. (2023). AUKUS Remarks. Transcript, Canberra: Commonwealth of Australia.

Porter, M. E. (1990). The competitive advantage of nations. Harvard Business Review, March–April, 73–91.

Productivity Commission. (2021a). Submission to the senate economics references committee inquiry into the Australian manufacturing industry. https://www.pc.gov.au/research/supporting/manufacturing-industry

Productivity Commission. (2021b). Vulnerable Supply Chains: Interim Report. Canberra: Australian Government Productivity Commission, Commonwealth of Australia.

PwC., & DESE. (2020). AUR Automotive, Retail, Service and Repair Training Package: Case for Change. Sydney: PwC.

Roberts, P. (2019). Manufacturing decline leaves Australia in the third world of exporters. Australian Manufacturing Forum, 14 October, https://www.aumanufacturing.com.au/manufacturing-decline-leaves-australia-in-the-third-world-of-exporters

Rutovitz, J., Briggs, C., & Langdon, R. (2022). To clean up Australia's power grid, we're going to need many thousand more skilled workers – And fast. The Conversation, 14 December.

Stanford, J. (2020a). A Fair Share for Australian Manufacturing: Manufacturing Renewal for the Post-COVID Economy. Canberra: Centre for Future Work at The Australia Institute.

Stanford, J. (2020b). Employment Aspects of the Transition from Fossil Fuels in Australia. Canberra: Centre for Future Work at the Australia Institute.

Vorrath, S. (2021). Australia storage start-up applies for li-ion battery recycling patents. Renew Economy, 16 August.

Wang, M. (2009). Manufacturing FDI and economic growth: Evidence from Asian economies. Applied Economics, 41(8), 991–1002.

Weller, S., & O'Neill, P. (2014). De-industrialisation, financialisation and Australia's macro-economic trap. Cambridge Journal of Regions, Economy and Society, 7, 509–526.

Worrall, L. (2023). Celebrating Australian sovereign capability – Sovereign capability and how to get it. @AuManufacturing, 13 March. https://www.aumanufacturing.com.au/celebrating-australian-sovereign-capability-sovereign-capability-and-how-to-get-it

Worrall, L., Spoehr, J., & Gamble, H. (2022). Innovation Procurement – Lessons for Australia. Adelaide: Australian Industrial Transformation Institute, Flinders University of South Australia.

Wood, T. (2022). Why Australia Needs a 21st Century Industry Policy. Melbourne: Grattan Institute.

CHAPTER 5

Economic Complexity

Rebuilding Industry through Innovation

Hamish Gamble

THE FUTURE OF WORK will be shaped by the future of industry. While many advanced economies around the world have experienced an absolute decline in the importance of manufacturing to their economies, the emergence of Industry 4.0 (Lasi et al., 2014) offers an opportunity to re-establish manufacturing bases. Industry 4.0 connects manufacturing with the digital economy through technologies such as artificial intelligence (AI), automation, and computerised systems. This connection enables manufacturing processes to be transformed from long-run bulk production to a highly agile, innovative, and responsive process using more customised, short run production techniques to meet the needs of customers. The interaction between manufacturing and the digital economy highlights the importance of developing an ecosystem where technology precipitates innovation, and where innovation is fostered and directed to provide economic growth and development and contributes to meeting society-level challenges such as climate change, and income inequality. Driving innovation efficiently and appropriately requires strong, targeted and evidence-based innovation and industry policy.

This chapter is concerned with economic complexity, which identifies the productive capabilities of a country based on the products it exports. The chapter will highlight the importance of economic complexity – as a tool to measure the structure of an economy and to identify opportunities for future economic development. It will also investigate the relationship

DOI: 10.1201/9781003393757-5

between economic complexity and the structure of the economy through a comparative analysis of Australia, Germany, and Canada. This will highlight how differences in economic complexity necessitate different policy approaches. A suggested policy approach will be presented for improving complexity in de-industrialised, low-complexity countries, contrasting with successful policy undertaken in other regions.

The chapter will proceed first by reviewing the history of innovation policy and the emergence of economic complexity as an important tool in the innovation policy space. Next, the key measures of economic complexity and their importance will be defined. Third, a comparative analysis will summarise how economic complexity relates to future economic growth, economic diversification, manufacturing capabilities, and export markets. The chapter will conclude with policy implications and lessons.

5.1 CHALLENGES AND OPPORTUNITIES

From a manufacturing and industrial development perspective, the impact of the COVID-19 pandemic on global and local supply chains has increased the focus of national governments on domestic industrial capabilities. Nations realised the importance of maintaining an industrial base with the capability to make the products and provide the services that are critical to maintaining domestic security, keeping citizens safe, and growing the economy. Decades of neoliberal economic policy focusing on trade liberalisation, privatisation, and deregulation have resulted in a downturn in manufacturing and the associated productive capabilities that it provides. Industry policy was sidelined following the oil shocks of the 1970s, with criticism of directional industry policy centring on the perception of policy-makers 'picking winners'. While the importance of industrial capabilities has been reaffirmed, the tendency to criticise industrial policy as picking winners has not changed.

For countries facing a downturn of traditional manufacturing, the quest for new industries and products to replace declining sectors is pertinent. For instance, in Australia, there has been a steady decline in the contribution of the manufacturing sector to Gross Domestic Product (GDP) (World Bank, 2021), which was punctuated by announcements in 2013 and 2014 that local automotive manufacturing would cease. Similar experiences have occurred in the rust belt in the United States (Alder et al., 2014). Even outside of manufacturing downturn, industry closure and decline will continue to impact regions – such as the closure of fossil fuel projects in regional communities in Australia.

The question remains – how can policy-makers, institutions, and governments best direct the industrial capabilities present in their region to build an economy that provides benefit for its citizens through improved living standards and can meet industrial challenges such as decarbonisation? Countering the argument of picking winners requires evidence for how and why specific industries have been chosen. To that end, an evidence-based methodology to select and prioritise industries for development is necessary.

5.2 HISTORY OF INNOVATION POLICY

Innovation policy has over time been influenced by various frames of thought. Schot and Steinmueller (2019) proposed three frames of innovation policy, while acknowledging that these frames often overlap. The first frame is associated with the end of the Second World War and focused on public investment in science and technology to fuel economic growth. This came as a response to the market failure of private investment being unable to maintain national esteem and military readiness. The second frame pertained to a complex national innovation system with relationships between businesses, universities, individuals, and entrepreneurs shaping innovation (Cirillo et al., 2019; Edquist, 2019). In the innovation ecosystem, the underlying network of government, university, and businesses has remained a core tenet of innovation policy (Etzkowitz & Leydesdorff, 2000). More recently, there is a growing call for a movement towards a third framing of innovation policy, which is more directional, and focuses on social, environmental, and reflective consequences beyond economic growth as measured by GDP. Instead, policy should direct innovation towards growing macroeconomic dysfunctions such as climate change, social inequity, excessive waste, and resource depletion (Mazzucato, 2016; Tylecote, 2019), which have been directly attributed to a lack of innovation policy by Pfotenhauer et al. (2019). Innovation policy based on this frame has been termed mission-oriented policy, and has a focus on the creation of new markets through fixing directional failures, rather than fixing market and systemic failures (Robinson & Mazzucato, 2019). The evolution of this frame of innovation policy is a response to the increasing emphasis on societal grand challenges, and the global trend towards the interconnection of industries and has been observed in both the National Aeronautics and Space Administration (NASA) and the European Space Agency (ESA) (Robinson & Mazzucato, 2019). Additionally, China has built innovation capabilities in the renewable sector through the photovoltaic industry (Shubbak, 2019) and wastewater treatment technologies (Yap & Truffer, 2019).

At the same time, innovation policy in Europe has developed a focus on the importance of location and regional knowledge. Smart specialisation policy has emerged as a means of directing regional economies to develop along place-based technological trajectories, guided by and building upon existing knowledge within the region (Dosi, 1982; Rigby & Essletzbichler, 1997). Smart specialisation is based on the concept that development in regions occurs more optimally by focusing on distinctive and original areas of specialisation, rather than by copying what has been successful in other regions (Foray et al., 2009). This is because knowledge is location-specific and what can work in one region will not necessarily work in other regions. The differences in economic and institutional structure shape possibilities for future development. In addition, focusing on activities which complement existing productive assets and activities will derive a greater benefit from increases in research and development (R&D) and innovation. Selecting activities in which a region is already strong increases the chances that a directional-based policy is successful. Outside of smart specialisation strategies in Europe, the link between industry development and location has also led to the development of special economic zones in China (Yeung et al., 2009), Mexico's Smart Diversification Strategy (Solleiro-Rebolledo et al., 2020), and the Supercluster Initiative in Canada (Doloreux & Frigon, 2021).

Despite the above examples, practical usage of smart specialisation policy has so far been limited, due to difficulties developing analytical tools to guide the policy directives. In attempting to rectify this, Balland et al. (2019) have developed a framework which links concepts of relatedness, knowledge complexity, and diversification to develop a smart specialisation policy tool which assesses the costs and benefits of alternative technological trajectories. They identify that methods based on the economic complexity literature as developed by Hidalgo and Hausmann (2009) can quantify the knowledge complexity of a region. Where Balland et al. (2019) use the number of patents by different technology classes to identify knowledge complexity, this chapter will use gross product exports by country.

5.3 ECONOMIC COMPLEXITY – A TOOL FOR SMART SPECIALISATION

Economic complexity is based on the idea that what a country makes reveals what it knows – that is, the existence of a product suggests that the knowledge required to create it also exists. Consider a simple product like an apple. The process to get an apple from the farmer to the supermarket involves knowledge of horticulture, pest control, logistics and refrigeration. The apple represents the knowledge embedded in the individuals who work along the value chain. A more complicated product such as a car requires a larger breadth of knowledge across a large network of industries and individuals. This knowledge is shared within and across industries – the farmer need not know how to build a refrigerator, and the automaker need not know how to produce steel, because the knowledge is held by other individuals, or other businesses. Individual knowledge is specialised, and collective knowledge is diversified.

Economic complexity has gained prominence as a method for identifying both the existing productive capabilities of a location (region, state, and country), as well as the connections between existing capabilities in a location, and potential future capabilities. It is also linked with innovation policy through its focus on sectors. Complexity methods also help to provide a quantitative base for modern policy efforts such as smart specialisation (Hidalgo, 2021). Economic complexity has been applied at both regional and national levels to quantify the structure of economies in the United States, China, Mexico, Canada, Russia, Brazil, Uruguay, Australia, Turkey, Spain, Italy, Paraguay, and the United Kingdom (see Hidalgo (2021) for an exhaustive list of related papers). However, the link between economic structure and policy directives has been explored less. Economic complexity methods have also been used to analyse and identify the growth opportunities of countries in specific areas – such as the green economy (Mealy & Teytelboym, 2020).

Economic complexity aims to quantify the level of productive knowledge present in an economy. Economies that can combine knowledge across many different industries are able to produce more products, and products which are more knowledge-intensive and require advanced qualifications and skills. Conversely, those economies which are simpler, have a narrower base of production and hence produce fewer and less complex products (Hausmann et al., 2013) that generate less demand for advanced qualifications and skills.

There are many different methods and data sources used to quantify the level of complexity, including product exports by country, patents by technology class, and payroll by industry. In a global ranking of the economic complexity index of countries, Hidalgo and Hausmann (2009) use gross product export data to calculate economic complexity, and develop the product space, which describes the relatedness and proximity between products. The availability and consistency of export data allows the evolution of complexity to be tracked over time, and for comparisons to be made simply between countries. As such, this approach is adopted here.

5.4 MEASURES OF ECONOMIC COMPLEXITY

Economic complexity methods produce many indicators describing the economic structure of a region, including diversity, ubiquity, proximity, complexity outlook gain, distance, complexity outlook index, product complexity index, and economic complexity index. However, the analysis which follows will focus on how differences in economic structure require differences in the policy response if aiming to (re)build industrial capabilities. To that end, the three measures of *economic complexity index, distance, and complexity outlook gain*, as described below, will be prioritised over other measures. These are selected as they respectively provide a quantitative description of how new products are related to existing capabilities, the benefit of building capabilities in a new product, and a summary measure of the structure of the economy. For a technical overview of all measures of economic complexity, see Hausmann et al. (2013).

5.4.1 Economic Complexity Index

The economic complexity index (ECI) is a measure of the level of knowledge embedded in a country, based on the products it exports with comparative advantage.[1] Complex countries are those which export many products with comparative advantage and export products which are rare. The complexity of a country and the complexity of products are calculated at the same time. This method first looks at the number of products exported with comparative advantage by each country, called diversity. The diversity is adjusted by how rare the products are in global trade, called ubiquity. At the same time, the rareness of products is adjusted by how many countries export that product. As each adjustment occurs, the calculations converge to a ranking of products – the product complexity index (PCI) and a ranking of countries (ECI).

5.4.2 Distance (Relatedness)

Distance describes how near a country is from the productive knowledge necessary to develop a new product. It is a measure of the proportion of knowledge that a country is *missing*. As such, a distance value of 0 indicates that all requisite knowledge is available to a country, and a distance value of 1 indicates that none of the requisite knowledge is available. Here, knowledge is quantified by *proximity*, which is a measure of how often two products are co-exported (Hausmann et al., 2013). That is, if many countries that export wine also export grapes, then the proximity between wine and grapes will be high. This indicates that that there is some shared knowledge or capability required to be competitive in the production of both products.

5.4.3 Complexity Outlook Gain (Benefit)

The Complexity Outlook Gain (COG) is the potential benefit in terms of future diversification to an economy from the development of a specific (and new) product. The COG represents the strategic value of the development of a product, based on how many potential high-complexity products it opens to the economy. That is, how the knowledge from the development of a new product can be applied to develop additional new products.

5.5 COMPARATIVE ANALYSIS

In this section, a comparison will be drawn between Australia, Canada, and Germany. This comparison will focus on the differences in economic complexity indicators – the economic complexity index, product distance as a measure of relatedness, and complexity outlook gain as a measure of economic benefit – as well as differences in the structure of the economy. The analysis of the economic structure will focus on the strength of the manufacturing sector, concentration among products exported, and the make-up of export baskets. These countries have been chosen because they span a significant range of economic complexity. The link between economic complexity and policy will also be expanded.

The Economic Complexity Index for Australia, Canada and Germany is shown in Figure 5.1. This data is derived using gross export data of 788 products by 249 countries between 1962 and 2020, measured by the Standard International Trade Classification (SITC). To ensure reliability of trade statistics, The Growth Lab at Harvard (2019) reduces[2] the data set to 133 countries as classified in the Atlas of Economic Complexity (Hausmann et al., 2013). Germany is selected as a country that has consistently maintained a high level of economic complexity and currently ranked 3rd highest as of 2020. Canada has a middling level of economic complexity, having declined from 24th in 1962 to 43rd in 2020, and Australia has a low level of economic complexity – having decreased from 37th in 1962 to stand now at 91st.

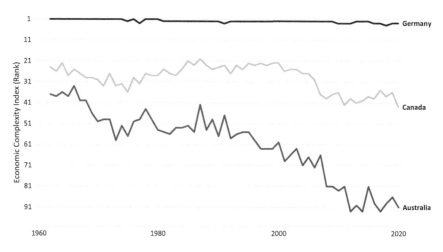

FIGURE 5.1   Economic complexity index (rank) for Germany, Canada, and Australia.

Source: Author's calculation, using data from The Growth Lab at Harvard, 2019.

The economic complexity of a country is indicative of its ability to increase economic complexity in the future. The economic complexity index explains about 78 percent of the variation in GDP[3] – highly complex countries tend to be the richest countries, and vice versa (Hausmann et al., 2013). The difference between a country's level of economic complexity and its GDP has been shown to predict future economic growth (Hidalgo & Hausmann, 2009) – where future economic growth is estimated to be lower in countries with a level of complexity lower than implied by their level of GDP. Countries with high economic complexity are more diversified – they are globally competitive in the production of more products. But they are also more specialised – they are the centres of highly complex industries (Hausmann et al., 2013).

Because economic complexity is a measure of productive capabilities, countries with a higher level of economic complexity have more productive capabilities and can more easily apply these capabilities to the development of new complex products. Conversely, countries with low economic complexity find the development of new complex products more difficult.

This is illustrated in Figure 5.2 which shows the relationship between distance (relatedness) and complexity gain (benefit) for Germany, Canada, and Australia. Each point represents a product as classified by the SITC.

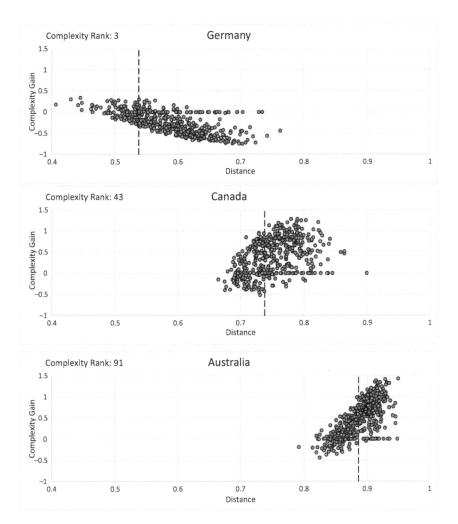

FIGURE 5.2 Developing a new product is easier when complexity is higher, but the benefit is lower.

Note: Dashed line represents the average distance to new products.
Source: Author's calculation, using data from The Growth Lab at Harvard, 2019.

Two things are immediately obvious – the *higher* the economic complexity, the *lower* the average distance to new products, as represented by the dashed vertical line for each country. The average distance is calculated as the arithmetic mean of the distance of all products which are not exported with comparative advantage for each country. These products are excluded because the benefit to a country from developing a product in which they are already competitive is zero by definition. All else equal, new opportunities are closer to the existing capability set of high economic complexity countries. Secondly, the relationship between benefit and relatedness is also dependent on economic complexity. For Germany, products that are closer to the existing capability set generate a higher complexity benefit. For Australia, this relationship is reversed – the products with the greatest complexity benefit are those farthest away from existing capabilities. This pattern has also been observed across regions in the European Union where regions with high knowledge complexity[4] find a positive relationship between the relatedness of existing knowledge to new technologies with higher complexity (Balland et al., 2019).

This relationship implies that more direct policy interventions may be necessary for economies with lower levels of economic complexity compared to countries with high levels of complexity. An intervention designed to improve complexity could focus on the development of a new sector, or specific products within a new sector. If these products are far away from the countries existing capabilities (as quantified by a distance nearer to 1), then development of these products is likely to be more costly and embody a greater degree of risk. Products with higher complexity gain will generate considerable complexity to the economy and build more capabilities. Given the differences in the relationship between complexity gain and distance, building complexity in a low economic complexity economy necessarily requires a strategy which has greater risk. Where Germany has many opportunities for building capabilities with a relatively low risk, Canada has some and Australia has only a few.

5.5.1 Economic Structure

As economic complexity is derived from export data, the most significant drivers of a country's economic complexity index are the products that it exports with comparative advantage. As such, it is important to consider the diversity and complexity of the products exported with comparative advantage. Table 5.1 shows the export diversity, export complexity, and export concentration of Australia, Canada, and Germany for 2020. Export diversity measures the number of products exported with comparative advantage, and export complexity measures the average complexity of the products exported with comparative advantage. Export concentration is measured by a modified Herfindahl–Hirschman Index (HHI) which is defined as the sum of the squared export share of each product exported

TABLE 5.1   Export Diversity and Complexity of Australia, Canada, and Germany

	Export Diversity	Export Complexity	Export Concentration
Australia	98	−0.11	0.10
Canada	188	−0.04	0.04
Germany	309	0.25	0.02

(Rhoades, 1993). A concentration of 1 indicates that the export market is dominated by 1 product, and a concentration of 0 indicates that the export market is equally distributed across all products. While concentration is not directly related to economic complexity, there is a strong correlation between the two of about 55 percent.

The combination of low diversity and high export concentration reveals Australia's reliance on a high volume of exports across a limited number of products. In 2020, almost one quarter of Australia's total export revenue was generated from iron ore exports, and another 10 percent from lignite coal. In Germany, the largest export is information and communication technology (ICT) services, followed by cars. Similarly, Canada's largest exports are ICT services and crude petroleum. The top 10 products exported by each country are available in the Appendix in Table A.1.

In Australia, the export basket is highly concentrated in agricultural and mining products which, with few exceptions, are low in complexity and represent the beginning of the value chain. Conversely, in Germany, the export basket contains many non-ubiquitous products which require significant value-add and have a high level of complexity. Both Canada and Germany export passenger motor vehicles – a highly complex product – but this is absent from the export basket of Australia following the closure of the automotive industry in 2017 (see also Dean and Beale, both in this volume). This further strengthens the case for maintaining and in Australia's case rebuilding this industry.

Similarly, manufacturing capabilities and the strength of the manufacturing sector in general are important dimensions to consider when developing a policy response to either maintain a high level of economic complexity or increase complexity from a low level. The relative size of the manufacturing sector is also strongly correlated with economic complexity. Figure 5.3 shows the proportion of GDP generated from the manufacturing sector for Germany, Canada, and Australia, and Figure 5.4 shows the relationship between the Economic Complexity Index and

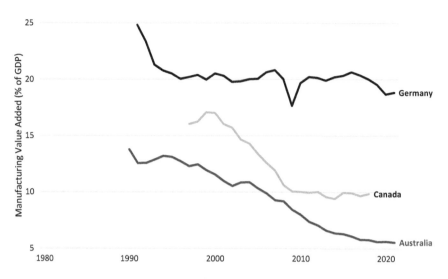

FIGURE 5.3   Value added by the manufacturing sector as a percent of gross domestic product.

Source: Author's calculations using data from World Bank, 2021.

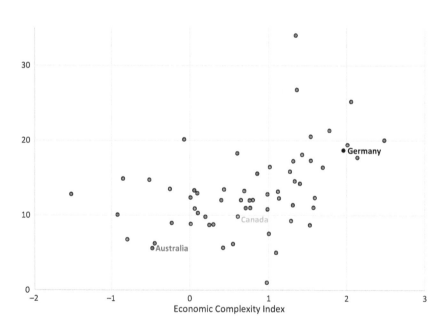

FIGURE 5.4   Economic complexity is strongly correlated with value added by the manufacturing sector.

Source: Author's calculations using data from The Growth Lab at Harvard, 2019; World Bank, 2021.

manufacturing value-added. Australia's manufacturing output is below 6 percent of total GDP, and manufacturing self-sufficiency as measured by imports of elaborately transformed manufactured goods as a ratio of manufacturing consumption ranks the lowest of all OECD countries at 71.5 percent (Stanford, 2020).

Overall, countries with low economic complexity are faced with barriers which make building economic complexity more difficult. They have a weaker manufacturing sector, are less diversified, have a more concentrated export basket, and, as such, have a higher reliance on few products for export revenue, and fewer complex opportunities close to existing capabilities. In combination, the policy response is more important when complexity is lower.

5.6 BUILDING ON ECONOMIC COMPLEXITY

Innovation and industrial policy in Australia have often been piecemeal – focused mostly on primary resource endowments and maintaining trade surpluses with industrialising Asian countries. Ultimately, industrial policy has been rejected at the national level, with exceptions and political concessions applied to intervene in industry closures and building a national defence capability. Initiatives to boost innovation do exist, but they have a horizontal focus – on research and translation, SMEs, and business environment issues, rather than prioritising the importance of industry verticals. In comparison, Smart specialisation approaches to industry development and innovation policy have been undertaken in Bavaria in Germany through the Bavarian Cluster Campaign which started in 2006. This transitioned research, technology development, and innovation policy from a very narrow focus on key sectors and technologies to a broad sectoral approach where sectors are identified based on regional needs, and potentials, and revised through economic development and technological evolution (Baier et al., 2013). In Germany more generally, there is a strong focus on the development and diffusion of high-performance production systems. The German government prioritises Industry 4.0 as a technology policy to achieve the fourth industrial revolution and is the first mover in Industry 4.0. High-end technology and business extension services are delivered through a network of institutions, and Industry 4.0 projects are funded jointly by industry and federal and state governments. In addition, the EU makes explicit use of public procurement to stimulate local industry development and innovation with a focus on sectors with the potential to yield technological advantage and spill overs. In Canada, a recently announced policy initiative focusing on Innovation Superclusters aims to strengthen existing clusters, and help innovative firms to access information, knowledge, and technology more productively (Doloreux & Frigon, 2021).

The policy and strategic implications of economic complexity, for advanced, low-complexity economies seeking an accelerated transition of manufacturing and industry as a basis for sustainable growth in living standards, are clear. First, the focus needs to be on promoting competitive advantage based on innovation, organisational superiority, and agility. Cost-based competition may not be a sustainable basis for industry growth in high-cost advanced economies. Second, the objective must be to create an environment conducive to the creation of a greater diversity of productive activities and capabilities, particularly network richness or complexity, by focussing on strengthening tacit, embedded and net-worked, non-traded sources of competitive advantage. Combining the technical with the organisational and strategic seeks to foment connected-ness and density to capitalise on the economic complexity created and to provide a platform of competitive advantage less likely to be replicated by competitors. Third, in developing new capabilities and moving up the value chain, a country or region needs to build on capacities and abilities it already has. This means targeting products close to the current set ('near-by' products) and targeting capability gaps to move up the value chain progressively. Because productive knowledge is embedded it is generally not realistic to envisage making things at a large distance from the existing set of capabilities.

5.6.1 Policy Options

The previous section showed that for countries with low economic complexity, there are fewer complex opportunities for development near the existing capabilities. While it is reasonable to expect that a country like Germany can continue to maintain its economic complexity with minimal interventions through a self-reinforcing cycle, the opposite is true for low-complexity countries, which will require active and interventionist policy to break the cycle. This conclusion is shared by Hausmann et al. (2013) who identify four strategic approaches to diversify into related products and improve economic complexity. These approaches are *strategic bets* (coordinate 'long jumps' into areas of strategic significance with the potential for future diversification), *parsimonious industrial policy* (address bottlenecks to help move into related products close to existing knowledge), *light touch* (leverage existing success to further build complex production), and *technological frontier* (focus development on novel products).

Compared to leading industrial nations, and even developing nations, Australia faces the negative impacts of path dependence. Deindustrialisation has limited the potential to leverage existing capabilities into new products. Australia's position in global value chains as a supplier of raw materials for offshore value adding is self-reinforcing. Therefore, the lever must be through direct and explicit policy to drive innovation and industrialisation. This policy can also assist in meeting other development goals in Australia, such as the decarbonisation agenda or building sovereign capabilities (Australian Industrial Transformation Institute, 2021; Worrall et al., 2021).

For deindustrialised or low-complexity countries, a key starting point is a 'knowledge foresighting' policy to identify areas of current and future competitive advantage, as well as gaps and opportunities in domestic supply chains (Green, 2020; Worrall, 2020) as is currently undertaken by the European Commission's Smart Specialisation Platform, building from the structured processes of Entrepreneurial Discovery. Such processes reduce the cost of exploring and creating new opportunities, while simultaneously increasing coordination between businesses, unions, academia, and government. Additionally, it reduces the risk of top-down selection of industrial opportunities. The knowledge foresighting develops sectoral roadmaps, with a focus on targeting complex products in key value chains, and reveals the areas of strategic significance as identified by the *strategic bets* approach.

For Australia, the obvious starting point is an analysis of the existing natural resource base to identify where investment into moving up the value chain can provide spillover benefits. Australia is uniquely positioned to take advantage of its geography and access to natural resources to build a competitive industry based on renewable energy via an active industry policy. This industry could focus on the development of lithium batteries, solar panels, or wind turbines, and the green economy more generally. Such development would necessarily increase Australia's capability in mineral processing which, given Australia's resource base, presents a significant opportunity also to move up the value chain in other industries and sectors. Resource endowments should be targeted for selected value chain strategies, from raw materials processing through to product manufacture. For example, investment in the processing of the ores is critical for entry into the lithium-ion value chain, and other green industries, but presently, Australia's comparative advantage is only at the raw materials end. Processing the ore is the next logical step in the value chain and the condition for any prospect of becoming a downstream manufacturer of batteries and battery packs. The same point applies to other ores that could join the virtuous circle of green energy powering the production of elements required in the green economy, while simultaneously rebuilding manufacturing capabilities (see Dean in this volume).

5.7 CONCLUSION

Economic complexity analysis reveals two important indicators for a country's industrial development – the structure of the economy and opportunities for future development. These insights provide evidence for identifying sectors which can be prioritised for development and form the basis of innovation and industrial policy. Additionally, the connections between existing capabilities and new opportunities suggest the importance of path dependency for future economic growth.

While economic complexity can reveal opportunities, it is up to local, state, and national governments, as well as policy-makers, to assess these opportunities and integrate them into actions that contribute to the well-being of citizens, and also to meet global challenges. The COVID-19 crisis showed how Australia's lack of economic complexity and industrial capabilities created an economy with low levels of self-sufficiency, which was vulnerable to external shocks and trade disruptions. This followed from a historic and long-lasting hollowing out of industrial policy, particularly at the national level. The promotion of purely market-based economically liberal policies has over time led to the capture of public policy and the state by the private sector. The importance of industry verticals and sectors, and building scale, has been lost.

An economic complexity analysis of Australia, Canada, and Germany highlighted how economic complexity implies a path dependency of future economic growth and diversification. For Australia, a country with low economic complexity and diminished manufacturing capabilities, national governments and policy-makers must refocus on industry verticals and sectors to build on the opportunities identified by economic complexity.

APPENDIX

TABLE A.1 Top 10 Products Exported from Australia, Canada, and Germany in 2020

Export Value	Product Complexity	Product
Australia		
70,787	−2.33	Iron ore and concentrates, not agglomerated
26,884	−1.71	Other coal, not agglomerated
22,138	−0.01	Special transactions, commodity not classified according to class
21,240	−1.86	Petroleum gases and other gaseous hydrocarbons, nes, liquefied
15,770	−2.20	Gold, non-monetary (excluding gold ores and concentrates)
5,451	−1.02	Bovine meat, fresh, chilled or frozen
3,874	−1.54	Aluminium ores and concentrates (including alumina)
3,018	−1.77	Copper ore and concentrates; copper matte; cement copper
2,265	−2.52	Crude petroleum and oils obtained from bituminous materials
2,252	−1.59	Meat of sheep and goats, fresh, chilled or frozen
Canada		
47,808	−2.52	Crude petroleum and oils obtained from bituminous materials
31,655	0.96	Passenger motor vehicles (excluding buses)
19,877	−0.01	Special transactions, commodity not classified according to class
16,727	−2.20	Gold, non-monetary (excluding gold ores and concentrates)
8,789	1.33	Other parts and accessories, for vehicles of headings 722, 781–783
7,524	0.07	Wood of coniferous species, sawn, planed, tongued, grooved, etc
7,490	−0.68	Petroleum products, refined
6,737	0.76	Medicaments (including veterinary medicaments)
5,371	−1.12	Aluminium and aluminium alloys, unwrought
5,022	−1.29	Petroleum gases, nes, in gaseous state

(Continued)

TABLE A.1 (*Continued*)

Export Value	Product Complexity	Product
Germany		
120,801	0.96	Passenger motor vehicles (excluding buses)
61,139	0.76	Medicaments (including veterinary medicaments)
53,622	1.33	Other parts and accessories, for vehicles of headings 722, 781–783
46,014	−0.01	Special transactions, commodity not classified according to class
33,687	1.68	Glycosides, glands, antisera, vaccines and similar products
32,624	0.77	Switches, relays, fuses, etc; switchboards and control panels, nes
24,081	2.09	Machinery for specialized industries and parts thereof, nes
20,808	0.43	Chemical products and preparations, nes
20,097	0.16	Aircraft of an unladen weight exceeding 15000 kg
14,957	0.60	Miscellaneous articles of plastic

Note: nes = not elsewhere specified
Source: The Growth Lab at Harvard (2019)

NOTES

1 Comparative advantage is a measure of the relative performance or competitiveness of a country in the production of a product based on gross exports. A country is said to have revealed comparative advantage in a product if the share of its exports in that product is greater than the proportion of that product's exports in global trade.
2 This process removes countries with population below 1.2 million, total trade below $1 billion, and other countries with data quality issues due to domestic circumstances.
3 After taking into account income generated from extractive industries which has more bearing on location than productive capabilities.
4 Knowledge complexity is analogous to economic complexity calculated using regional patent applications by technological domain.

REFERENCES

Alder, S., Lagakos, D., & Ohanian, L. (2014). Competitive pressure and the decline of the Rust Belt: A macroeconomic analysis.

Australian Industrial Transformation Institute. (2021). Manufacturing transformation: High value manufacturing for the 21st Century. F. U. o. S. Australia.

Baier, E., Kroll, H., & Zenker, A. (2013). Templates of smart specialisation: Experiences of place-based regional development strategies in Germany and Austria.

Balland, P.-A., Boschma, R., Crespo, J., & Rigby, D. L. (2019, September 02). Smart specialization policy in the European Union: Relatedness, knowledge complexity and regional diversification. Regional Studies, 53(9), 1252–1268. https://doi.org/10.1080/00343404.2018.1437900

Cirillo, V., Martinelli, A., Nuvolari, A., & Tranchero, M. (2019, May 01). Only one way to skin a cat? Heterogeneity and equifinality in European national innovation systems. Research Policy, 48(4), 905–922. https://doi.org/10.1016/j.respol.2018.10.012

Doloreux, D., & Frigon, A. (2021). The innovation superclusters initiative in Canada: A new policy strategy? Science and Public Policy, 49(1), 148–158. https://doi.org/10.1093/scipol/scab071

Dosi, G. (1982). Technological paradigms and technological trajectories: A suggested interpretation of the determinants and directions of technical change. Research Policy, 11(3), 147–162.

Edquist, C. (2019). Towards a holistic innovation policy: Can the Swedish National Innovation Council (NIC) be a role model? Research Policy, 48(4), 869–879.

Etzkowitz, H., & Leydesdorff, L. (2000). The dynamics of innovation: From National Systems and "Mode 2" to a Triple Helix of university–industry–government relations. Research Policy, 29(2), 109–123.

Foray, D., David, P. A., & Hall, B. (2009). Smart specialisation – The concept. Knowledge Economists Policy Brief, 9(85), 100.

Green, R. (2020, April 14). A new deal for manufacturing – Five building blocks for a new plan. Australian manufacturing forum.

Hausmann, R., Hidalgo, C. A., Bustos, S., Coscia, M., Simoes, A., & Yildirim, M. A. (2013). The atlas of economic complexity: Mapping paths to prosperity. MIT Press. https://books.google.com.au/books?id=cp-NAgAAQBAJ

Hidalgo, C. A. (2021). Economic complexity theory and applications. Nature Reviews Physics, 3(2), 92–113.

Hidalgo, C. A., & Hausmann, R. (2009). The building blocks of economic complexity. Proceedings of the National Academy of Sciences, 106(26), 10570–10575. https://doi.org/10.1073/pnas.0900943106

Lasi, H., Fettke, P., Kemper, H.-G., Feld, T., & Hoffmann, M. (2014). Industry 4.0. Business & Information Systems Engineering, 6, 239–242.

Mazzucato, M. (2016). From market fixing to market-creating: A new framework for innovation policy. Industry and Innovation, 23(2), 140–156.

Mealy, P., & Teytelboym, A. (2020). Economic complexity and the green economy. Research Policy, 51(8), 103948. https://doi.org/10.1016/j.respol.2020.103948

Pfotenhauer, S. M., Juhl, J., & Aarden, E. (2019, May 01). Challenging the "deficit model" of innovation: Framing policy issues under the innovation imperative. Research Policy, 48(4), 895–904. https://doi.org/10.1016/j.respol.2018.10.015

Rhoades, S. A. (1993). The Herfindahl-Hirschman index. Federal Reserve Bulletin, 79, 188.

Rigby, D. L., & Essletzbichler, J. (1997). Evolution, process variety, and regional trajectories of technological change in US manufacturing. Economic Geography, 73(3), 269–284.

Robinson, D. K. R., & Mazzucato, M. (2019, May 01). The evolution of mission-oriented policies: Exploring changing market creating policies in the US and European space sector. Research Policy, 48(4), 936–948. https://doi.org/10.1016/j.respol.2018.10.005

Schot, J., & Steinmueller, W. E. (2019, May 01). Transformative change: What role for science, technology and innovation policy?: An introduction to the 50th Anniversary of the Science Policy Research Unit (SPRU) special issue. Research Policy, 48(4), 843–848. https://doi.org/10.1016/j.respol.2018.12.005

Shubbak, M. H. (2019, May 01). The technological system of production and innovation: The case of photovoltaic technology in China. Research Policy, 48(4), 993–1015. https://doi.org/10.1016/j.respol.2018.10.003

Solleiro-Rebolledo, J. L., García-Martínez, M. B., Castañón-Ibarra, R., & Martínez-Salvador, L. E. (2020). Smart specialization for building up a regional innovation agenda: The case of San Luis Potosí, Mexico. Journal of Evolutionary Studies in Business, 5(1), 81–115.

Stanford, J. (2020). A fair share for Australian manufacturing: Manufacturing renewal for the post-COVID economy. C. f. F. Work.

The Growth Lab at Harvard, U. (2019). International trade data (SITC, Rev. 2) Version V6) Harvard Dataverse. https://doi.org/10.7910/DVN/H8SFD2

Tylecote, A. (2019). Biotechnology as a new techno-economic paradigm that will help drive the world economy and mitigate climate change. Research Policy, 48(4), 858–868.

World Bank. (2021). Manufacturing, value added (% of GDP) – OECD members. World Bank national accounts data, and OECD National Accounts data files. https://data.worldbank.org/indicator/NV.IND.MANF.ZS?locations=OE

Worrall, L. (2020, May 11). We learned we don't have an industry policy. Australian manufacturing forum.

Worrall, L., Gamble, H., Spoehr, J., & Hordacre, A.-L. (2021). Australian sovereign capability and supply chain resilience – Perspectives and options. F. U. o. S. Australia.

Yap, X.-S., & Truffer, B. (2019, May 01). Shaping selection environments for industrial catch-up and sustainability transitions: A systemic perspective on endogenizing windows of opportunity. Research Policy, 48(4), 1030–1047. https://doi.org/10.1016/j.respol.2018.10.002

Yeung, Y.-M., Lee, J., & Kee, G. (2009). China's special economic zones at 30. Eurasian Geography and Economics, 50(2), 222–240.

CHAPTER **6**

Just Transitions

Just for Whom? Lessons from Australia's Automotive Closure

Gemma Beale

THE 'JUST TRANSITION' CONCEPT has evolved from 1970s trade union demands primarily concerned with environmentally toxic worksites into a mainstream policy tool and research focus. It is now well established that the global transition to a carbon-neutral economy, and its ensuing economic and environmental challenges, will impact jobs, consumption, and service provision (IPCC, 2022). Accordingly, the just transition agenda now includes a broader conceptualisation of both risk and justice for the workers who will be affected by energy transition *and* by climate change.

This chapter is specifically concerned with just transition as it relates to job losses and industry responses to decarbonisation in the form of transition support for workers. It first provides historical and contemporary context about the just transition movement. Then it draws on the 2017 closure of the Australian automotive manufacturing industry, the most recent example of a mass unemployment event in Australia, to argue that the combination of widespread precarious employment in Australia, and the likelihood that climate change and energy transition will lead to a situation of continuing and concurrent employment disruptions mean place-based transition solutions are no longer suitable.

6.1 HISTORICAL CONTEXT

The International Labour Organization (ILO) attributes the first use of the phrase 'just transition' to American trade union leader Tony Mazzocchi who, in 1993, referred to it when campaigning for a 'superfund for workers'

DOI: 10.1201/9781003393757-6

to support workers who were displaced by the environmental protection policies introduced in the 1990s (ILO, 2018). He, like many early advocates for a just transition, was concerned with the impact of toxic chemicals and contaminated work environments on workers' health, the environment, and jobs (ILO, 2018; Stevis et al., 2020).

The concept is a direct response to conceptions of environmentalism that tended to pit workers' interests against environmental interests in the so-called 'jobs versus environment conflict' (Goods, 2013, p. 14; see also Galgoczi, 2020). This alleged conflict depicts policy interventions required for the transition to a carbon-neutral economy as antithetical to labour interests grounded in the logic of exponential growth (Goods, 2013). It argues that, with cheap energy the foundation of industrial growth, slowing or reducing energy production, even when the latter is environmentally damaging, is inescapably tied to job losses.

The contemporary conceptualisation of just transition responds to this tension by seeking to redistribute the burden of climate change so that it does not disproportionately impact workers and their communities through (green) job creation and transition support (Goods, 2013, 2020; Stevis et al., 2020). This is encapsulated in the ILO's Just Transition Framework which calls for a coherent country-specific combination of 'macroeconomic, industrial, sectoral and labour policies' with 'the aim to generate *decent jobs* along the entire supply chain' [emphasis added] (ILO, 2018, p. 3).

According to the ILO's Framework, there are two core dimensions to just transition: the outcome, which includes decent work for all and the eradication of poverty, and the process, which requires a managed transition with meaningful social dialogue at all levels to make sure the burden is shared fairly (ILO, 2018). Two central components of the union movement's original approach are evident in this conceptualisation; that there is a public responsibility to facilitate and actively support a just transition that should not be reduced to 'welfare', and an understanding that, as a planned transition, decarbonisation is unlike ordinary transitions and therefore requires dedicated and holistic policy approaches (ILO, 2018). These holistic policy approaches must include comprehensive economy wide strategies that are aware of – and able to counteract – asymmetrical global power relations (Newell & Mulvaney, 2013). Such an intervention requires government to mediate the (often) competing business interests with the environmental and economic interests of poor and working people. Consequently, advocates argue that it is vital that just transition policies are an *integral and embedded* component of sustainable development policy frameworks rather than an add-on to existing climate policy (IPCC, 2022).

Regarding the role of unions, scholars have argued that the just transition agenda is a natural extension of a core aim of the labour union movement to influence the distribution of benefits and harms through recognition and participation (Goods, 2020; Morena et al., 2020). This relationship is clearest in the three core principles of just transition identified by Stevis and Felli (2014): redistribution, recognition, and participation, where redistribution seeks to guarantee the burden of transition is borne evenly by society; recognition ensures that the workers and communities most directly affected are explicitly accounted for in transition efforts; and participation means guaranteeing that all sections of society, including unions and representatives from industry, participate in the planning and undertaking of transitions.

Put simply, the just transition agenda in the context of action on climate change and sustainability is about balancing the problems of energy justice with the need to rapidly reduce greenhouse emissions (Galgoczi, 2020; Newell & Mulvaney, 2013). It aims to protect jobs in vulnerable industries from simply being moved to less-regulated countries and seeks to ensure adequate support is provided when job losses are unavoidable.

A recurring problem of just transition rhetoric, research, and policy has been the difficulty of identifying what that balance means in practice, threatening failure to define and agree upon who is factored into the calculations and what exactly is meant by 'just' (Bainton et al., 2021; Galgoczi, 2020; Goods, 2020; ILO, 2018; Newell & Mulvaney, 2013). It is complex in part because it requires energy insecurity and energy poverty be tackled spatially and temporally – by accounting for the uneven distribution within and between nations *and* between current and future generations. Although this complexity has led to suggestions that a widely adoptable definition is 'premature' (Jermain et al., 2022, p. 2) in order to move the agenda forward, some consensus is necessary.

6.2 DEFINING 'JUST'

Although it is difficult to separate the broader temporal and socioeconomic context and demands of just transition agenda, here I primarily focus on its application in the Australian context. Within that, the chapter specifically explores the principle that the burden of economic redistribution, necessary to mitigate catastrophic global warming, should not fall disproportionally on workers and their communities (ILO, 2018; Morena et al., 2020; Newell & Mulvaney, 2013).

Since the mid-2010s there has been a gradual growth in research on the subject that has increased sharply in recent years. The resurgence in academic interest in just transitions mirrors the contemporary interest in worker and community displacement and disadvantage. Although interest has increased, the majority of the literature has tended to focus on (the important task of) economic and industrial transformation (Abram et al., 2022; Evans & Phelan, 2016; Filipović et al., 2022; Heffron, 2021; IISD, 2022; ILO, 2018). There has been comparatively limited discussion of the practical components of workers' transition support (Jermain et al., 2022).

As such it is necessary to turn to the literature on industry closures and large-scale job loss. The individual, family, and community impacts of mass unemployment events including closures and large-scale layoffs should not be underestimated. Existing literature tells us that the loss of a major employer can have a detrimental impact at local and national levels (Barber & Hall, 2008; Beer & Evans, 2010; Beer & Thomas, 2007; Burgan & Spoehr, 2013; Ranasinghe et al., 2014), and that job loss, especially in the case of industry closure, can have serious and often lasting inter-generational, psychosocial effects on workers and their families and communities (Beer et al., 2006; Chapain & Murie, 2008; Jolley et al., 2011; Newman et al., 2009). As such, workers' transition programmes that seek to mitigate these negative impacts are a core component of large-scale closures (Bowman & Callan, 2017; Davies et al., 2017). Transition support tends to include a combination of information about job opportunities, resume support, funding for retraining, and information about community and health services.

Section 6.3 uses the recent closure of the Australian automotive manufacturing industry as a case study for best practice worker transition support.

6.3 LEARNING FROM THE CLOSURE OF AUSTRALIAN AUTOMOTIVE MANUFACTURING INDUSTRY

In October 2017, car manufacturer Holden, part of the General Motors Company, produced its last red Commodore vehicle model and, in doing so, marked the end of 70 years of motor vehicle assembly operations in Australia (Barbaro & John, 2014). It followed closures in Victoria of Toyota's Altona plant in the same month, and Ford's engine and assembly plants a year earlier (Australian Government, 2020).

The closure of Australia's automotive manufacturing industry was significant. The industry had played a pivotal role in the development of the nation's broader manufacturing industry and was a key generator of secure full-time employment and skill-based career paths for workers (Clibborn et al., 2016). Automotive manufacturing was one of the country's most vertically developed, integrated, and complex value chains (Spoehr, 2015; Stanford, 2017; Worrall et al., 2021). It was considered a 'jewel' of industrial policy-makers because it anchored complex supply chains and acted as a trendsetter for advanced technology and innovation, and wages and employment conditions (Barnes, 2021; Beer, 2018; Beer et al., 2019). The loss of the industry has not only led to the loss of secure and ongoing work, but it also seriously impacted Australia's advanced manufacturing capabilities and sovereign self-sufficiency (Stanford, 2020; Worrall et al., 2021).

Following the announcement of the closure, a suite of federal, state, and company-funded programmes was put in place to assist automotive manufacturing and supply-chain workers transition into new jobs (Bowman & Callan, 2017). Automotive manufacturing workers and affected supply-chain workers were eligible for the South Australian state government's automotive supply chain worker transition programme (also known as 'Drive Your Future'), administered by Northern Futures Inc., a community-based not-for-profit organisation, and the Australian Government's Automotive Industry Structural Adjustment Program (AISAP), administered through the private employment service provider Job Network (Bowman & Callan, 2017; Nous Group, 2013). The 1,500 Holden workers employed on site in 2014 were also automatically incorporated into Holden's Transition Program (Bowman & Callan, 2017). Each programme offered varying levels of assistance in finding information about job opportunities, identifying transferable skills and skills gaps, funds for retraining, referrals to health services, and ongoing support and mentoring (Australian Government, 2020; Bowman & Callan, 2017; DIS, 2018). These programmes were demonstrably informed by existing literature on the importance of comprehensive support programmes, as well as the closure of another car plant, Mitsubishi, in South Australia, in 2006.

The closure of the automotive manufacturing industry was distinct from past closures in Australia in that although it happened during a period of relative economic stability, there had been a clear and well-documented growth in precarious and insecure work at the time, partly attributed to the growth in casual and non-standard employment contracts in Australia over the three preceding decades (Campbell & Burgess, 2018; Carney & Stanford, 2018).

6.4 DEFINING PRECARITY

Despite substantial attention being paid to precarious employment over the last 30 years, a commonly accepted definition is yet to be found (Alberti et al., 2018; Benach et al., 2014; Kreshpaj et al., 2020; Paraskevopoulou, 2020; Standing, 2011). The lack of consensus is partly attributed to discrepancies in employment regulation and legislation that make it difficult to identify and compare precariousness across regulatory borders (OECD, 2015); and partly to what has been called a conceptual slippage in meaning (Alberti et al., 2018; Anderson, 2010; Campbell & Price, 2016; della Porta et al., 2015). As a result, precarious work is most often defined in contrast to 'standard' work, which is full-time, ongoing work, with paid leave entitlements (Burgess & Campbell, 1998; Lee et al., 2018; Wu et al., 2020).

Although a consensus is yet to be reached on a singular definition of precarious work, it has been widely accepted that a unidimensional definition of precarious work as exclusively employment insecurity fails to capture the depth and breadth of precarity (Burrows, 2013; Campbell & Burgess, 2018; Tweedie, 2013). As such, there has been a trend towards a multi-dimensional definition for precarious employment that includes job insecurity, irregular hours, poor or highly variable wages, reduced rights and entitlements, and limited control over-working conditions (Fournier, 2009; Kalleberg, 2018; Kreshpaj et al., 2020).

The growth of precarious work in Australia and across the industrialised world over the last three decades has been well documented (Campbell & Burgess, 2018; Howell & Kalleberg, 2019; Kalleberg, 2011, 2018; Lewchuk, 2017; Wayne & Michelynn, 2014). Research from the OECD (2015, p. 135) looking at the distribution of work, wages and skills shows that, in most OECD countries, standard work has 'disappeared' for those in the middle of the wage or skills distribution, while non-standard jobs have increased. The same research shows that employment losses in 'middle-skill' occupations were in standard work while both high- and low-skill jobs tended to be in non-standard arrangements (OECD, 2015, p. 137). Non-standard employment has risen in 19 out of 21 countries surveyed by the European Labour Force Survey (Laß & Wooden, 2020).

The main indicator that the Australian Bureau of Statistics (ABS) uses to track insecure employment in Australia is workers' access to paid sick and annual leave. As of August 2022, 2.7 million Australian employees[1] or

23 percent of employees did not have access to paid leave (ABS, 2022). The true number is likely to be higher as a growing number (and proportion) of Australian workers hold second and third jobs, which are likely to be casual or otherwise precarious, but are not counted in official statistics (Burgess et al., 2008).

Figure 6.1 shows that the share of casual employment has remained high since the early 1990s (ABS, 2022). The growth of casual contracts spans industries and occupations (Burgess et al., 2008; Campbell & Burgess, 2018).

High rates of precarious employment for workers in transition is especially concerning given that, much like factory and industry closure, it has been linked with an increase in the rates of poor individual and community physical, psychosocial, and mental health outcomes (Bardasi & Francesconi, 2004; Bhattacharya et al., 2021; Clarke et al., 2007; Grzywacz & Dooley, 2003; Keuskamp et al., 2014; Kim et al., 2008; McNamara et al., 2011; Schneider & Harknett, 2019). It poses such a risk to individual, familial, and community health outcomes that it is now considered a

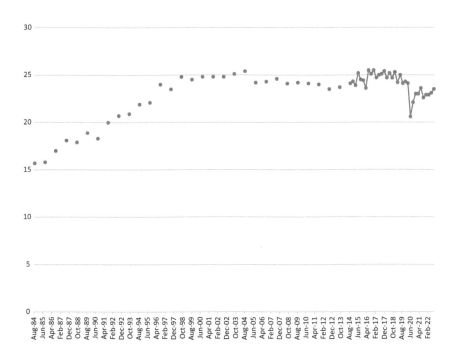

FIGURE 6.1   Share of casual employment.

Source: author, using data from ABS, 2022.

social determinant of health (Benach & Muntaner, 2007; Benach et al., 2014). The ordinary risks for workers in transition are exacerbated by high rates of insecure work (Beale, 2022).

6.5 PRECARITY AND TRANSITION

This case study draws from a longitudinal investigation into South Australian automotive workers' transition experiences conducted by the author, between 2018 and 2021, which found that workers struggled to find work of equal or greater value. The study employed a fixed-panel framework that followed the same group of workers to gather detailed information on changes in their characteristics, perspectives, and employment circumstances over time. Seventy-nine one-on-one interviews were conducted in three waves at six-month intervals, with 28 former South Australian automotive manufacturing workers (Smith et al., 2009). This method was used to help ensure that the findings formed through the case study would be of use for future instances of large-scale job loss.

In response to the lack of consensus around the definition of precarious work, and in order to gather as accurate and holistic an understanding of the interplay between precarious work and industry closure as possible, Beale (2022) developed a qualitative Framework of Employment In/Security grounded in the four objective components of precarious employment in the extant literature: employment insecurity (which includes risk of job loss and loss of hours; limited opportunity for promotion; and contract renewal predictability), economic insecurity (including low and fluctuating wages, and wage theft), work-time insecurity (predictability and consistency of hours and shifts; adequacy of hours and control over hours worked), and access to rights and entitlements (including contract type and paid leave – given rights and entitlements vary significantly across regulatory borders, this relies on the National Employment Standards set out in the Australian Fair Work Act 2009 (Australian Government, 2009)). This framework captures components that can be overlooked or obscured when relying on purely quantitative of precarious work data, such as national employment figures, which tend to limit their definitions to contract-type alone.

Through the application of the longitudinal, qualitative framework the study confirmed that precarious work poses a significant risk to workers' transition experiences following large-scale job loss (Beale, 2022). In the almost three years (29 months) following the closure of the Holden car manufacturing plant, the only participants not to experience at least one component of precarious work were the participants who were unable to secure *any* work during this period. It found a high incidence of financial insecurity and poor mental health for participants who did not find enough suitable work. This finding is shared by a large-scale multi-year study of Victorian automotive workers conducted by Barnes and Weller (2020) that found less than 50 percent of retrenched workers found permanent full-time work after the closure. Although my research (2022) does not claim that the instances of precarious work would be identically replicated across the automotive cohort, the design and application of the qualitative Framework for Employment In/Security does show that precarious work is a much more significant concern than research from previous closures suggested.

Larger investigations into the same closure conducted by Irving et al. (2022) and Barnes (2021) – as part of an Australian Research Council-funded longitudinal study called Future Work, Future Communities – found a significant percentage of retrenched automotive workers shifted into less-secure work and reported a drop in job quality, hours worked, income, and quality of life. This stands in contrast to the accepted wisdom informed by the Mitsubishi closure in the early 2000s – that one third of workers found full-time work, one third were unemployed or underemployed, and one third had left the workforce (Beer et al., 2006) – and to research conducted by ACIL Allen Consulting on behalf of the Australian Federal government that found 53 percent of former automotive workers found full-time work (Australian Government, 2020).

Traditional worker support programmes are designed to operate in prevailing employment landscapes, without capacity to stimulate job creation. In other words, for conventional programmes to be effective, there needs to be enough jobs – preferably good quality jobs – already available to ensure laid-off workers can find secure work. The just transitions literature, to date, has concentrated on the importance of creating good quality *green* jobs, but the findings from the automotive closures show the importance of increasing the quality of work across industry sectors as retrenched workers move into work outside the green energy sectors (Barnes, 2016, 2021; Barnes & Weller, 2020; Beale, 2022). This is particularly important given the knowledge that the employment impacts of decarbonisation and climate change are likely to impact the whole economy (IPCC, 2022, 2023).

More broadly an understanding of prevailing economic conditions and prospects is critical to determining the duration and type of support provided by transition programmes (Beale 2022). So too is the quality of work that is available.

6.6 MOVING PAST TEMPORALLY AND GEOGRAPHICALLY LIMITED PROGRAMMES

Until recently large-scale layoffs were relatively rare and tended to be confined to individual factories or companies. Workers support programmes have, consequently, been devised for rare, and temporally and geographically limited closures. The closure of the automotive industry was no different. There were two South Australian transition support centres, one in Adelaide's north and one in the south, where the majority of auto workers and auto companies were based (Australian Government, 2020). The centres opened in early 2014, shortly after Holden announced it would close in 2017, and they shut down in early 2019, 15 months after Holden's closure. An allowance offered to incentivise workers to retrain was withdrawn six months later, at the end of the 2018/2019 financial year.

Past closures have consistently found that transition support programmes need to run for an extended period because problems do not tend to emerge until '18 months to two years' after operations cease (Henderson & Shutt, 2004, p. 34). This has been attributed to workers delaying seeking help, finding their first endeavour into new employment unsuccessful, or experiencing a 'grieving period' that inhibits their ability to make plans (Nous Group, 2013, p. 15). Evidence from earlier closures also indicates that workers have the best employment outcomes if they retrain before a closure (Davies et al., 2017). However, workers from the South Australian automotive industry reported finding it difficult – if not impossible – to retrain while they were still working full-time (Beale, 2022). Moreover, participant employment outcomes were not static or linear and the reality of the transition programmes ending after 18 months meant the most vulnerable workers found themselves forced into the government's generic employment programme.

Finally, it is worth noting that traditional transition support programmes have relied heavily on the goodwill of private companies. At the time of the automotive closure, for example, Australia was a strong consumer market for Holden, Ford, and Toyota. As such, the companies had a vested interest in maintaining goodwill in the community. This is less likely if affected companies do not need to maintain a consumer market – as in the case with some primary industries – or as closures and layoffs become a normalised component of the employment landscape.

6.7 EMPLOYMENT SUPPORT IN TIMES OF DE-CARBONISATION

In the context of a just transition agenda, the suitability of temporally limited and place-based solutions needs to be questioned. Given the high rates of insecure work and climate change leading to more frequent, widespread, and concurrent disruptions to employment (IPCC, 2022, 2023), conventional approaches to employment emergencies may have had their day.

The current transition model, where support for workers is implemented incident by incident, no longer appears fit for purpose. It is now widely accepted that the global transition to a carbon-neutral economy, necessary to halt climate catastrophe, will impact every aspect of manufacturing, consumption, and service provision and the contemporary understanding of just transition reflects that (ILO, 2018; Newell & Mulvaney, 2013). The Paris Agreement, a landmark, legally binding international commitment made by 196 Nations in 2015 to limit global warming to below 2 degrees Celsius compared to pre-industrial levels exemplifies the seriousness of the threat. Its implementation requires economic and social transformation on a global scale from all signatories, including Australia. The centrality of decent work to that transformation is embedded in Goal 8 of the United Nations' Sustainable Development Goals (SDG) (UNDP, 2023).

In addition to the dual complexity of decarbonisation and industrial transformation, climate scientists have warned that the impact of increased natural disasters will be unpredictable and will likely leave no industry untouched (IPCC, 2022, 2023). Likewise, the COVID-19 pandemic has reminded policymakers of the dangers of 'unknown-unknowns' having catalysed an unprecedented global economic crisis that exposed and exacerbated existing vulnerabilities and inequalities in the Australian labour market (Clibborn, 2021; Pennington & Stanford, 2020). Just transition policies must be prepared for concurrent and consecutive employment disruptions that are not confined to primary resource industries. Natural disasters, like industry closure, have been shown to have long-lasting effects on employment (Venn, 2012). It will become illogical for just transition policy to have government intervene in employment support services one company, or one incident, at a time.

6.8 A BRIEF LOOK ACROSS BORDERS

The ILO (2015, p. 17) outline active labour market policies in their 'Guidelines for a just transition' that, among other things, encourages governments to use innovative strategies to 'strengthen public employment services to further develop their role as transition agents'. The ILO guidelines suggest such services should provide information, guidance, matching services, and targeted subsidies for workers to retrain, which is consistent with the closure support offered to automotive workers (Australian Government, 2020; Bowman & Callan, 2017; Callan et al., 2020; ILO, 2015).

When we look to the specifics of the worker support components of the international just transition agenda, we see that support still tends to follow best practice principles of individual closures, where worker support programmes are deployed closure by closure. The recurring examples of worker transition support in the literature of the Ruhr Valley, in Germany and the coal phase-out in Alberta, Canada, follow this overarching model (Mertins-Kirkwood & Hussey, 2020; Reitzenstein et al., 2020). In each instance, a local transition support authority is established, and funding for retraining and career counselling, among other things, is made available for workers directly affected by the closure. The only example the author could find of a broader, nationwide approach to the workers just transition support was in Scotland, where the Scottish Just Transition Commission is in the process of examining how an entire workforce could be transitioned away from employment dependent on fossil fuels (Mercier, 2020). However, that process is still underway and, in practice, Scotland's last coal-fired power station to close in Longannet, Fife in 2018 was approached in a similar fashion to the examples above and the automotive closure in Australia (Mercier, 2020). This can, in part, be attributed to the comparatively recent interest and pursuit of just transition frameworks.

6.9 CONCLUSION

Effective transition programmes need to be responsive to their overarching employment and policy contexts, yet existing programmes are ill equipped for our current and future circumstances. Learning the lessons of the automotive closure is vital if Australia is to successfully meet our climate and social development goals. The central lesson of the South Australian automotive closure is that Australia's employment landscape is dominated by insecure employment. Incorporating best practice transition support into an ongoing national employment support programme would better accommodate workers who delay seeking assistance or need further assistance when the first job they find is unsuitable or insufficient. A nationally accessible programme would also be better suited to future employment disruptions. One of the persistent political barriers to an ambitious decarbonisation agenda is the fear of widespread job loss. To address this fear, workers and their communities need to be reassured that adequate support will be available to them regardless of location or employment type. For example, research into closures has also consistently found incorporating formal and informal peer-to-peer support to be incredibly valuable (Australian Government, 2020; Callan et al., 2020; Davies et al., 2017).

We know that large-scale job loss, especially in the case of industry closure, can have serious and often lasting inter-generational, psychosocial effects on workers and their families and communities. As such, it is vital that interventions, including workers transition support, be robust and nationally consistent. A just transition policy agenda must include a broad understanding of both risks and justice for those who will be affected by the transition to a low-carbon economy.

The closure of the automotive industry raises a range of questions about the suitability of traditional transition support services. The most significant of these is the impact of precarious work on workers employment transitions. It shows that, in Australia, precarious work poses a serious threat to the successful employment transitions of workers following large-scale job loss. The ILO's Just Transition Framework underlines a need 'to generate decent jobs along the entire supply chain' (2018, p. 3) and the automotive closure shows us that such an aim should not be restricted to jobs in the energy sector. Improving the quality of employment, across the board, should be a central component of the transition agenda. Precarious work represents an underlying risk that is exacerbated during times of crisis and the just transition agenda will be flanked by crisis.

Considering the lessons of the automotive closure in the context of a holistic just transitions agenda, it is evident that traditional place-based worker transition programmes, already limited in their scope, will not be suitable for the large-scale disruptions to employment that will be brought by decarbonisation, climate change and automation.

NOTE

1 Increased from 2.4 million in the previous year (ABS, 2021).

REFERENCES

Abram, S., Atkins, E., Dietzel, A., Jenkins, K., Kiamba, L., Kirshner, J., Kreienkamp, J., Parkhill, K., Pegram, T., Ayllón, S. M. L. (2022). Just Transition: A whole-systems approach to decarbonisation. *Climate Policy*, 1–17. https://doi.org/10.1080/14693062.2022.2108365

ABS. (2021). Working arrangements. *Australian Bureau of Statistics*. https://www.abs.gov.au/statistics/labour/earnings-and-work-hours/working-arrangements/latest-release

ABS. (2022). Working arrangements. *Australian Bureau of Statistics*. https://www.abs.gov.au/statistics/labour/earnings-and-work-hours/working-arrangements/latest-release

Alberti, G., Bessa, I., Hardy, K., Trappmann, V., & Umney, C. (2018). Against and beyond precarity: Work in insecure times. *Work, Employment and Society*, 32(3), 447–457. https://doi.org/10.1177/0950017018762088

Anderson, B. (2010). Migration, immigration controls and the fashioning of precarious workers. *Work, Employment & Society*, 24(2), 300. https://doi.org/10.1177/0950017010362141

Australian Government. (2009). *Fair Work Act 2009*. https://www.legislation.gov.au/Details/C2017C00323

Australian Government. (2020). *The transition of the Australian car manufacturing sector*. Wallis and ACIL Allen Consulting. https://www.dewr.gov.au/whats-next/resources/transition-australian-car-manufacturing-sector-outcomes-and-best-practice-summary-report

Bainton, N., Kemp, D., Lebre, E., Owen, J. R., & Marston, G. (2021). The energy-extractives nexus and the just transition. *Sustainable Development*, 29(4), 624–634. https://doi.org/10.1002/sd.2163

Barbaro, B., & John, S. (2014). Closing the motor vehicle industry: The impact on Australia.

Barber, A., & Hall, S. (2008). Birmingham: Whose urban renaissance? Regeneration as a response to economic restructuring. *Policy Studies*, 29(3), 281–292. https://doi.org/10.1080/01442870802159871

Bardasi, E., & Francesconi, M. (2004). The impact of atypical employment on individual wellbeing: Evidence from a panel of British workers. *Social Science & Medicine*, 58(9), 1671–1688. https://doi.org/10.1016/S0277-9536(03)00400-3

Barnes, T. (2016). *Transition to where? Thinking through transitional policies for Victoria's automotive manufacturing industry* (Library Fellowship Paper, Issue. https://www.parliament.vic.gov.au/publications/research-papers/send/36-research-papers/13609-transition-to-where

Barnes, T. (2021). Pathways to precarity: Work, financial insecurity and wage dependency among Australia's retrenched auto workers. *Journal of Sociology*, 57(2), 443–463. https://doi.org/10.1177/1440783320925151

Barnes, T., & Weller, S. A. (2020). Becoming precarious? Precarious work and life trajectories after retrenchment. *Critical sociology*, 46(4–5), 527–541. https://doi.org/10.1177/0896920519896822

Beale, G. (2022). *Recalibrated expectations: A qualitative longitudinal investigation into precarious work and industry closure.* Adelaide: Flinders University. https://theses.flinders.edu.au/view/3a69134b-8afa-4b16-8f6a-52e65c618496/1

Beer, A. (2018). The closure of the Australian car manufacturing industry: Redundancy, policy and community impacts. *Australian Geographer, 49*(3), 419. https://doi.org/10.1080/00049182.2017.1402452

Beer, A., Baum, F., Thomas, H., Cutler, C., Zhang, G., Jolley, G., Ziersch, A., Verity, F., MacDougall, C., & Newman, L. (2006). An evaluation of the impact of retrenchment at Mitsubishi focussing on affected workers, their families and communities: Implications for human services policies and practices.

Beer, A., & Evans, H. (2010). A tale of two cities: auto plant closures and policy responses in Birmingham and Adelaide. In A. Beer & H. Evans (Eds.), *The impacts of automotive plant closure: A tale of two cities* (pp. 1–5). New York, NY: Routledge.

Beer, A., & Thomas, H. (2007). The politics and policy of economic restructuring in Australia: Understanding government responses to the closure of an automotive plant. *Space and Polity, 11*(3), 243–261. https://doi.org/10.1080/13562570701811569

Beer, A., Weller, S., Barnes, T., Onur, I., Ratcliffe, J., Bailey, D., & Sotarauta, M. (2019). The urban and regional impacts of plant closures: New methods and perspectives. *Regional Studies, Regional Science, 6*(1), 380–394. https://doi.org/10.1080/21681376.2019.1622440

Benach, J., & Muntaner, C. (2007). Precarious employment and health: Developing a research agenda. *Journal of Epidemiology and Community Health, 61*(4), 276–277. https://doi.org/10.1136/jech.2005.045237

Benach, J., Vives, A., Amable, M., Vanroelen, C., Tarafa, G., & Muntaner, C. (2014). Precarious employment: Understanding an emerging social determinant of health. In J. E. Fielding (Ed.), *Annual review of public health, Vol 35* (Vol. 35, pp. 229–253). https://doi.org/10.1146/annurev-publhealth-032013-182500

Bhattacharya, A., Ray, T., Bhattacharya, A., & Ray, T. (2021). Precarious work, job stress, and health-related quality of life. *American Journal of Industrial Medicine, 64*(4), 310–319. https://doi.org/10.1002/ajim.23223

Bowman, K., & Callan, V. J. (2017). Brief for a longitudinal study of automotive manufacturing and supply chain workers (unpublished).

Burgan, B., & Spoehr, J. (2013). *The contribution of GMH Elizabeth operations to the south Australian economy and the potential impacts of closure.* https://digital.library.adelaide.edu.au/dspace/bitstream/2440/123007/1/Burgan_Contribution_P2013.pdf

Burgess, J., & Campbell, I. (1998). The nature and dimensions of precarious employment in Australia. *Labour & Industry: A Journal of the Social and Economic Relations of Work, 8*(3), 5–21. https://doi.org/10.1080/10301763.1998.10669175

Burgess, J., Campbell, I., & May, R. (2008). Pathways from casual employment to economic security: The Australian experience. *Social Indicators Research, 88*(1), 161–178. https://doi.org/10.1007/s11205-007-9212-5

Burrows, S. (2013). Precarious work, neo-liberalism and young people's experiences of employment in the Illawarra region. *Economic and Labour Relations Review, 24*(3), 380–396. https://doi.org/10.1177/1035304613498189

Callan, V. J., Bowman, K., Fitzsimmons, T. W., & Poulsen, A. L. (2020). Industry restructuring and job loss: Towards a guiding model to assist the displaced older worker. *Journal of Vocational Education & Training, ahead-of-print*(ahead-of-print), 1–25. https://doi.org/10.1080/13636820.2020.1744693

Campbell, I., & Burgess, J. (2018). Patchy progress? Two decades of research on precariousness and precarious work in Australia. *Labour & Industry - A Journal of the Social and Economic Relations of Work, 28*(1), 48–67. https://doi.org/10.1080/10301763.2018.1427424

Campbell, I., & Price, R. (2016). Precarious work and precarious workers: Towards an improved conceptualisation. *Economic and Labour Relations Review, 27*(3), 314–332. https://doi.org/10.1177/1035304616652074

Carney, T., & Stanford, J. (2018). The dimensions of insecure work: A factbook. *The Australian Institute Centre for Future Work.*

Chapain, C., & Murie, A. (2008). The impact of factory closure on local communities and economies: The case of the MG Rover Longbridge closure in Birmingham. *Policy Studies, 29*(3), 305–317. https://doi.org/10.1080/01442870802159962

Clarke, M., Lewchuk, W., de Wolff, A., & King, A. (2007). 'This just isn't sustainable': Precarious employment, stress and workers' health. *International Journal of Law and Psychiatry, 30*(4), 311–326. https://doi.org/10.1016/j.ijlp.2007.06.005

Clibborn, S. (2021). Australian industrial relations in 2020: COVID-19, crisis and opportunity. *Journal of Industrial Relations, 63*(3), 291–302. https://doi.org/10.1177/00221856211012813

Clibborn, S., Lansbury, R. D., & Wright, C. F. (2016). Who killed the Australian automotive industry: The employers, government or trade unions? *Econ Pap, 35*(1), 2–15. https://doi.org/10.1111/1759-3441.12127

Davies, A. R., Homolova, L., Grey, C. N. B., & Bellis, M. A. (2017). Mass unemployment events (MUEs) – Prevention and response from a public health perspective. *Public Health Wales, Cardiff,* 1–31. http://www.wales.nhs.uk/sitesplus/documents/888/Watermarked%20PHW%20Mass%20Unemployment%20Report%20E%2815%29.pdf

della Porta, D., Silvasti, T., Hänninen, S., & Siisiäinen, M. (2015). The precarization effect. In D. della Porta, S. Hänninen, M. Siisiäinen, & T. Silvasti (Eds.), *The new social division: Making and unmaking precariousness.* London: Palgrave Macmillan UK. https://doi.org/10.1057/9781137509352

DIS (2018). *Automotive industry structural adjustment program.* Department of Industry and Skills https://www.business.gov.au/assistance/automotive-industry-structural-adjustment-programme

Evans, G., & Phelan, L. (2016). Transition to a post-carbon society: Linking environmental justice and just transition discourses. *Energy Policy, 99,* 329–339. https://doi.org/10.1016/j.enpol.2016.05.003

Filipović, S., Lior, N., & Radovanović, M. (2022). The green deal – Just transition and sustainable development goals Nexus. *Renewable & Sustainable Energy Reviews, 168.* https://doi.org/10.1016/j.rser.2022.112759

Fournier, G. (2009). Precarious Employment: Understanding Labour Market Insecurity in Canada Edited by Leah F. Vosko Montréal: McGill-Queen's University Press, 2006, 485 p., ISBN 0-773529-61-6 (bd.). *Relations industrielles (Québec, Québec)*, *64*(1), 167. https://doi.org/10.7202/029544ar

Galgoczi, B. (2020). Just transition on the ground: Challenges and opportunities for social dialogue. *European Journal of Industrial Relations*, *26*(4), 367–382. https://doi.org/10.1177/0959680120951704

Goods, C. (2013). A just transition to a green economy: Evaluating the response of Australian unions. *Australian Bulletin of Labour*, *39*(2), 13–33.

Goods, C. (2020). Australian business: Embracing, reconceptualising, or ignoring a just transition in Australia. In E. Morena, D. Krause, & D. Stevis (Eds.), *Just transitions* (1 ed., pp. 76–94). Pluto Press.

Grzywacz, J. G., & Dooley, D. (2003). "Good jobs" to "bad jobs": Replicated evidence of an employment continuum from two large surveys. *Social Science & Medicine*, *56*(8), 1749–1760. https://doi.org/10.1016/S0277-9536(02)00170-3

Heffron, R. J. (2021). *Achieving a just transition to a low-carbon economy*. Springer International Publishing AG.

Henderson, R., & Shutt, J. (2004). Responding to a coalfield closure: Old issues for a new regional development agency? *Local economy*, *19*(1), 25–37. https://doi.org/10.1080/0269094032000168451

Howell, D. R., & Kalleberg, A. L. (2019). Declining job quality in the United States: Explanations and evidence. *Rsf-the Russell Sage Journal of the Social Sciences*, *5*(4), 1–53. https://doi.org/10.7758/rsf.2019.5.4.01

IISD. (2022). *Making good green jobs the law: How Canada can build on international best practice to advance just transition for all*. International Institute for Sustainable Development. https://www.iisd.org/publications/green-jobs-advance-canada-just-transition

ILO. (2015). *Guidelines for a just transition towards environmentally sustainable economies and societies for all*. International Labour Organization. https://www.ilo.org/wcmsp5/groups/public/@ed_emp/@emp_ent/documents/publication/wcms_432859.pdf

ILO. (2018). *Just transition towards environmentally sustainable economies and societies for all*. https://www.ilo.org/wcmsp5/groups/public/---ed_dialogue/---actrav/documents/publication/wcms_647648.pdf

IPCC. (2022). *Climate change 2022: Mitigation of climate change*. Intergovernmental Panel on Climate Change. https://www.ipcc.ch/report/ar6/wg3/downloads/report/IPCC_AR6_WGIII_FullReport.pdf

IPCC. (2023). *Synthesis report of the IPCC sixth assessment report*. Intergovernmental Panel on Climate Change. https://report.ipcc.ch/ar6syr/pdf/IPCC_AR6_SYR_SPM.pdf

Irving, J., et al. (2022). Plant closures in Australia's automotive industry: Continuity and change. *Regional Studies, Regional Science*, *9*(1), 5–22.

Jermain, D. O., Ren, Z. J., Foster, S. B., Pilcher, R. C., & Berardi, E. J. (2022). Coal in the 21st century: Integrating policy with practice for just transitions. *Electricity Journal*, *35*(10), Article 107220. https://doi.org/10.1016/j.tej.2022.107220

Jolley, G., Newman, L., Ziersch, A., & Baum, F. (2011). Positive and negative impacts of job loss on family life: The perceptions of Australian car workers. *Australian Journal of Social Issues, 46*(4), 411–433. https://doi.org/10.1002/j.1839-4655.2011.tb00227.x

Kalleberg, A.L. (2011). *Good jobs, bad jobs: The rise of polarized and precarious employment systems in the United States, 1970s–2000s.*

Kalleberg, A.L. (2018). *Precarious lives: Job insecurity and well-being in rich democracies.* Cambridge, UK: Polity Press.

Keuskamp, D., Ziersch, A. M., Baum, F., & LaMontagne, A. D. (2014). Precarious employment, psychosocial working conditions, and health: Cross-sectional associations in a population-based sample of working Australians.

Kim, M. H., Kim, C. Y., Park, J. K., & Kawachi, I. (2008). Is precarious employment damaging to self-rated health? Results of propensity score matching methods, using longitudinal data in South Korea. *Social Science & Medicine, 67*(12), 1982–1994. https://doi.org/10.1016/j.socscimed.2008.09.051

Kreshpaj, B., Orellana, C., Burstrom, B., Davis, L., Hemmingsson, T., Johansson, G., Kjellberg, K., Jonsson, J., Wegman, D. H., & Bodin, T. (2020). What is precarious employment? A systematic review of definitions and operationalizations from quantitative and qualitative studies. *Scandinavian Journal of Work Environment & Health, 46*(3), 235–247. https://doi.org/10.5271/sjweh.3875

Laß, I., & Wooden, M. (2020). Trends in the prevalence of non-standard employment in Australia. *Journal of Industrial Relations, 62*(1), 3–32. https://doi.org/10.1177/0022185619873929

Lee, C., Huang, G.-H., & Ashford, S. J. (2018). Job insecurity and the changing workplace: Recent developments and the future trends in job insecurity research. *Annual Review of Organizational Psychology and Organizational Behavior, 5*(1), 335–359. https://doi.org/10.1146/annurev-orgpsych-032117-104651

Lewchuk, W. (2017). Precarious jobs: Where are they, and how do they affect well-being? *The Economic and Labour Relations Review, 28*(3), 402–419. https://doi.org/10.1177/1035304617722943

McNamara, M., Bohle, P., & Quinlan, M. (2011). Precarious employment, working hours, work-life conflict and health in hotel work. *Applied Ergonomics, 42*(2), 225–232. https://doi.org/10.1016/j.apergo.2010.06.013

Mercier, S. (2020). *Four case studies on just transition: Lessons for Ireland*, Research Series Paper No.15 (May 2020)., Available at SSRN: https://ssrn.com/abstract=3694643

Mertins-Kirkwood, H., & Hussey, I. (2020). A top-down transition: A critical account of Canada's government-led phase-out of the coal sector. In E. Morena, D. Krause, & D. Stevis (Eds.), *Just transitions: Social justice in the shift towards a low-carbon world* (1 ed.). Pluto Press.

Morena, E., Krause, D., & Stevis, D. (2020). *Just transitions: Social justice in the shift towards a low-carbon world.* Pluto Press.

Newell, P., & Mulvaney, D. (2013). The political economy of the "just transition". *Geographical Journal, 179*(2), 132–140. https://doi.org/10.1111/geoj.12008

Newman, L. A., MacDougall, C. J. M., & Baum, F. E. (2009). Australian children's accounts of the closure of a car factory: Global restructuring and local impacts. *Community, Work & Family, 12*(2), 143–158. https://doi.org/10.1080/13668800902778934

Nous Group. (2013). *Lessons learnt from large firm closures – Main report.* https://docs.education.gov.au/documents/lessons-learnt-large-firm-closures-vol-1-main-report

OECD. (2015). *In it together: Why less inequality benefits all.* OECD. https://www.oecd-ilibrary.org/docserver/9789264235120-en.pdf?expires=1527572409&id=id&accname=ocid177318a&checksum=47B73ED3BEB5C2FC0BB3F956F5ABDD79

Paraskevopoulou, A. (2020). Gender and Precarious Work. In K. F. Zimmermann (Ed.), *Handbook of labor, human resources and population economics* (pp. 1–18). Springer International Publishing. https://doi.org/10.1007/978-3-319-57365-6_30-1

Pennington, A., & Stanford, J. (2020). Rebuilding after COVID-19 will need a sustained national reconstruction plan. *Journal of Australian Political Economy, 2020*(85), 164–174.

Ranasinghe, R., Hordacre, A.-L., & Spoehr, J. (2014). Impact of the auto industry closure workplace futures survey playford and Salisbury wave 2. Australian Workplace Innovation and Social Research Centre, University of Adelaide.

Reitzenstein, A., Schulz, S., & Heilmann, F. (2020). The story of coal in Germany: A model for just transition in Europe? In E. Morena, D. Krause, & D. Stevis (Eds.), *Just transitions: Social justice in the shift towards a low-carbon world* (1st ed.). Pluto Press.

Schneider, D., & Harknett, K. (2019). Consequences of routine work-schedule instability for worker health and well-being. *American Sociological Review, 84*(1), 82–114. https://doi.org/10.1177/0003122418823184

Smith, P., Lynn, P., & Elliot, D. (2009). Sample design for longitudinal surveys. In P. Lynn (Ed.), *Methodology of longitudinal surveys.* John Wiley & Sons, Incorporated. https://doi.org/10.1002/9780470743874

Spoehr, J. (2015). Far from the Car – The case for transformational change in response to the closure of the automotive manufacturing industry. *WISeR, The University of Adelaide.* http://www.flinders.edu.au/fms/AITI/Documents/wiser201506_far_from_the_car.pdf

Standing, G. (2011). *The precariat: the new dangerous class.* Bloomsbury Academic.

Stanford, J. (2017). Automotive surrender: The demise of industrial policy in the Australian vehicle industry. *The Economic and Labour Relations Review: ELRR, 28*(2), 197–217. https://doi.org/10.1177/1035304617709659

Stanford, J. (2020). *A fair share for Australian manufacturing: Manufacturing renewal for the Post-COVID economy.* https://d3n8a8pro7vhmx.cloudfront.net/theausinstitute/pages/3332/attachments/original/1595693276/A_Fair_Share_for_Australian_Manufacturing.pdf?1595693276

Stevis, D., & Felli, R. (2014). Global labour unions and just transition to a green economy. *International Environmental Agreements: Politics, Law and Economics, 15*(1), 29–43. https://doi.org/10.1007/s10784-014-9266-1

Stevis, D., Morena, E., & Krause, D. (2020). Introduction: The genealogy and contemporary politics of just transitions. In E. Morena, D. Krause, & D. Stevis (Eds.), *Just transitions: social justice in the shift towards a low-carbon world* (1 ed.). Pluto Press.

Tweedie, D. (2013). Precarious work and Australian labour norms. *Economic and Labour Relations Review*, *24*(3), 297–315. https://doi.org/10.1177/10353 04613494521

UNDP. (2023). Sustainable development goals. *United Nations Development Programme.* https://www.undp.org/sustainable-development-goals

Venn, D. (2012). Helping displaced workers back into jobs after a natural disaster. https://doi.org/10.1787/5k8zk8pn2542-en

Wayne, L., & Michelynn, L. (2014). Precarious employment and social outcomes. *Just labour.* https://doi.org/10.25071/1705-1436.4

Worrall, L., Gamble, H., Spoehr, J., & Hordacre, A.-L. (2021). Australian sovereign capability and supply chain resilience – Perspectives and options. https://www.flinders.edu.au/content/dam/documents/research/aiti/Australian_sovereign_capability_and_supply_chain_resilience.pdf

Wu, C.-H., Wang, Y., Parker, S. K., & Griffin, M. A. (2020). Effects of chronic job insecurity on big five personality change. *Journal of Applied Psychology.* https://doi.org/10.1037/apl0000488

CHAPTER 7

Being Safe from and with Robots

Work Health and Safety in the Age of the Intelligent Machine

Valerie O'Keeffe and Sara Howard

INTRODUCING TECHNOLOGY, IN THIS CASE robotics, provides opportunities to improve work by redesigning processes, potentially benefitting productivity, quality and safety. Inevitably new technology changes tasks and jobs. This chapter summarises robotic applications in workplace settings within Australia and around the world and considers the health and safety challenges these present. The term 'robot' is very familiar, yet conceptions of robots and their available forms are diverse. In this chapter, we take a broad description of robots, acknowledging that they can be stationary (i.e., the robot pedestal/base does not move) or mobile (such as unmanned aerial vehicles or drones, quadruped robots and automated guided vehicles (AGVs)). Robots can be operated by a human locally or at a distance (tele-operated), 'smart' (fitted with artificial intelligence (AI) and autonomous) or 'dumb' (non-autonomous); and used for industrial or service purposes. Examination of robot uptake by country also highlights important drivers of this technology adoption, which are generally linked to addressing workforce shortages. The chapter concludes by exploring safety hazards and emerging issues associated with human–robot interactions. Managing risks highlights the importance of work design (addressing physical and psychosocial factors, including perceived safety). Successful mitigation requires a systems approach that evaluates interactions between people, tasks, technologies, environment and work organisation.

DOI: 10.1201/9781003393757-7

7.1 ROBOTICS TECHNOLOGY

In lay terms, a robot can be described as a multipurpose piece of equipment that replaces human effort, is automatically operated, is physically mobile in its environment and can execute tasks with speed and precision (Dobberstein, 2022; LaFrance, 2016; Moravec, n.d.; TechTarget Network, n.d.).

Non-autonomous robots act on pre-programmed information created by the programmer, and are designed to perform specific tasks in well-defined and controlled environments such as those often found in industrial and manufacturing settings (Smids, Nyholm, & Berkers, 2020). In contrast, autonomous robots are 'told what to do' but contain a learning model and feedback loop (enabled by computer vision, sensors and machine learning). These components of AI ensure the possibility of automatic learning using huge volumes of data giving them context awareness and facilitating independent decision making, without direct human input (Jarota, 2021). Autonomous robots are typically applied to less structured service settings like concierge robots in hotels (Nippon, 2018) and delivery robots distributing and registering patient medications in hospitals (Smids et al., 2020).

Robots constitute one method of delivering automation (i.e., technology that reduces the need for human intervention in a process) which occurs on a spectrum from no automation (fully manual processes) to fully automated (involving no human assistance), incorporating various levels of automation, as described by Adriaensen et al. (2022) and Gopinath and Johansen (2019). Importantly, a system that is fully automated does not equate to an autonomous system, since it may operate without ongoing human involvement, but lack intelligence.

Robots tend to be categorised as industrial or service, depending on their intended application. An industrial robot can be defined as 'an automatically controlled, reprogrammable, multipurpose manipulator, programmable in three or more axes, which can be either fixed in place or mobile for use in industrial automation applications' (International Organisation for Standardisation, 2012). Globally, industrial robot adoption rates tend to be strongly correlated with the presence of automotive manufacturing (Leigh, Lee, & Kraft, 2022). Currently, there are more than three million industrial robots operating in factories around the world, and they are most likely found in electrical/electronics, automotive and metal and machinery businesses assisting with manual handling, welding and assembly (International Federation of Robotics, 2022b).

Advancements in industrial robotics tend to focus on the application of collaborative robots (Javaid, Haleem, Singh, Rab, & Suman, 2022). Collaborative robots, or 'cobots', are:

> speed and force limited industrial robotic arms that are designed with reduced pinch-points, smooth joint-shell designs, and include built-in safety sensors. They are typically smaller and less powerful than traditional industrial robotic arms and correspondingly have reduced payloads and slower operation. Such design elements enable a cobot to stop if it collides with an operator or item in the workspace.
>
> (Howard et al., 2021, p. 2)

Cobots can be viewed as a source of competitive advantage, with Howard et al. (2021) summarising the constituents of their value proposition. Since 2017, the market share of cobots relative to traditional industrial robots has been growing steadily (International Federation of Robotics, 2022b), reaching approximately 22,000 installations in 2020, predominantly in the electronics and automotive industries (Placek, 2022).

The development of industrial robots and smart capabilities such as AI is increasing the uptake of robots across businesses (Sostero, 2020) where a business is 'more likely to adopt robots when it is located in a region with a large number of existing robot users and robot-related skilled labour' (Leigh et al., 2022, p. 1041). While robots have been most prolific in manufacturing, 'the service sector is the current technological frontier of automation' (Sostero, 2020, p. ii). A service robot can be defined as a 'robot that performs useful tasks for humans or equipment excluding industrial automation applications' (International Organisation for Standardisation, 2012). In a professional setting, robots tend to be used in commercial tasks and operated by trained personnel (International Organisation for Standardisation, 2012). In 2019, around 360,000 professional service robots were sold to enterprises (Stewart et Casey, & Wigginton, 2019). The most common applications for professional service robots in 2021 included transportation and logistics, hospitality, medical and healthcare, professional cleaning and agriculture (International Federation of Robotics, 2022b).

7.2 UPTAKE OF ROBOTS IN THE WORKPLACE

The extent of robot adoption is commonly measured by robot density – the number of industrial robots installed as a share of manufacturing workers (Atkinson, 2018; International Federation of Robotics, 2021). The

TABLE 7.1   Top 5 Leading Nations in Robot Density (Based on 2020 Data)

Country	Number of Robots Installed per 10,000 Employees
South Korea	932
Singapore	605
Japan	390
Germany	371
Sweden	289
Australia	83

Source: International Federation of Robotics (2021), Stanford (2020).

global average in 2020 was 126 robots per 10,000 employees, nearly twice
the average of 66 per 10,000 in 2015 (International Federation of Robotics,
2021). Compared to other industrialised countries, Australia has a relatively low uptake of robots (see Table 7.1), although there is large variation
in adoption rates between countries. The following sections will review
contemporary, innovative applications of robotics in workplaces across
the five leading countries in robot density (see Table 7.1) and compare
these with Australian applications.

7.3 INTERNATIONAL PERSPECTIVES

Robots have been adopted across industries in diverse applications and
countries, as illustrated in Table 7.2. The use cases provided are by no
means exhaustive, and where numerous applications exist, examples are
selected to portray breadth and variety of use. The context of uptake in
each country is briefly discussed.

7.3.1 South Korea

Robots are frequently found in Korean manufacturing companies (Jee-
Hee, 2021), including in the production of hybrid and electric vehicle
batteries (Market Prospects, 2020), but they are increasingly found in
healthcare, agriculture and defence (Lee, 2022). High levels of robot adoption are likely influenced by labour shortages and expenses (Hosokawa,
2022) stemming from South Korea's extremely low fertility rate (McCurry,
2023), making the technology price-competitive.

7.3.2 Singapore

Typically, Singaporeans dislike engaging in '3D jobs' – those that are dirty,
dangerous and demanding (or difficult or demeaning) – making robotic
systems well-suited solutions (NCS, 2022). Furthermore, Singapore is a

TABLE 7.2   Examples of Robotics Applications in Top Five Leading Nations (Based on Robot Density in Manufacturing Industries)

Company	Application	Technology	Outcome
South Korea			
LG Electronics (Assembly Magazine, 2022)	Assembly– Appliances: refrigerators, washers and dryers	Six axis robots complete welding & screwdriving; AGV transport parts and finished appliances	Increased productivity (by 25%) and safety (prevent human engagement in physically demanding and repetitive duties), decreased defects
CJ Logistics (Nikkei Asia, 2022)	Warehousing and logistics: Packing and shipping services for online retailer (Naver)	101 robots lift and move 630 shelves on 7,000 square metre floor	Shelves with items to pack move to workers – reduces worker waiting times. Efficiency has improved by 55%, reduced cost of shipping & handling for consumers
The Agency for Defence Development (applied research of prototype) (Kim, 2022)	Defence – reconnaissance missions and disaster site exploration	Modular robot with Autonomous Tunnel Exploration – detects underground risks and generates a high-resolution 3D map of the area (AI software allows for recognition, judgement and exploration functions)	Robot can be controlled remotely. Prevent/limit human exposure to harsh conditions (e.g., caves, hazardous facilities)
Initiative of provincial government (Eun-Ji, 2022)	Agriculture – crop cultivation and harvesting	Wearable robotic devices: fork (assist with lifting objects from floor to waist height), vest (assist reaching upward) or chair (supports posture when in a sitting position)	Reduce human workload/effort, prevent fatigue and musculoskeletal disorders and improve income of farmers

(Continued)

TABLE 7.2 (*Continued*)

Company	Application	Technology	Outcome
Myongji Hospital (Ang, 2022)	Healthcare & care management	'PIO', AI-driven care robot, stimulates attachment and emotion in dementia patients	For patients – relieve depression and improve emotional stability and cognitive ability. For health professionals – reduce workload
Woowa Brothers (Nikkei Asia, 2022)	Food delivery	'Dilly Drive' small robot drives to restaurant, employee loads it with food order, robot delivers to consumer, coordinating access to lobbies and elevators	Piloting service in outskirts of Seoul (awaiting review of traffic laws and safety regulations as not currently allowed on sidewalk)
Robo Arete (Robert Chicken) (Kyoung-Son, 2021)	Chef/cooking	Robot arm can cook 40–50 portions of chicken per hour. Human receives order and packs it	Increased productivity, prevent human exposure to high temperatures (170 degrees Celsius) and increased consistency in quality
Singapore			
Gammon (Reuters, 2022)	Construction – surveying	'Spot' four-legged robot scans sections of mud and gravel to check on work progress	Reduced labour requirements from 2 to 1 employee
Public Library (Lee, 2020)	Information service – inspection/ quality control	Shelf-Reading Robot, scans labels on 100,000 books (30% of its daily collection) at night to determine if in right place and in right order and provides report identifying any errors for manual correction by human	Reduces routine, labour-intensive work and reduces workers' postural and eye strain risks. Allows staff to engage in higher-value tasks (interacting with and assisting patrons)

KK Women's and Children's Hospital (Changi General Hospital, 2015)	Healthcare & care management	Robotic bottle dispensing system at Emergency Pharmacy – can autoload, pick, assemble and label medication bottles. In combination with RFID tags, can track and deliver medication	Enhanced efficiency of dispensing (dispense up to 1,800 bottles per day) allowing pharmacists to focus on safety checks and patient education, improving overall patient experience
National Gallery (National Gallery Singapore, 2021)	Tourism	TEMI, an autonomous robot guide, introduces visitors to selected artworks in the museum	Improved customer convenience/ experience. Provides additional capacity for visitors who have missed a scheduled, human-delivered tour
Solar Clean International (Solar Clean International, n.d.)	Cleaning	Remote-controlled, autonomous, intelligent robot cleans solar panels in a range of locations (e.g., high rise buildings, floating ocean panels)	Improved safety, quality and efficiency
Germany			
Ford (Cologne plant) (ETAuto, 2016)	Automotive	Cobots assist production workers to fit shock absorbers	Productivity and quality improvements, reduced injury risks (previously requiring workers to lift heavy parts overhead)
Klinikum Chemnitz (HealthTech, n.d.)	Medical – surgical assistance	Versius Surgical Robot System supports medical teams to conduct minimal access surgery (i.e., laparoscopic or keyhole surgery)	Reduces strain on surgeon during long and complex surgeries

(Continued)

TABLE 7.2 (*Continued*)

Company	Application	Technology	Outcome
Edeka supermarkets (Zhao, 2021)	Retail – Customer service	Humanoid robot 'Pepper' stands near the checkout and reminds employees and shoppers to wear masks and follow social-distancing rules. Customers can also ask product-related questions (e.g., current sale items, available stock lines)	Allows employees to focus on higher-value activities
Japan			
Fujita Works (Universal Robots, 2023)	Manufacturing – sheet metal work	Welding process divided into pre-welding (undertaken by workers) and permanent welding (completed by cobots)	Improve work efficiency and reduce physical burden on workers, increase job satisfaction
Kalm Dairy (Rich, 2019)	Agriculture – food production	Eight robots milk more than 400 cows, three times a day. Cows wear sensors on collar to indicate time for milking, automated gates corral cows into stalls where robots attach suction cups to cows' teats. Computers track the volume of milk streaming into tanks	Prevented closure of dairy farm due to lack of workforce availability (had already merged with other local dairies)
Office building in Shinagawa (Lufkin, 2020)	Professional services – security	Ugo, a police bot, does a routine patrol around the building every two hours, sharing vision from its built-in camera with human guards elsewhere in the building	Increased efficiency and flexibility of resource deployment

Dawn Avatar café (Albrecht, 2018; BBC, 2018)	Food – dining	Teleoperated robots (transmit audio and video via internet) to take food orders and serve food	Enable individuals with severe physical disabilities (e.g., amyotrophic lateral sclerosis) to participate in the workforce.
International Space Station (Australian Associated Press, 2013)	Space – companionship	Kirobo, an astronaut humanoid robot (34 cm tall, weighing 1 kg) who speaks Japanese, sent into space to accompany the first Japanese commander of the International Space Station	Enhance human well-being in isolated settings
Sweden			
TNG (Savage, 2019)	Professional services – recruitment	Tengai (robot head), poses all interview questions in an identical way, in the same tone and order and provides transcript to recruiter/manager for appraisal	Reduce subjectivity/unconscious bias in interviews
Boliden (Goodman, 2017)	Mining	Teleoperated loader to collect rock containing silver, zinc and lead	Prevents human operator from inhaling dust and exhaust fumes.
FT-Produktion (The Robot Report Staff, 2019)	Manufacturing – metal fabrication	3 or 4 cobots execute high-volume production runs, overseen by one operator	Eliminated monotonous manual tasks with operators able to focus on smaller production runs with greater variation in tasks and increased job satisfaction
BillerudKorsnas (Palmer, 2019)	Manufacturing – pulp and paper	Using AI systems to monitor massive amounts of data from machines to determine how long to cook wood chips before they turn into pulp	Reduction in tedious tasks, humans can focus on value-add tasks

geographically small city, nation and state whose labour market relies heavily on foreign workers. In 2010, approximately 35% of Singapore's labour force were foreign-born (Yeoh & Lin, 2012). Travel and migration restrictions imposed by the COVID-19 pandemic increased the impetus for companies to adopt technology and automation as a key part of the response to a reduction of 235,700 foreign workers between December 2019 and September 2021 (Teo, 2022). Technology was also seen as a solution to mitigate the spread of disease and improve safety in the workplace, as illustrated in a recent 'Workplace Smart Cleanliness' study that found 75% of workers in Singapore believed robots 'are an ideal complement to janitorial staff in ensuring the cleanliness of their workspace' (Onag, 2022, para 1).

7.3.3 Germany

Several German automobile companies (e.g., Audi, Volkswagen) utilise cobots to assist with various car assembly processes (Liuima, 2016). As creators of the term 'Industrie 4.0', a concept intended to capture the widespread integration of information and communication technology in industrial production; (Winter, n.d.), it is not surprising that Germany is a leading adopter of robotics. The strategic and forward-thinking approach of German government and business towards technology has enabled Germany to be an 'automation superpower' (Prakash, 2017). Ethical and legal considerations are at the forefront of policy development, guiding the testing and implementation of technology. Examples include delegating liability for autonomous cars on the autobahn and malfunctioning robotic arms, as well as monitoring cyber-security and surveillance risks (Prakash, 2017).

7.3.4 Japan

Japan is the world's number one producer of industrial robots, delivering nearly half of the global supply (International Federation of Robotics, 2022a). Like other countries, Japan's uptake is driven by labour shortages, although this is exacerbated by the nation's domestic orientation – 'we don't accept many immigrants, so robots are more suitable' (Matsui cited by Lufkin (2020, para. 11)), with the population preferring automation to immigration (Lufkin, 2020). Additionally, Japan's popular culture has long embraced robots and viewed them as lovable entities, unlike western cultures, where they are often portrayed as menacing and something to be feared (Lufkin, 2020). Again, led by the automotive sector, Toyota Motor Hokkaido (which manufactures car transmissions, axles and components) has incorporated cobots to improve the parts-feeding process (Universal Robots, 2023).

7.3.5 Sweden

Like Germany, Sweden has a strong automotive industry with positive, progressive attitudes towards technology. Volvo has undertaken development of an autonomous trash-collecting robot (Savov, 2015) and Scania AB was the first truck manufacturer to automate the application of cab door linings (Scania, 2016). The Swedish mindset is to protect workers over jobs; thus, they focus on (re)training humans and tend not to fear technology (Goodman, 2017). In a 2017 survey conducted by the European Commission, 80% of Swedes welcomed robots and AI, perhaps a product of their employee-funded job security council that supports workers to pursue new roles if their job is negatively affected by robots (Foundry4, 2019).

7.3.6 Australia

Australia's relatively sluggish adoption of robotics is likely to have been hindered by the cessation of its automotive industry around 2018, when production lines for Mitsubishi, Ford, Holden and Toyota all moved offshore to take advantage of lower productions costs (Valadkhani, 2016). Some argue that government policy and decision-making over a longer period have resulted in Australian manufacturers becoming less competitive:

> In fact, the eventual demise of the industry was inevitably set in the late 1940s when the sector was established behind substantial government assistance, therefore masking forever the necessity for it to be outward-looking, and internationally competitive on price, quality and innovation.
>
> (Scales, 2017, Para 3)

Despite this broader context, Australian industry is increasingly engaging with robotics and AI, recognising its value proposition in terms of competitive advantage and sovereign capability (Spoehr et al., 2020). The pandemic, political instability and conflict, combined with global disruption to supply chains, have starkly highlighted the vulnerabilities of Australian manufacturing, driving technology adoption (Australian Industry Group, 2021).

Manning et al. (2021) described seven use cases of robotics in manufacturing sites located in South Australia, including electronic components and appliances, and wine packaging. Table 7.3 provides a sample of these and other robotics applications across Australia, many of which are showcased in roadmaps developed by the Australian Centre for Robotic Vision

TABLE 7.3 Innovative Applications of Robots in Australian Settings

Company	Application	Technology	Outcome
Victoria International Container Terminal, Port of Melbourne (Edwards, 2017)	Freight management – container handling facility	One Terminal, the world's first fully automated container handling terminal	Increased safety, reduce bottlenecks/turnaround times
New Royal Adelaide Hospital (Barouch, 2018; Fleet, 2017)	Healthcare – housekeeping services and sample processing	25 AGVs – transport around 1,800 trolleys (of linen, waste, meals and pharmacy supplies); Lab automation – blood/urine, etc. samples placed robotically into an incubator where they are photographed, and results read digitally	Reduced manual work with more time to focus on patient care; clinicians receive lab results 40% more quickly
NSW National Parks and Wildlife (Spires, 2020)	Ecological assessments	Remote pilot operates drone to complete thermal scanning and multispectral mapping to measure destruction from bushfires	Cost-effective and efficient way to collect data. The majority of terrain is too dangerous for humans to complete on ground
Boeing (Keay, 2018)	Manufacturing – machining	Cobot arm for machining of rivets in aviation components to achieve correct height	Reduced repetitive work and musculoskeletal strain for workers. Reductions in rework rates/damaged parts
REDARC (Manning et al., 2021)	Manufacturing – assembly	Automated cobot for assembly, labelling and transport of PCB boards	Increased productivity by 52%, allowing workers to focus on higher-value tasks

FBR (Keay, 2022)	Construction – mobile block laying	Fully autonomous robot Hadrian X[a] used to build houses without human involvement	Elimination of repetitive work and associated stress, injury due to exposure to cement and sand dust. Faster construction periods, less waste and higher bricklayer satisfaction
MPC Kinetic (Keay, 2022)	Construction – digging trenches to bury a range of pipelines (oil, gas, water)	Fully autonomous excavator robot achieved by retrofitting autonomous capability to existing excavators allowing upgrading of pipelines	Reduced capital expenditure and increased productivity. Skilled excavator operators can now focus on higher complexity tasks and new roles such as Robotic Equipment Operators (rather than repetitive work).
Rio Tinto (Pilbara, WA) (Keay, 2018)	Mining – transportation	Rio Tinto deployed the world's first fully autonomous water trucks (Rio Tinto, 2021), adding to fleet of autonomous trucks transporting ore and waste	Water consumption can be tracked, dust suppression made more efficient, thereby reducing waste and increasing productivity
Woodside Energy (Nickel West site, WA) (Keay, 2022)	Oil & gas – inspection and patrol tasks	Robots include Robonaut 2 system (humanoid robot that can grasp objects, flip switches and high-five crew members[b]) and 'Ripley' (a Husky unmanned ground vehicle (UGV)[c] with two bespoke robotic arms added)[d]	Improved on and offshore safety through reduced worker exposure to harsh working conditions

(Continued)

TABLE 7.3 *(Continued)*

Company	Application	Technology	Outcome
Blueprint Lab (Australia-based advanced robotic designer and manufacturer) (Keay, 2022)	Maritime – inspection and retrievals under harsh environments	A remotely operated robotic arm designed for underwater retrievals (e.g., for US Navy) and pipe and tank inspections (e.g., for oil and gas and marine environments)	Under trial – reduced worker exposure to harsh working conditions

[a] www.fbr.com.au
[b] https://robots.ieee.org/robots/robonaut/#~:text=Robonaut%202%20is%20a%20humanoid,members%20after%20successfully%20performing%20tasks
[c] https://clearpathrobotics.com/husky-unmanned-ground-vehicle-robot/
[d] https://www.youtube.com/watch?v=r8BwBYAZsxQ

(Keay, 2018) and Robotics Group Australia (Keay, 2022). Australia currently has fewer published examples of robotic systems used in professional services than leading countries.

7.4 KEEPING SAFE WITH AND FROM ROBOTS

The introduction of technology will inevitably alter the design of work, workspaces and workplaces, having significant impact on individual, team and organisational performance. How work is designed makes the difference (Smids et al., 2020) between whether workers experience positive or negative changes physically, mentally, socially and culturally. Adopting a human factors and ergonomics (HFE[1]) approach (i.e., examining interactions between people, their tasks, tools and technologies, the physical environment in which they work and the social and cultural context of the organisation which determines how work is done) is essential for understanding and designing work matched to human capacities and limitations (Dempsey, Wogalter, & Hancock, 2000) as well as motivation, all of which are necessary for wellbeing and safety.

Robots can be dangerous when in close contact with humans. Between 1992 and 2015, America's National Institute for Occupational Safety and Health identified 61 robot-related workplace deaths, with accidents typically occurring under non-routine operating conditions (e.g., programming, maintenance and setup) where an unexpected event occurs (Anderson Whittaker, 2018). Safety incidents are likely to increase given operators' greater exposures to technology (e.g., cobots, AGVs, drones), through working in closer proximity and for longer periods. Amazon, an American multinational e-commerce company, provides an early example of this where data from a sample of fulfilment warehouses (across multiple states) indicates that worker injury frequency and severity are greater in those warehouses utilising robots (Kraus, 2019).

More intelligent, autonomous robots may provide additional complexities in understanding how they may malfunction and how to mitigate consequences. For example, in 2015, a maintenance technician working in a Michigan car parts plant was killed – not by performing maintenance tasks on the robot – she was caught by surprise and crushed to death when a robot unexpectedly moved into the cell she was working in (a section which was meant to be 'off-limits' to that robot and separated by safety doors) and loaded a trailer attachment assembly part on top of her (Agerholm, 2017). A similar, but lower-risk, outcome was experienced in Singapore, where TEMI, an autonomous robot guide working in the

National Gallery (see Table 7.2), guided a group of children into a room they did not have permission to enter, until the group was stopped by a human colleague (Dobberstein, 2022).

Undertaking a comprehensive risk assessment is critical to prevent and minimise harm to humans and other assets when adopting robotic systems. When working with robots (and advanced technologies more generally), safety hazards and their impact on human performance can be divided into three main domains – physical, cognitive and social and cultural.

7.4.1 Physical

Traditionally, working safely around robots has been focused on physical safety, largely controlled through separation by physical barriers such as safety cages. Modern smaller, lighter and force-limited cobots enable operators to work in closer proximity and are commonly deployed to reduce the physical demands of repetitive work, high loads and awkward postures (Pearce, Mutlu, Shah, & Radwin, 2018). Automated robots also prevent or minimise human exposure to harsh and dangerous environments, where workers may be exposed to dust, fumes, radiation or explosive environments that are exacerbated by long periods of work (Pauliková, Gyurák Babeľová, & Ubárová, 2021). Physical impacts to operators working with robots typically include musculoskeletal disorders from repetitive motions (Pearce et al., 2018), constrained motions from some haptic interfaces that restrict users' movements to maintain precision (Jafari, Adams, & Tavakoli, 2016), impacts from collision and crushing, and penetrating injuries from sharp attachments (Pauliková et al., 2021). Risk control strategies targeting physical safety hazards when operating a robot system are summarised in Table 7.4.

7.4.2 Cognitive

Working with complex robotic systems with variable automation levels and operational modes (both within and between robots) and, at times, opaque programming and AI capability can create increased mental processing, frustration, stress and fatigue for human operators (Fratczak, Goh, Kinnell, Justham, & Soltoggio, 2021). Such failure to detect or understand information or problems and lack of awareness to changes in the task environment can lead to errors and accidents (Fratczak et al., 2021; Kaber & Endsley, 2004). For example, diminished situational awareness and distraction could trigger a safety-stop on equipment where the

TABLE 7.4   Safety Requirements When Operating a Robot System

Operation Mode	Description
Speed and separation monitoring	Applies to the execution of coexistent tasks and is based on the principles of contact/collision avoidance. Robot system and operator can move simultaneously in the same collaborative workspace if safe distances relative to the robot system are assured.
Power and force limiting	Applies to the execution of cooperative and collaborative tasks and requires intrinsically safe design. Robot system and operator can use the workspace concurrently with contact between the two permissible due to limited power and force.
Hand guiding	Applies to the execution of cooperative and collaborative tasks where controlling the robot through a hand-guiding device is appropriate. Robot system is allowed to work in a non-collaborative mode without the presence of an operator. Once robot system has achieved a safety-rated monitored stop, the operator can enter the workspace to hand guide the robot.
Safety-rated monitored stop	Applies to the execution of collaborative tasks, although more accurately refers to the transition between collaborative and non-collaborative operation. Allows robot system to discontinue its motion in a collaborative workspace and may only restart when the operator is not present.

Source: Based on: Adriaensen et al. (2022), International Organisation for Standardisation (2011), (2016) and Vicentini (2020).

operator has unintentionally entered the robotic workspace (Gopinath & Johansen, 2019). It is essential that the technology (through well-designed interfaces and feedback) and the workplace (through instruction, information and training) support staff so they can easily identify the current operating mode of robots, know when and how to change the mode, and understand the function of each mode (Sarter & Woods, 1995).

7.4.3 Social and Cultural

Successful adoption of technology relies on its acceptance by the intended end users, who need a willingness to learn new information and skills (Lee, Kozar, & Larsen, 2003; Yousafzai, Foxall, & Palliseter, 2007). This willingness is influenced by gender, age, intelligence, interest, prior knowledge and experience, motivation, degree of control and self-efficacy (confidence in ability to successfully use technology) (Simsek, 2012). Lack of acceptance of robots (or any technology) can result in people 'delaying, obstructing, under-utilising or sabotaging its use' (Leonard-Barton, 1988, p. 604).

Highly relevant to successful robotics uptake is trust. Humans tend to perceive robots as lacking adequate human-like mental models and identity, impairing their capacity to interact and build trust with humans (Groom & Nass, 2007). Fear, shock and surprise can be felt when humans do not know what to expect from a robot's behaviour, particularly when anticipating its motion. When a robot has high levels of autonomy and intelligence, trust can be eroded as humans may feel discouraged and resentful where their performance is compared to that of the robot, and the human appears less competent (Smids et al., 2020). Ease of use (including providing information on robot status, guidance and feedback on human actions, and space for the human to move relative to the robot) is an important feature of robotic systems (Benos, Bechar, & Bochtis, 2020) that can mitigate lack of trust and promote willingness for human–robot interaction (Fang, Ong, & Nee, 2014).

To take advantage of the opportunities presented by intelligent robotic technologies, work should be designed to assist robots becoming team members. Increasing workers' experience of the robot as having a personality can promote a sense of cohesion that increases team interactions and overall performance. Where AI and robots augment human performance through collaboration, more mundane tasks can be transferred to robots, allowing humans to perform higher-value, creative and socially oriented work. Increasing human trust in robots again highlights the importance of manufacturers designing technology that takes account of human perceptions and expectations that maximise usability (Bröhl, Nelles, Brandl, Mertens, & Nitsch, 2019). Designing tasks, processes and jobs to ensure technologies integrate successfully tends to augment, rather than diminish, human performance (Welfare, Hallowell, Shah, & Riek, 2019).

From a broader social and cultural perspective, resistance to working with robots may also arise due to recognition that technology 'may upset the balance and distribution of roles, responsibilities, and, consequently, existing power relations within the organisation' (Leonardi, 2009 p. 408). Poorly selected and integrated technology may fail to meet the needs of actual work practices resulting in employees deviating from formal procedures, creating safety and other unintended consequences (Ferneley & Sobreperez, 2006).

Recent efforts to support safe human–robot interactions in the workplace include the development of various guidelines and checklists for use when designing and implementing cobots (e.g., NSW Government, 2022). These resources target hazard reduction at the source, supplemented by workers adopting safe practices. Robots are made safer when fundamental design features are made safer, for example, incorporating lower force capacities, collision avoidance systems and softer outer shells to reduce impact forces. In an example of such engineering controls, a German start-up (Cobotect GmbH) focuses on better safeguarding robotics systems and the parts they use with airbag technology that cushions potentially dangerous automated parts, preventing injury to the worker as well as allowing robots to work faster. The company has developed a prototype where a robotic arm has an airbag attached to its gripper that can inflate and deflate (Sachgau, 2017).

7.5 ROBOTS AND HUMAN BEHAVIOUR

Through increasing autonomy and intelligence, robots have transformed from being tools that assisted and followed instructions, to tools that instruct their users what to do, even influencing how users think and behave. Effective collaboration requires an individual to take the perspective of the co-worker, through understanding their goals and anticipating their actions (Fratczak et al., 2021). Humans have the capacity to 'read' non-verbal visual cues to anticipate the actions of other humans (Duarte et al., 2018) but struggle to do so with automated robots. At the simplest level of interaction, studies examining human anticipation of robot movements have found overall reaction times and error rates improve when the position of the work piece being manipulated (stimulus) and the required responses (human and robot reactions) are spatially compatible and allow the human to follow the action. This stimulus–response relationship is important to keep in mind when reconfiguring collaborative workstations because human–robot orientation changes (Salm-Hoogstraeten & Müsseler, 2021).

Remarkably, robots fitted with AI are now learning how to identify and use human vulnerabilities to influence human decision making (Whittle, 2021). AI neural network systems combined with deep reinforcement learning (similar to how humans learn) have been used to develop and test models with humans by playing computer games. In each game the machine learned from participant responses and identified their vulnerabilities, then used this information to lead the human participants towards specific actions (Whittle, 2021). Such intelligence in robots can be used for positive applications like influencing people to adopt positive behaviour patterns (e.g., eating a healthy diet) as well as steering people away from harmful choices in certain situations. Likewise, smart technologies can be used for unethical purposes, highlighting the need to develop good policy frameworks to govern their use (see the CSIRO AI Ethics Framework[2]).

Considering the dark side of individual human behaviour, collaborating with smart robots can elicit feelings of resentment, frustration and anger culminating in human to robot abuse. People are more likely to be abusive when frustrated by not being able to understand robot behaviour; or if they feel manipulated or belittled; meaning that smart robots should always be programmed to be polite. Studies have demonstrated that the higher level of intelligence or mindfulness humans perceive in a robot, the lower the degree of abuse directed at it (Bartneck & Hu, 2008; Keijsers & Bartneck, 2018). Robots can generate empathetic responses from people, either by mimicking empathetic behaviours or by monitoring a user's emotional state to trigger empathetic responses. Robots have even been shown to provoke bystander intervention in a study where a robot was knocked over by a researcher after giving feedback (in either an indifferent or an empathetic manner) to a participant performing a memory task. All participants intervened to support the robot by raising it, while 56% also intervened verbally to chastise the researcher for aggression towards the robot. Significantly more participants intervened to help the robot when it was empathetic than when it was indifferent (Tan, Vázquez, Carter, Morales, & Steinfeld, 2018).

Mimicking many characteristics of a living animal, the quadruped robot, Spot (Boston Dynamics), is often shown in YouTube videos being kicked to demonstrate its stability. While robots are not living beings, humans tend to attribute human or life-like qualities to them, particularly when designed to emulate living beings (Sharkey, 2015).[3] There is much ethical debate whether mistreatment of life-like robots can increase aggressive and cruel behaviours to living beings through desensitisation (e.g., see Chessman, 2018). Many of the preceding examples refer to laboratory settings but raise questions about what roles humans, as individuals and as a society, want to grant robots, and the degree of influence robots can exert. Such questions always lead back to the humans who design, build and deploy such technologies with the intent of achieving specific behaviours. It is these people – designers, programmers and users of technology – who shape the forms of human interaction and their consequences (Hildt, 2021), again reinforcing the need for ethical frameworks to govern applications.

7.6 EMERGING APPLICATIONS AND FUTURE DIRECTIONS

7.6.1 Physical Factors

Current emerging applications addressing physical HFE factors are focused on improving the scheduling of human–robot collaborative subtasks and motion planning (i.e., designing robot movement to avoid obstacles and achieve precision critical for autonomous vehicles, or correctly placing bolts into casings). Task design is the source of HFE risk factors and fundamental to targeting risks at the source. Improving the dynamics of human–robot collaboration can reduce the risk of musculoskeletal injuries and collisions, while improving sequencing and productivity (Gualtieri, Rauch, & Vidoni, 2021). Promising investigations aim to develop intelligent assistance that will enable robotic task sharing while optimising assembly sequencing, simultaneously monitoring and responding to reduce operator physical strain (Pearce et al., 2018).

Such real-time robot assisted ergonomics continuously observes the human's posture and initiates cooperative robot movements in response, bringing the human posture back to acceptable limits. Using an algorithmic framework and sensors, the cooperating robot always adapts the environment (e.g., by changing the orientation of the workpiece) to increase comfort for the user, creating dynamic adjustment of human working postures (Shafti et al., 2019). To date, robots have not had the autonomy to plan their assistance in lifting and positioning tasks, so incorporating HFE parameters into cobots' decision-making processes is likely to improve the performance of human workers, even in currently accepted high-risk work environments (van der Spaa, Gienger, Bates, & Kober, 2020).

7.6.2 Cognitive Factors

Developments addressing cognitive factors focus on improving the acceptability of the interaction process between humans and robots to reduce stress and high mental effort while sharing workspaces with robots (Gualtieri et al., 2021). Intelligent machines have potential to learn complex human skills like precision planning, perception and flexibility, allowing robots to detect the non-verbal intentions of others and to judge the likelihood they will achieve their goals (Lopez-de-Ipina et al., 2023). The ASIMO robot can distinguish between multiple faces and voices at once and predict human behaviour.[4] The aim of intelligent systems is to jointly understand the type and level of collaboration required between human and robot operators, creating efficient human–robot teams.

The robot system extracts knowledge about the environment and uses it to provide smart interactive support for humans and robots to interact, while providing intelligent control. This human–robot integration reduces cognitive loading on the human, improving levels of stress and fatigue (Lopez-de-Ipina et al., 2023).

Other promising areas of research use natural language processing (NLP), integrated with augmented reality (AR), which can help translate human verbal and non-verbal communication to robotic systems (Haase & Schönheits, 2021; Liu & Zhang, 2019). Amazon's Alexa voice system is one example, having been used to control industrial robots with natural language (Kapadia, Staszak, Jian, & Goldberg, 2017). The study of Haase and Schönheits (2021) used AR to provide input and a feedback interface enabling an operator to control multiple robots concurrently with natural language instructions. NLP has the advantage of enabling hands-free operation to verbally control the robot with higher levels of intuitive behaviour, reducing cognitive demands and improving user satisfaction. NLP is also enabling robots like Pepper[5] to sense emotion in people and respond appropriately.

As transparency and usability become increasingly important for human–robot interaction, there is growing attention on developing design guidelines to improve cognitive ergonomics. Gualtieri et al. (2021) developed and trialled guidelines incorporating the HFE systems approach to human–robot collaboration. Key criteria include workstation layout, robot system features, robot systems performance factors and organisational characteristics. Trial results show humans achieving higher levels of cognitive performance and improved assembly quality.

7.6.3 Social and Cultural Factors

At the social and cultural levels, economies and jobs will change with the rise of robots (Leigh et al., 2022). Work transformation will stimulate changes in workforce structure, suggesting many Australian workers will shift to more portfolio and freelance work (Haljkowicz et al., 2016). The future of work after widespread robot adoption is likely to displace some jobs but most jobs will be changed, with higher-value new jobs also being created. The profile of the workforce may change with older workers and those with disabilities having greater participation enabled by automated technology, as illustrated in a Japanese example of cafe service Table 7.2. Using robots and AI, the workers take orders, instruct the robot to clear tables and interact with customers, increasing the independence and capacity of workers with disability to earn wages and contribute to society.

Automated robotic welding, assembly and warehousing are likely to see more extensive 'lights out' manufacturing become a reality, where machining cells can be set up with robots to operate around the clock without human intervention (Tilley, 2017). The need for humans to run production processes can be overcome by use of AI, AGVs, data analytics, predictive maintenance, programmable logic controllers, robot sensors and vision systems.[6] Theoretically the technology to implement 'lights out' manufacturing currently exists, but the business case does not yet support removal of humans in assembly operations. Current advances in autonomous robots, AI and NLP may provide greater flexibility in manufacturing operations, making 'lights out' manufacturing viable into the future.

7.7 IMPLICATIONS OF ROBOT TECHNOLOGY FOR THE DESIGN OF WORK

Installing a cobot into the workplace is like introducing a new team member. At the individual and team levels, Baltrusch et al. (2022, p. 737) suggest that robots should follow the practices of good team members, as highlighted in their five design guidelines: support me, don't judge me, don't scare me, don't surprise me and acknowledge my preferences. Successful technology adoption, particularly for cobots, relies on humans trusting the robot is safe. Safety encompasses physical and psychosocial safety, which relies on three forms of design (Baltrusch et al., 2022). Collaboration design refers to the design of interaction, including allocation, sequencing and timing of activities; robot design, addressing the features of the robot itself, including appearance; and workplace design, addressing the interplay of factors in the physical and psychosocial environments. These design features are relevant to the micro-level of tasks, and job design at the macro level, that is, the configuration of tasks and activities into whole jobs. Task content in jobs influences workers' degree of autonomy and variety, impacting overall satisfaction, safety, well-being and work performance.

The design of satisfying and effective jobs begins by matching technology to business goals. Achieving these goals relies on successfully configuring tasks that are meaningful (require workers to use a variety of skills, contribute to a clear outcome and add value to the overall goals of the organisation). Introducing technology should also ameliorate risks, an important feature of good job design (by reducing hazardous exposures, e.g., repetition, noise, dust), rather than introducing new hazards (monotony, stress, human–robot collisions and feelings of isolation) (Howard, O'Keeffe, Hordacre, & Spoehr, 2022). The introduction of robots has generated much concern about the loss of jobs, or creation of boring jobs (Taylor et al., 2019), highlighting the importance of social support at work. Structuring tasks and teams to be interdependent promotes opportunities for social connection, practical support and learning (Howard et al., 2022). Performance feedback is also an important element of social support, and, while working with intelligent robots, may come from the robot itself. Feedback should always be constructive and respectful, and provided by supervisors. Its purpose is to support workers improve performance and understand the value of their work in the broader context of the organisation (Parker & Grote, 2022).

New skills and knowledge will be essential as technology modifies jobs. Success in the technology-rich future workplace will require a mix of skills, including technical (hard) skills (i.e., technology know-how, skills in business and manufacturing processes) balanced with non-technical (soft) skills, referring to personal, social and methodical competences (Galaske, Arndt, Friedrich, Bettenhausen, & Anderl, 2018). Individuals combining technical and non-technical skills are described as being 'T-shaped' (Bodell, 2020), where the horizontal head of the 'T' refers to their breadth of interpersonal and organisational skills that enable them to effectively collaborate and translate knowledge to other contexts. Such T-shaped workers combine generalist and specialist skills, making them flexible and versatile (Howard et al., 2022). New jobs in the future of work will require digital literacy and skills, and include work involving programming, business data analysis, cloud architecture and software development, robotics systems engineering and cybersecurity management.

Finally, the structure of work in society has long been regulated through legislative frameworks comprising standards, codes of practice and guidance to ensure safety and security of individuals, workforces and society. Technology adoption is changing work, calling for renewed regulation and standards targeted at three levels – for the design and use of technology itself (e.g., International Organisation for Standardisation, 2011 standards for the safe design and use of robotics),[7] for the design of work (including industrial relations and work health and safety laws (e.g., Jain, Hassard, Leka, Di Tecco, & Iavicoli, 2021) and policy for governance, describing law for the protection of public and societal safety and wellbeing. Societal implications are evident in emerging literature on cybersecurity (e.g., Fuster & Jasmontaite, 2020) and use of AI (e.g., Taeihagh, 2021; Wirtz, Weyerer, & Kehl, 2022) and autonomous systems, including robots (e.g., Tan & Taeihagh, 2021).

7.8 CONCLUSION

Adoption of robotics in one industry and geographical location often prompts innovation and adoption in others, with benefits across economies. Robotics is no longer limited to industrial applications with professional service robots rapidly expanding in retail, hospitality and healthcare. Like any technology, intelligent robot systems can be used for beneficial (improving safety, quality and wellbeing) and detrimental purposes (dehumanising work, job losses, spying and warfare). Outcomes depend on the people making decisions about design and implementation. This potential highlights the need for policy-makers to determine standards governing the use of advanced technologies at three levels: society, workplace and technology. In the workplace, realising benefits requires focus on the dynamics of human-technology interaction in terms of physical, cognitive and social and cultural factors and providing foundations for good job design, skill development and enhanced system performance.

NOTES

1 The terms 'human factors' and 'ergonomics' are often used interchangeably, but, in this chapter, we refer to the collective term. The International Ergonomics Association defines ergonomics (and human factors) as 'the scientific discipline concerned with understanding the interactions between humans and other elements of a system'. It also refers to the profession that 'applies theory, principles, data, and methods to design with the intent to optimise human well-being and overall system performance' (https://iea.cc/about/what-is-ergonomics/)

2 https://www.csiro.au/en/research/technology-space/ai/ai-ethics-framework

3 https://edition.cnn.com/2015/02/13/tech/spot-robot-dog-google/index.html

4 https://www.pocket-lint.com/gadgets/news/134820-real-life-robots-that-will-make-you-think-the-future-is-now/

5 https://www.pocket-lint.com/gadgets/news/134374-pepper-the-emotion-reading-robot-that-feels-sells-out-in-60-seconds/

6 https://www.assemblymag.com/articles/94982-lights-out-automation-fact-or-fiction

7 https://www.iso.org/standard/51330.html

REFERENCES

Adriaensen, A., Costantino, F., Di Gravio, G., & Patriarca, R. (2022). Teaming with industrial cobots: A socio-technical perspective on safety analysis. *Human Factors and Ergonomics in Manufacturing & Service Industries, 32*, 173–198. https://doi.org/10.1002/hfm.20939

Agerholm, H. (2017). Robot 'goes rogue and kills woman on Michigan car parts production line. https://www.independent.co.uk/news/world/americas/robot-killed-woman-wanda-holbrook-car-parts-factory-michigan-ventra-ionia-mains-federal-lawsuit-100-cell-a7630591.html

Albrecht, C. (2018). Cafe in Japan uses robots to create jobs for people with disabilities. https://thespoon.tech/cafe-in-japan-uses-robots-to-create-jobs-for-people-with-disabilities/

Anderson Whittaker, N. (2018). NIOSH tackles safety of workplace robots. https://myosh.com/blog/2018/02/13/niosh-tackles-safety-workplace-robots/

Ang, A. (2022). South Korea's Myongji Hospital to develop robots that support dementia patients. https://www.healthcareitnews.com/news/asia/south-koreas-myongji-hospital-develop-robots-support-dementia-patients

Assembly Magazine. (2022). Automation boosts output by 25 percent at LG appliance assembly plant. https://www.assemblymag.com/articles/97384-automation-boosts-output-by-25-percent-at-lg-appliance-assembly-plant

Atkinson, R. D. (2018). Which nations really lead in industrial robot adoption? https://www2.itif.org/2018-industrial-robot-adoption.pdf

Australian Associated Press. (2013). Japan sends 'Astro Boy' to space. https://www.sbs.com.au/news/article/japan-sends-astro-boy-to-space/3bdijjs9s

Australian Industry Group. (2021). Australian supply chains: State of play. https://www.aigroup.com.au/news/reports/2021/australian-supply-chains-state-of-play/

Baltrusch, S., Krause, F., de Vries, A., van Dijk, W., & de Looze, M. (2022). What about the human in human robot collaboration? A literature review on HRC's effects on aspects of job quality. *Ergonomics*, *65*(5), 719–740. https://doi.org/10.1080/00140139.2021.1984585

Barouch, J. (2018). The new royal Adelaide hospital: Futuristic and state-of-the-art. https://totalfacilities.com.au/technology/new-royal-adelaide-hospital-futuristic-state-art/#:~:text=A%20fully%20automated%20microbiology%20lab,around%2040%20percent%20more%20quickly

Bartneck, C., & Hu, J. (2008). Exploring the abuse of robots. *Interaction Studies*, *9*(3), 415–433. https://doi.org/10.1075/is.9.3.04bar

BBC. (2018). Japanese cafe uses robots controlled by paralysed people. https://www.bbc.com/news/technology-46466531

Benos, L., Bechar, A., & Bochtis, D. (2020). Safety and ergonomics in human-robot interactive agricultural operations. *Biosystems Engineering*, *200*, 55–72. https://doi.org/10.1016/j.biosystemseng.2020.09.009

Bodell, L. (2020). Why T-shaped teams are the future of work. https://www.forbes.com/sites/lisabodell/2020/08/28/futurethink-forecasts-t-shaped-teams-are-the-future-of-work/?sh=19f4ab6f5fde

Bröhl, C., Nelles, J., Brandl, C., Mertens, A., & Nitsch, V. (2019). Human–robot collaboration acceptance model: Development and comparison for Germany, Japan, China and the USA. *International Journal of Social Robotics*, *11*(5), 709–726. https://doi.org/10.1007/s12369-019-00593-0

Changi General Hospital, S. H. (2015). KKH introduces new robotic bottle dispensing system for better efficiency and patient experience. https://www.cgh.com.sg/news/announcements/kkh-bds-opas

Chessman, C. F. (2018). Not quite human: Artificial Intelligence, animals, and the regulation of sentient property. *Animals, and the Regulation of Sentient Property.* https://doi.org/10.2139/ssrn.320080

Dempsey, P. G., Wogalter, M. S., & Hancock, P. A. (2000). What's in a name? Using terms from definitions to examine the fundamental foundation of human factors and ergonomics science. *Theoretical Issues in Ergonomics Science, 1*(1), 3–10. https://doi.org/10.1080/146392200308426

Dobberstein, L. (2022). At 9 for every 100 workers, robots are rife in Singapore – So we decided to visit them. https://www.theregister.com/2022/01/05/singapore_robot_holiday/#:~:text=Singapore's%20robots%20are%20ubiquitous.,at%20night%20while%20Singapore%20slumbers

Duarte, N. F., Raković, M., Tasevski, J., Coco, M. I., Billard, A., & Santos-Victor, J. (2018). Action anticipation: Reading the intentions of humans and robots. *IEEE Robotics and Automation Letters, 3*(4), 4132–4139. https://doi.org/10.1109/LRA.2018.2861569

Edwards, D. (2017). 'World's first' fully automated port terminal opens in Melbourne. https://roboticsandautomationnews.com/2017/09/11/worlds-first-fully-automated-terminal-opens-in-melbourne/14021/

ETAuto. (2016). Workers at Ford's Germany plant work hand in hand with robots. https://auto.economictimes.indiatimes.com/news/industry/workers-at-fords-germany-plant-work-hand-in-hand-with-robots/53237606

Eun-Ji, B. (2022). Robots, AI to ease labor shortages in agricultural sector. https://www.koreatimes.co.kr/www/nation/2022/12/281_322845.html;%20https://www.healthcareitnews.com/news/asia/south-koreas-myongji-hospital-develop-robots-support-dementia-patients

Fang, H., Ong, S.-K., & Nee, A. Y. (2014). Novel AR-based interface for human-robot interaction and visualization. *Advances in Manufacturing, 2*, 275–288. https://doi.org/10.1007/s40436-014-0087-9

Ferneley, E. H., & Sobreperez, P. (2006). Resist, comply or workaround? An examination of different facets of user engagement with information systems. *European Journal of Information Systems, 15*(4), 345–356. https://doi.org/10.1057/palgrave.ejis.3000629

Fleet, N. (2017). New royal Adelaide hospital: Futuristic NRAH features robots, state-of-the-art hi-tech equipment. https://www.adelaidenow.com.au/rah/new-royal-adelaide-hospital-futuristic-nrah-features-robots-stateoftheart-hitech-equipment/news-story/f966f535c051f792956f976c889c4ac5

Foundry4. (2019). 5 countries with the most robots in manufacturing. https://foundry4.com/5-countries-with-the-most-robots-in-manufacturing

Fratczak, P., Goh, Y. M., Kinnell, P., Justham, L., & Soltoggio, A. (2021). Robot apology as a post-accident trust-recovery control strategy in industrial human-robot interaction. *International Journal of Industrial Ergonomics, 82*, 103078. https://doi.org/10.1016/j.ergon.2020.103078

Fuster, G. G., & Jasmontaite, L. (2020). Cybersecurity regulation in the European Union: The digital, the critical and fundamental rights. *The ethics of cybersecurity*, 97–115. https://doi.org/10.1007/978-3-030-29053-5_5

Galaske, N., Arndt, A., Friedrich, H., Bettenhausen, K. D., & Anderl, R. (2018). Workforce management 4.0-assessment of human factors readiness towards digital manufacturing. *Paper presented at the Advances in Ergonomics of Manufacturing: Managing the Enterprise of the Future: Proceedings of the AHFE 2017 International Conference on Human Aspects of Advanced Manufacturing*, July 17–21, 2017, The Westin Bonaventure Hotel, Los Angeles, California, USA 8.

Goodman, P. S. (2017). The robots are coming and Sweden is fine. https://www.nytimes.com/2017/12/27/business/the-robots-are-coming-and-sweden-is-fine.html

Gopinath, V., & Johansen, K. (2019). Understanding situational and mode awareness for safe human-robot collaboration: Case studies on assembly applications. *Production Engineering*, 13, 1–9. https://doi.org/10.1007/s11740-018-0868-2

Groom, V., & Nass, C. (2007). Can robots be teammates?: Benchmarks in human–robot teams. *Interaction Studies*, 8(3), 483–500. https://doi.org/10.1075/is.8.3.10gro

Gualtieri, L., Rauch, E., & Vidoni, R. (2021). Emerging research fields in safety and ergonomics in industrial collaborative robotics: A systematic literature review. *Robotics and Computer-Integrated Manufacturing*, 67, 101998. https://doi.org/10.1016/j.rcim.2020.10199

Haase, T., & Schönheits, M. (2021). Towards context-aware natural language understanding in human-robot-collaboration. *Paper presented at the 2021 IEEE 17th International Conference on Automation Science and Engineering (CASE)*. https://doi.org/10.1109/CASE49439.2021.9551482

Haljkowicz, S., Reeson, A., Rudd, L., Bratanova, A., Hodgers, L., Mason, C., & Boughen, N. (2016). *Tomorrow's digitally enabled workforce: Megatrends and scenarios for jobs and employment in Australia over the next twenty years*. Brisbane.

HealthTech. (n.d.). German hospitals integrate Versius Robotic System into their operating rooms. https://healthtech.eu/news/german-hospitals-integrate-versius-robotic-system-into-their-operating-rooms/

Hildt, E. (2021). What sort of robots do we want to interact with? Reflecting on the human side of human-artificial intelligence interaction. *Frontiers in Computer Science*, 3, 671012. https://doi.org/10.3389/fcomp.2021.671012

Hosokawa, K. (2022). South Korean industry embraces robots to ease labor crunch. https://asia.nikkei.com/Business/Technology/South-Korean-industry-embraces-robots-to-ease-labor-crunch

Howard, S., O'Keeffe, V., Hordacre, A.-L., & Spoehr, J. (2022). *Manufacturing work by design: Pillars of successful integration of Industry 4.0 technology into jobs*. Adelaide, South Australia: https://www.flinders.edu.au/content/dam/documents/research/aiti/manufacturing_work_by_design.pdf

Howard, S., Rajagopalan, A., Manning, K., O'Keeffe, V., Hordacre, A.-L., & Spoehr, J. (2021). From ship to shore. Reducing the barriers to collaborative robot uptake in shipbuilding and manufacturing through human factors. https://www.flinders.edu.au/content/dam/documents/research/aiti/imcrc-human-factors/from_ship_to_shore_report.pdf

International Federation of Robotics. (2021). Robot density nearly doubled globally. https://ifr.org/ifr-press-releases/news/robot-density-nearly-doubled-globally

International Federation of Robotics. (2022a). Japan is world's number one robot maker. https://ifr.org/ifr-press-releases/news/japan-is-worlds-number-one-robot-maker

International Federation of Robotics. (2022b). World robotics 2022. https://ifr.org/downloads/press2018/2022_WR_extended_version.pdf

International Organisation for Standardisation. (2011). ISO 10218-1, Robots and robotic devices - Safety requirements for industrial robots - Part 1: Robots. https://www.iso.org/standard/51330.html

International Organisation for Standardisation. (2012). Robots and robotic devices - Vocabulary. ISO 8373:2012. https://www.iso.org/obp/ui/#iso:std:iso:8373:ed-2:v1:en

International Organisation for Standardisation. (2016). ISO/TS 15066 Robots and robotic devices - Collaborative robots. https://www.iso.org/standard/62996.html

Jafari, N., Adams, K. D., & Tavakoli, M. (2016). Haptics to improve task performance in people with disabilities: A review of previous studies and a guide to future research with children with disabilities. *Journal of Rehabilitation and Assistive Technologies Engineering*, 3. https://doi.org/10.1177/2055668316668147

Jain, A., Hassard, J., Leka, S., Di Tecco, C., & Iavicoli, S. (2021). The role of occupational health services in psychosocial risk management and the promotion of mental health and well-being at work. *International Journal of Environmental Research and Public Health*, 18(7), 3632. https://doi.org/10.3390/ijerph18073632

Jarota, M. (2021). Artificial intelligence and robotisation in the EU - Should we change OHS law? *Journal of Occupational Medicine and Toxicology*, 16. https://doi.org/10.1186/s12995-021-00301-7

Javaid, M., Haleem, A., Singh, R. P., Rab, S., & Suman, R. (2022). Significant applications of Cobots in the field of manufacturing. *Cognitive Robotics*, 2, 222–233. https://doi.org/10.1016/j.cogr.2022.10.001

Jee-Hee, K. (2021). The robots are rising faster in Korea than elsewhere. https://koreajoongangdaily.joins.com/2021/01/27/business/economy/robot-robot-density-industrial-robot/20210127192306995.html

Kaber, D. B., & Endsley, M. R. (2004). The effects of level of automation and adaptive automation on human performance, situation awareness and workload in a dynamic control task. *Theoretical Issues in Ergonomics Science*, 5(2), 113–153. https://doi.org/10.1080/1463922021000054335

Kapadia, R., Staszak, S., Jian, L., & Goldberg, K. (2017). EchoBot: Facilitating data collection for robot learning with the Amazon echo. *Paper presented at the 2017 13th IEEE Conference on Automation Science and Engineering (CASE)*. https://doi.org/10.1109/COASE.2017.8256096

Keay, S. (2018). A robotics roadmap for Australia, 2018. https://apo.org.au/sites/default/files/resource-files/2018-06/apo-nid176691_1.pdf

Keay, S. (2022). A robotics roadmap for Australia, 2022. https://roboausnet.com. au/wp-content/uploads/2021/11/Robotics-Roadmap-for-Australia-2022_ compressed-1.pdf

Keijsers, M., & Bartneck, C. (2018). Mindless robots get bullied. *Paper presented at the Proceedings of the 2018 ACM/IEEE International Conference on Human-Robot Interaction.* https://doi.org/10.1145/3171221.3171266

Kim, B. (2022). South Korea develops robot for autonomous tunnel exploration. https://www.defensenews.com/unmanned/2022/06/24/south-korea-develops-robot-for-autonomous-tunnel-exploration/

Kraus, R. (2019). Robots at Amazon warehouses might make workplace injuries worse. https://sea.mashable.com/tech/7637/robots-at-amazon-warehouses-might-make-workplace-injuries-worse

Kyoung-Son, S. (2021). A dream made of fried chicken and a robot arm. https://koreajoongangdaily.joins.com/2021/05/24/business/tech/chicken-robot-franchise/20210524190100427.html

LaFrance, A. (2016). What is a robot? The question is more complicated than it seems. https://www.theatlantic.com/technology/archive/2016/03/what-is-a-human/473166/

Lee, J. (2020). Behind-the-scenes: Robots in S'pores's libraries do the manual work so humans don't have to. https://mothership.sg/2020/10/nlb-robots/

Lee, J. Y. (2022). Robots roll into South Korea, making it the most automated country in the world. https://nextrendsasia.org/robots-roll-into-south-korea-making-it-the-most-automated-country-in-the-world/#:~:text=In%20 South%20Korea%2C%20the%20service,agriculture%20and%20even%20 national%20defence

Lee, Y., Kozar, K. A., & Larsen, K. R. (2003). The technology acceptance model: Past, present, and future. *Communications of the Association for Information Systems, 12*(1), 50. https://doi.org/10.17705/1CAIS.01250

Leigh, N. G., Lee, H., & Kraft, B. (2022). Disparities in robot adoption among U.S. manufacturers: A critical economic development challenge. *Industry and Innovation, 29*(9), 1025–1044. https://doi.org/10.1080/13662716.2021.2007 757

Leonard-Barton, D. (1988). Implementation characteristics of organisational innovations: Limits and opportunities for management strategies. *Communication Research 15*(1), 603–631.

Leonardi, P. M. (2009). Why do people reject new technologies and stymie organizational changes of which they are in favor? Exploring misalignments between social interactions and materiality. *Human Communication Research, 35*(3), 407–441. https://doi.org/10.1111/j.1468-2958.2009.01357.x

Liu, R., & Zhang, X. (2019). A review of methodologies for natural-language-facilitated human–robot cooperation. *International Journal of Advanced Robotic Systems, 16*(3). https://doi.org/10.1177/1729881419851402

Liuima, J. (2016). Industry 4.0: German car industry introduces collaborative robots. https://www.euromonitor.com/article/industry-4-0-german-car-industry-introduces-collaborative-robots#:~:text=Audi%20was%20one%20 of%20the,have%20Mercedes%2DBenz%20and%20Opel

Lopez-de-Ipina, K., Iradi, J., Fernandez, E., Calvo, P. M., Salle, D., Poologaindran, A., ... Requejo, C. (2023). HUMANISE: Human-inspired smart management, towards a healthy and safe industrial collaborative robotics. *Sensors*, *23*(3), 1170. https://doi.org/10.3390/s23031170

Lufkin, B. (2020). What the world can learn from Japan's robots. https://www.bbc.com/worklife/article/20200205-what-the-world-can-learn-from-japans-robots

Manning, K., Jang, R., Rajagopalan, A., Spoehr, J., Hordacre, A.-L., & Moretti, C. (2021). Robotics and the digital shipyard. https://www.flinders.edu.au/content/dam/documents/research/aiti/imcrc-human-factors/robotics_and_the_digital_shipyard.pdf

Market Prospects. (2020). The development strategy of the smart robot industry under the framework of South Korea Industry 4.0. https://www.market-prospects.com/articles/smart-robot-industry-of-south-korea

McCurry, J. (2023). South Korea's birthrate sinks to fresh record low as population crisis deepens. https://www.theguardian.com/world/2023/feb/22/south-koreas-birthrate-sinks-to-fresh-record-low-as-population-crisis-deepens

Moravec, H. P. (n.d.). Robot technology. https://www.britannica.com/technology/robot-technology

National Gallery Singapore. (2021). National Gallery Singapore accelerates the convergence of arts and technology through new innovation lab. https://www.nationalgallery.sg/sites/default/files/pdf/%5BMedia%20Release%5D%20National%20Gallery%20Singapore%20Accelerates%20the%20Convergence%20of%20Art%20and%20Technology%20through%20New%20Innovation%20Lab.pdf

NCS. (2022). Singapore robotics: all you need to know. https://www.ncs.co/en-sg/knowledge-centre/singapore-robotics/

Nikkei Asia. (2022). South Korean industry embraces robots to ease labor crunch. https://kr-asia.com/south-korean-industry-embraces-robots-to-ease-labor-crunch

Nippon. (2018). World's first robot-staffed hotels make business travel inroads. https://www.nippon.com/en/guide-to-japan/gu900045/

NSW Government. (2022). Working safely with collaborative robots. https://www.centreforwhs.nsw.gov.au/Projects/working-safely-with-collaborative-robots

Onag, G. (2022). 75% of Singapore workers give cleaning cobots a nod. https://futureiot.tech/75-of-singapore-workers-give-cleaning-cobots-a-nod/

Palmer, A. (2019). Robots are taking on jobs humans consider to be 'too boring', Swedish company claims. https://www.dailymail.co.uk/sciencetech/article-7016139/Robots-taking-jobs-humans-consider-boring-Swedish-company-claims.html

Parker, S. K., & Grote, G. (2022). Automation, algorithms, and beyond: Why work design matters more than ever in a digital world. *Applied Psychology*, *71*(4), 1171–1204. https://doi.org/10.1111/apps.12241

Pauliková, A., Gyurák Babeľová, Z., & Ubárová, M. (2021). Analysis of the impact of human–cobot collaborative manufacturing implementation on the occupational health and safety and the quality requirements. *International*

Journal of Environmental Research and Public Health, 18(4), 1927. https://doi.org/10.3390/ijerph18041927

Pearce, M., Mutlu, B., Shah, J., & Radwin, R. (2018). Optimizing makespan and ergonomics in integrating collaborative robots into manufacturing processes. *IEEE transactions on automation science and engineering, 15*(4), 1772–1784. https://doi.org/10.1109/TASE.2018.2789820

Placek, M. (2022). Collaborative robots worldwide – Statistics & facts. https://www.statista.com/topics/8062/collaborative-robots-worldwide/

Prakash, A. (2017). German robotics remains a policy priority. https://www.roboticsbusinessreview.com/consumer/german-robotics-remains-policy-priority/

Reuters. (2022). From baristas to inspectors: Singapore's robot workforce plugs labour gaps. https://www.tbsnews.net/world/baristas-inspectors-singapores-robot-workforce-plugs-labour-gaps-429534

Rich, M. (2019). Japan loves robots, but getting them to do human work isn't easy. https://www.nytimes.com/2019/12/31/world/asia/japan-robots-automation.html

Rio, Tinto. (2021). Rio Tinto to deploy world's first fully autonomous water trucks at Gudai-Darri. https://www.businesswire.com/news/home/20210621005358/en/

Sachgau, O. (2017). How one German company is making workplace robots safer for humans. https://www.insurancejournal.com/news/international/2017/09/18/464667.htm

Salm-Hoogstraeten, S.V., & Müsseler, J. (2021). Human cognition in interaction with robots: Taking the robot's perspective into account. *Human Factors, 63*(8), 1396–1407. https://doi.org/10.1177/0018720820933764

Sarter, N. B., & Woods, D. D. (1995). How in the world did we ever get into that mode? Mode error and awareness in supervisory control. *Human Factors, 37*(1), 5–19. https://doi.org/10.1518/001872095779049516

Savage, M. (2019). Meet Tengai, the job interview robot who won't judge you. https://www.bbc.com/news/business-47442953

Savov, V. (2015). Volvo's ROAR robots will take all the heavy, smelly lifting out of trash collection. https://www.theverge.com/2015/9/16/9336229/volvos-robots-roar-trash-collection

Scales, B. (2017). The rise and fall of the Australian car manufacturing industry. https://www.afr.com/opinion/bill-scales-the-rise-and-fall-of-the-australian-car-manufacturing-industry-20171018-gz3ky4

Scania. (2016). The cab factory of the future. https://www.scania.com/group/en/home/newsroom/news/2016/the-cab-factory-of-the-future.html

Shafti, A., Ataka, A., Lazpita, B. U., Shiva, A., Wurdemann, H. A., & Althoefer, K. (2019). Real-time robot-assisted ergonomics. *Paper presented at the 2019 International Conference on Robotics and Automation (ICRA)*. https://doi.org/10.48550/arXiv.1805.06270

Sharkey, N. (2015). Is it cruel to kick a robot dog? https://edition.cnn.com/2015/02/13/tech/spot-robot-dog-google/index.html

Simsek, A. (2012). *Individual differences*. In N. Seel (Ed.), *Encyclopaedia of the sciences of learning*. https://doi.org/10.1007/978-1-4419-1428-6_370

Smids, J., Nyholm, S., & Berkers, H. (2020). Robots in the workplace: a threat to - or opportunity for – Meaningful work? *Philosophy & Technology, 33,* 503–522. https://doi.org/10.1007/s13347-019-00377-4

Solar Clean International. (n.d.). Commercial and industrial solar panel cleaning. https://solarcleanint.com/

Sostero, M. (2020). Automation and Robots in Services: Review of data and taxonomys. https://joint-research-centre.ec.europa.eu/publications/automation-and-robots-services-review-data-and-taxonomy_en

Spires, J. (2020). NSW, Australia uses drones after bushfires to collect data. https://dronedj.com/2020/10/16/nsw-australia-uses-drones-after-bushfires-to-collect-data/

Spoehr, J., Jang, R., Manning, K., Rajagopalan, A., Moretti, C., Hordacre, A.-L., … Worrall, L. (2020). The digital shipyard: Opportunities and challenges. https://www.flinders.edu.au/content/dam/documents/research/aiti/The_Digital_Shipyard_Opportunities_and_Challenges.pdf

Stanford, J. (2020) The Robots are NOT Coming (And why that's a bad thing…). *The Australia Institute.* https://australiainstitute.org.au/wp-content/uploads/2020/12/Robots-are-Not-Coming-Formatted.pdf

Stewart, D., Casey, M., & Wigginton, C. (2019). Robots on the move: Professional service robots set for double-digit growth. *Technology, media, and telecommunications predictions 2020.* https://www.deloitte.com/global/en/our-thinking/insights/industry/technology/technology-media-and-telecom-predictions/2020/professional-service-robots.html

Taeihagh, A. (2021). Governance of artificial intelligence. *Policy and Society, 40*(2), 137–157. https://doi.org/10.1080/14494035.2021.1928377

Tan, S. Y., & Taeihagh, A. (2021). Governing the adoption of robotics and autonomous systems in long-term care in Singapore. *Policy and Society, 40*(2), 211–231. https://doi.org/10.1080/14494035.2020.1782627

Tan, X. Z., Vázquez, M., Carter, E. J., Morales, C. G., & Steinfeld, A. (2018). Inducing bystander interventions during robot abuse with social mechanisms. *Paper presented at the Proceedings of the 2018 ACM/IEEE international conference on human-robot interaction.*

Taylor, C., Carrigan, J., Noura, H., Ungur, S., van Halder, J., & Dandona, G. (2019). Australia's automation opportunity: Reigniting productivity and inclusive income growth. https://www.mckinsey.com/au/our-insights/australias-automation-opportunity-reigniting-productivity-and-inclusive-income-growth

TechTarget Network. (n.d.). Definition robot. https://www.techtarget.com/searchenterpriseai/definition/robot

Teo, T. (2022). From baristas to inspectors: Singapore's robot workforce plugs labour gaps. https://www.reuters.com/technology/baristas-inspectors-singapores-robot-workforce-plugs-labour-gaps-2022-05-30/

The Robot Report Staff. (2019). Swedish machine shop boosts capacity with cobot cell. https://www.therobotreport.com/swedish-machine-shop-universal-robots/

Tilley, J. (2017). Automation, robotics and the factory of the future. https://www.mckinsey.com/capabilities/operations/our-insights/automation-robotics-and-the-factory-of-the-future#/

Universal Robots. (2023). Doing more with less: The driving forces accelerating cobot automation in Japan. https://www.universal-robots.com/blog/doing-more-with-less-the-driving-forces-accelerating-cobot-automation-in-japan/

Valadkhani, A. (2016). Collapse of Australian car manufacturing industry. https://www.swinburne.edu.au/news/2016/10/collapse-of-australian-car-manufacturing-industry/

van der Spaa, L., Gienger, M., Bates, T., & Kober, J. (2020). Predicting and optimizing ergonomics in physical human-robot cooperation tasks. *Paper presented at the 2020 IEEE International Conference on Robotics and Automation (ICRA).*

Vicentini, F. (2020). Terminology in safety of collaborative robotics. *Robotics and Computer-Integrated Manufacturing, 63*, 101921. https://doi.org/10.1016/j.rcim.2019.101921

Welfare, K. S., Hallowell, M. R., Shah, J. A., & Riek, L. D. (2019). Consider the human work experience when integrating robotics in the workplace. *Paper presented at the 2019 14th ACM/IEEE international conference on human-robot interaction (HRI).*

Whittle, J. (2021). AI can now learn to manipulate human behaviour. https://theconversation.com/ai-can-now-learn-to-manipulate-human-behaviour-155031

Winter, J. (n.d.,). What is Industry 4.0? https://blog.isa.org/what-is-industry-40

Wirtz, B. W., Weyerer, J. C., & Kehl, I. (2022). Governance of artificial intelligence: A risk and guideline-based integrative framework. *Government Information Quarterly, 39*(4), 101685. https://doi.org/10.1016/j.giq.2022.101685

Yeoh, B., & Lin, W. (2012). Rapid growth in Singapore's immigrant population brings policy changes. https://www.migrationpolicy.org/article/rapid-growth-singapores-immigrant-population-brings-policy-challenges

Yousafzai, S. Y., Foxall, G. R., & Palliseter, J. G. (2007). Technology acceptance: A meta analysis of the TAM: Part 1. *Journal of Modelling in Management, 2*(3), 251–280. https://doi.org/10.1108/17465660710834453

Zhao, Z. (2021). The rising acceptance of robots in Germany and workers' automation angst. https://www.aicgs.org/2021/01/the-rising-acceptance-of-robots-in-germany-and-workers-automation-angst/

CHAPTER 8

Workplace Relations with AI in Mind

What Is Likely to Change?

Andreas Cebulla and Zygmunt Szpak

THE CONCEPT OF INDUSTRY 4.0 has shaped our understanding and practice of the digital transformation of production processes in the last decade. It describes the growing use of technological devices to facilitate real-time communication and integrate previously distinct, parallel, spatially and procedurally separate activities in joint production processes (Xu et al. 2021; Sniderman et al., 2016). More recently, we have seen the conceptual development of Industry 4.0 into Industry 5.0, which promises to deliver greater social benefits and is grounded in a significant effort to base technology and work on ethical principles (Longo et al., 2020). Whereas under Industry 4.0, automation (such as the use of robots) might compete with human labour rather than complement it (Demir et al., 2019), under Industry 5.0, automation technologies merge with human labour in the process of "physical-digital harmonising" (Hanelt et al., 2021, p. 1167). In this scenario, Industry 5.0 offers a human-centred, rather than a technology-centred, focus, giving more consideration to human flourishing, collaboration rather than competition between labour and capital and the involvement of workers in businesses' digital transition processes (e.g., Breque De Nul & Petridis, 2021).

Digital transformation is increasingly being equated with the use of artificial intelligence (AI) and, more specifically, machine learning (ML) in the production and delivery of goods and services. The definitions of AI are multiple and occasionally contested (see, for example, Chhillar &

DOI: 10.1201/9781003393757-8

151

Aguilera, 2022). However, in the conventional application of the term, it describes enhanced computing capacity and the emergence of methods that are no longer guided by human instructions but function unsupervised. These advances enable organisations to exploit the "big data" they collect to improve work processes quasi-instantaneously through workforce planning, product enhancement and optimisation of service operations (PWC, 2021; McKinsey Analytics, 2021). The technologies include interconnected combinations of wearables for real-time monitoring of workers and simultaneous prediction of safety risks, optimal resource allocation, and equipment failure and maintenance (Patel et al., 2022). The new phase of industrial digitalisation differs from the previous one because the increased use and better capabilities of artificial intelligence create new ways to combine technologies. We use the term "advanced digitalisation" to describe a new stage in technology where robots, collaborative robots and tools that use artificial intelligence to imitate human thinking, emotions and actions are combined in many different ways.

8.1 POTENTIAL, CHALLENGES AND HAZARDS OF AI

The chorus in the technology of business and management spheres is that AI will be the game changer in economic and business development (Bughin & Zeebroeck, 2018; KPMG, 2019), and that any business delaying its adoption may well become a commercial laggard, threatened with extinction. These claims acknowledge the organisational complexity of working with AI in production and business management (e.g., Deloitte Insights, 2019), yet typically assess these aspects from a commercial perspective alone, paying less attention to effects on the people working in those businesses.

A prominent rationale for remodelling work processes using advanced digital technology, such as AI-supported tools, is to increase efficiency in production (e.g., Wilson, 2013). Proponents of Industry 5.0 also perceive AI and the technological advances it promises as providing new opportunities for applying higher-level human critical thinking skills to production processes. In that view, humans take on more responsible tasks whilst, under their supervision, machines are left to look after the more monotonous, repetitive tasks as human–machine interactions become more prominent (Breque De Nul & Petridis, 2021, p. 41, referring to Atwell, 2017).

In reality, such smart transition may not be as seamless as implied. For one, the technology may not be as robust as we like to believe. In many application domains, AI is still in need of further development. AI's deficiencies are demonstrated by reports of accidents involving AI (Arnold & Toner, 2021). The debate about the economic potential (Chui et al., 2022) but also social risks (Huang et al., 2023) posed by the OpenAI text bot, ChatGPT, is an example that AI tools are human designs with human flaws.

Moreover, like any technology and technological change (Barley, 1986; Burri, 2008), AI may assist with and augment the performance of tasks, but it may also replace those same tasks. The literature on the impacts of AI on workplaces has picked up on this in its exploration of AI-facilitated automation displacing workers (Frey & Osborne 2017, Brynjolfsson et al., 2018). When not concerned with displacement, the literature has explored the harm AI may cause by subjecting workers to anonymous and autonomous performance monitoring, often concerned with accelerating the speed of service delivery and especially, but no longer solely, witnessed in the gig economy (Moore, 2018; Kellogg et al., 2019; Marmo et al., 2022).

Last but certainly not least, AI has been found to be used for ethically suspect purposes as organisations impose AI technology on unsuspecting service users as (1) experimental tools (Cyphers, 2021; Ward, 2021), (2) for reasons of market manipulation (Jeffries & Yin, 2021) or (3) political capture (Grassegger & Krogerus, 2017).

8.2 INTRA-ORGANISATIONAL IMPACTS OF AI

Digitalisation of work processes often involves re-arranging or fragmenting human activity. Examples include recruitment using sentiment analysis, AI monitoring performance and allocating workloads, and automated warehousing and machine maintenance. This advanced digitalisation shifts the boundaries of personal (data) privacy, but also of common job descriptions, content and expertise, requiring new role assignments as the operation and management of the AI and the use to which it is put then change established working practices (Faraj et al., 2018). Time previously allocated to tasks that are now automated gets re-assigned, while the servicing of the AI is delegated up or down the organisational structure (Pepito & Locsin, 2018). When digital automation criss-crosses intra-organisational boundaries, inherited in-work relationships may need to adjust.

Advanced digitalisation thus potentially disrupts and displaces conventional social interactions and social relationships with human–machine interactions (Smids et al., 2020; also see O'Keeffe & Howard in this volume) when "space [...] is filled by automated, calculative routines that shape organizational decisions and practices" (Bartley et al., 2019, p. 5). Bartley et al. (2019, p. 8) refer to this phenomenon as "algorithmic distance", naming "predictive analytics and artificial intelligence for micro-targeted advertising, fraud detection, market segmentation, speech and facial recognition, and hiring of employees" as examples.

The data required for and acquired by predictive analytics and AI are taken from customers, clients and, in commercial and other organisations, employees. The growth in employee data acquisition, collection and retention by such organisations, facilitated by AI-assisted technologies, such as wearables or cobots, extends the realm and changes the nature of the scientific management of workplaces. In an earlier study (Cebulla et al., 2021, 2022), fieldwork with experts in AI, computer science and workplace health and safety identified aspects of workplace operations that AI was most likely to change, namely job control and workload, supervisor/peer and more general organisational relations. The study also found that employee privacy was likely to be reduced, raising the likelihood of workplace harm.

More specifically, job control and workload were expected to be affected by AI where job tasks and responsibilities were taken over by algorithms, thus changing job activities with respect to quantity (speed), quality (task range and complexity) or workers' autonomy over how and when to perform job tasks. This is more likely to occur where AI systems remain opaque so that their users remain uncertain as to the reliability of AI recommendations, especially where they may contradict personal experience and expertise. AI systems may also interfere with established accountability structures, where they disrupt established lines of responsibility.

In a similar vein, supervisor/peer and organisational relations change when AI systems step into established communication patterns, causing algorithmic distance within organisations. This occurs when automated monitoring systems are used to quantify performance or in automated review processes measuring employee, machine or process-related performances. In these instances, the need to check with colleagues for a second opinion disappears. For some, this may be a positive experience;

for others, it may lead to or increase isolation in the workplace (Nurski and Hoffman, 2022). The insertion of AI into organisational relationships risks breaching the psychological contracts between employees and employers, reducing employee engagement and job satisfaction (Braganza et al., 2021).

Finally, AI tools pose challenges to privacy and harm where they threaten the security of personal data (De Stefano, 2019) or induce behavioural changes that advantage those familiar with how an AI works over others. Simple manipulations, already documented in the context of quantified and quantifying performance review systems (Stelmaszak & Aaltonen, 2018; Aboubichr & Conway, 2023), can be used to distinguish oneself from familiar co-workers and anonymous competitors alike, as already widely witnessed in the gig economy (Jarrahi & Sutherland, 2019; Downs et al., 2010). The introduction of AI tools can also lead workers to adopt active strategies of reappropriating agency in how to perform tasks in their job. At times, this may compromise the function of AI tools as recommendations are ignored, as, for instance, observed amongst bank employees expected to refer to AI-generated predictions of consumer behaviour and associated product needs when communicating with their customers (Perez et al., 2022).

The sociological literature has also raised the spectre of changing earnings capacity of employees as AI reshapes the hiring of different skills sets. Although mainly discussed in the context of the macro-economy (e.g., Acemoglu & Restrepo, 2022), this reshaping may equally affect relative earnings at the micro-level of the business using AI (Barth et al., 2020), although the available evidence is currently equivocal (Domini et al., 2022). The determination of who, on one hand, operates the new technology and has access to and knowledge of its functionality, and who, on the other hand, is subjected to the operations of the new technology, shifts intra-firm skill demands. In turn, this modifies existing intra-organisational hierarchies, extending to reward structures and questions of job status, as low-skill labour costs are cut to fund investment in new hiring for higher skilled occupations (as discussed in Diessner et al. (2022) in relation to German manufacturing). Workers may experience these new challenges negatively, lowering their job engagement (Braganza et al., 2021) and already leading to calls for a greater role of industrial psychologists to help worker to negotiate the new, highly automated workplaces (Oosthuizen, 2022).

8.3 A TIMELINE OF AI RISKS AND HAZARDS

In their review of AI ethical risks, Morley et al. (2020) found that the literature discussed AI risks as occurring mainly during the early development stages of an AI system. Our own study (Cebulla et al., 2021) supported this conclusion: participants found it easiest to name risks that emerge during the early conceptualisation of an AI tool. These included risks of job loss and employee displacement; poorly communicated innovation objectives resulting in uncertainty and resistance to change; inadequate consideration of effects on prevailing moral, ethical or social principles; and inadequate testing of the new tool, and reliance of unrepresentative training data.

However, our research also showed awareness of the risks associated with activities during the later stages of AI development and actual operation. Such risks included the consideration given to the interconnectivity and interoperability of the tool; differential effects on worker status, privileging those with access to and understand of the tool; discontinuity of service or business (in the case of system failures, including systems going offline or other failures undetected because of a lack of awareness of AI biases) and physical workplace impacts, most apparent with respect to AI integration in co-working arrangements that require active and aware coordination of movement.

AI workplace risks and hazards may be best understood as additive and indeed cumulative, insofar as each risk is rooted in prior decisions with potentially lasting impacts. That research concluded that there was cause for a process of systematic, continuous AI risk and hazard review. Our suggestion at the time was for businesses to consider a strategic approach to assessing workplace risk of AI. As illustrated in Figure 8.1, this would involve early consideration of potential adverse effects and their avoidance, thus maximising benefits of AI over potential losses; ensuring effective communication of the purpose and functioning of AI, and identifying ethical, moral and social principles that the use of AI may affect. During subsequent development, appropriate structures and processes should be put into place to ensure that issues identified in the initial ideation phase remain in focus, monitored, and are addressed. During the eventual operations phase of the AI, these structures and processes are subjected to regular review and, where necessary, revision, resulting in a robust system designed to maintain and develop the competent use of AI, coordinated within and by the workforce, and secured with reliable quality insurance.

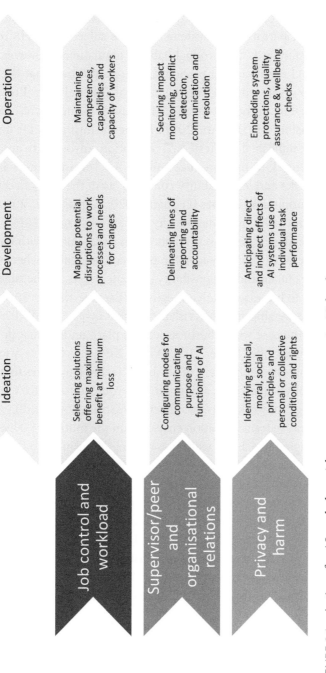

FIGURE 8.1   Actions for AI workplace risk assessment processes in AI development.

Source: Cebulla et al., 2023.

8.4 MAKING AI SAFE AT WORK

Like workplace practices more akin to Industry 4.0, those conducted with AI, such as the use of intelligent personal assistants (chatbots, time management or task performance systems) may be subject to WHS regulation, new ISO standards and product liability regulations. However, there is no specific AI regulation in place for now – a position that is changing rapidly, however, with the introduction of General Data Protection Regulation (GDPR) in the European Union and growing interest in ethical and responsible AI (Dignum, 2019). In the meantime, in the absence of such firmly established and tested AI regulation, anyone with appropriate programming skills may produce and sell AI. This introduces a range of workplace risks and legal liability concerns, as in the case of accidents involving autonomous machines (Dignam, 2020; Waring et al., 2020), and the need for human AI-override capacity (Etzioni & Etzioni, 2016).

A conventional view is to assess AI adoption risks – along with business risks more generally – from a leadership perspective as this is where strategic decisions are taken and responsibility ultimately rests. But because digitalisation leads to increased interconnectivity (Baethge-Kinsky, 2020; Dery et al., 2017), a leadership-focussed risk assessment may be insufficient. This is particularly the case where business leaders place undue trust in AI, in the pursuit of profits (de Cremer, 2022; Walsh, 2019). It is then easy to overlook the risk that the deployment of advanced technology poses to human cognitive and physical activity, as it gradually erodes a workforce's "experiential knowledge" of work processes (Baethge-Kinsky, 2020, p. 10).

The collaborative transformation envisaged in the Industry 5.0 literature may be challenging to achieve without a revamp of business strategies and commercial philosophy. Advancing the digitalisation of workplaces creates new risks to business operations in general as well as worker health and safety as organisations aim to become more "malleable" (Hanelt et al., 2021, p. 1161) to exploit fully and flexibly the new opportunities that AI adoption promises. Thus, whilst much of the current debate about the future of work focuses on the need for employees to demonstrate "resilience and adaptability" (Trenerry et al., 2021, p. 3), the same flexibility will need to be expected from the entire business processes if Industry 5.0 is to be achievable.

8.5 WORKFORCE ENGAGEMENT AS RISK MANAGEMENT

Krzywdzinski et al. (2022b) found that workers expect new AI technologies to contribute to workplace health, safety and stress prevention, and seek evidence of that effect. From a managerial point of view, this calls for adequate feedback controls to be put in place to record the AI systems' human (Industry 5.0) and organisational (Industry 4.0) impacts. The feedback concerns the assessment and response to evidence of technostress (Tarafdar et al., 2015; Graveling, 2020); or the speed, sequencing or monitoring of work, posing new endurance challenges (e.g., Jarrahi et al., 2021) and other often unforeseen side effects of increased workplace efficiency (e.g., Mayer et al., 2020). The functioning of AI systems requires continued monitoring via a practical, tested system of checks and balances, clear accountabilities and a readiness to intervene to ensure that worker well-being and safety expectations are being met.

Sanderson et al. (2021, p. 5) stress the importance of "diverse perspectives and collaborative teams in the design, development and use of AI technology" to promote the beneficent use of AI. Helper et al. (2019) and Ammanath and Blackman (2021) similarly conclude that addressing AI risks requires an internal capacity that "empowers shop-floor workers to combine their local knowledge with digital tools" (Helper et al., 2019, p. 35). Ammanath and Blackman (2021) also emphasise engaging "trusted and influential members across various functions" to work together. Empowering such collaborative capacity across organisations may be challenging to achieve when it involves delegating, sharing or surrendering decision-making responsibilities (Fountaine et al., 2019), which managers may be reluctant to do (Holmström & Hällgren, 2021). Yet, these principles are critical contributors to worker identification with business innovation and restructure as they affect their roles and responsibilities (Ranganathan, 2021). In practice, therefore, appropriate processes of AI risk management involve different organisational levels, from management and data managers to any affected business sections, including units (for instance, in the internal process chain) steps removed from the area immediately affected by the AI system. Formalised structures facilitate such communication, encouraging coordination and consensus that regulate the use of digital technology in workplaces without necessarily curtailing it (Global Deal, 2021; Krzywdzinksi et al., 2022; Lloyd & Payne 2023).

Organisations will require the support – and consent – of their workforce in implementing AI, especially where the AI tools are trained on data provided by that same workforce, such as facial or voice recognition data, or sentiment analysis tools (van den Broek et al., 2021; Fregin et al., 2020). Without such consent reached through communication and consultation, it may be unlikely that a workforce dependably commits to the organisation (Waring et al., 2020). Negotiating this consensus "would also prove pivotal in implementing the 'human-in-command' approach at the workplace" (De Stefano,

2019, p. 45), that is, ensuring that humans retain autonomy and are supported, but not dictated to, by machine predictions.

8.6 NATIONAL FRAMEWORKS OF EMPLOYMENT PROTECTION AND WORKER CONSULTATION

Legal frameworks for worker representation facilitate human-centricity in the workplace. Workplace consultation is not a given, nor is collective bargaining. Both strengthen workers' position in the workplace in that they provide employees with a voice, rights to consultation and negotiation that go beyond an entitlement to be kept informed. Collective agreements today go beyond their traditional primary role as a mechanism for wage negotiation and wage setting. In the age of big data and growing prevalence of people analytics in business, collective agreements may increasingly be used to co-determine the use and protection of employee data, and the management and accountability for surveillance in the workplace (De Stefano & Taes, 2022; Doellgast & Wagner, 2022). Without nationally legislated employment rights and representation, however, such collaboration risks being left to chance and goodwill rather than a matter of expected practice.

To date, the countries with the highest levels of AI skills penetration in the workforce, often matched by their government's AI readiness, have a

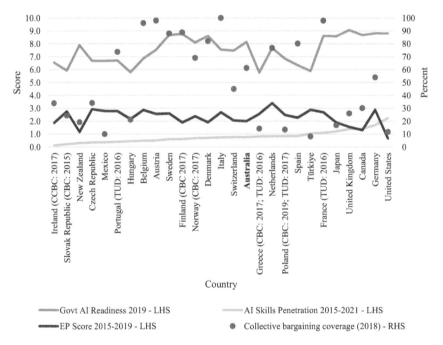

FIGURE 8.2   Employment protection, collective bargaining, AI skills penetration and Government AI Readiness, selected OECD countries.

mixed track record in employment protection and collective bargaining. Figure 8.2 plots AI skills penetration reported by members of the social media platform LinkedIn against OECD country rankings of employment protection and collective bargaining coverage, and an index of government's AI readiness produced annually by Oxford Insights since 2017. Thus, for instance, the United States (US) and Germany, which record amongst the highest levels of AI skills penetration amongst OECD countries, have quite different levels of collective bargaining coverage and employment protection; Germany scoring higher on both accounts than the US.

Australia occupies a middling position internationally. The country's AI skills penetration is below the mid-point of the range. The same is true for its employment protection score, as estimated by the OECD, which resembles that of Japan, another leader in AI skills penetration. However, in terms of collective bargaining, Australia sits above the approximate trend line, somewhere between Germany (with a higher AI skills penetration) and Finland (with a lesser AI skills penetration).

8.7 SOCIAL DIALOGUE AND COLLECTIVE AGREEMENTS IN THE AGE OF AUTOMATION

Australia's Fair Work Act 2009 requires business to consult their workforce before making major workplace changes likely to affect employees covered by a modern award or an enterprise agreement or in relation to its obligations arising under workplace health and safety (WHS) legislation. Major workplace change includes restructuring, redundancies, changes to rosters or working hours, retraining requirements or, most relevant in the present context, the transfer of employees to other work or other work locations. The little we know about how these obligations are implemented suggests a diversity of approaches, varying in the intensity and frequency, as well as their formality and the authority or voice or influence that workers are granted in such consultations (Simao et al., 2021; Ayers, 2018).

In Europe, the data suggest that business and unions make constructive use of employee representation to work out mutually acceptable ways of accommodating advanced digitalisation. Thus, a study by Belloc et al. (2020) of 20,000 European establishments located in 28 countries found employee representation correlated with robot usage and software-based artificial intelligence tools for data analytics. The authors are careful not to suggest a causal link of one direction or another but argue that existing collaborative arrangements support improved job design and working conditions, which "in turn [may] reduce workers' hostility towards automation and facilitates its introduction" (Belloc et al., 2020: 16). In their review of European labour law and its application, specifically in Germany, Klengel and Wenckebach (2021, p. 163) make a similar point when they conclude that "works councils [...] prove in practice not to be impeders, but often even drivers of digitalisation, or at least actors who put the use of AI systems on a more rational basis". A Canadian case study of five assembly plants, however, also notes that the extent to which unions and employees may influence technology adoption also depends on their respective internal cohesion and the competitive position of the enterprise in question; a weak market position may enable enterprises to extract concessions from labour to the latter's detriment (Rutherford & Frangi, 2020). Nissim and Simon (2021) similarly note that unions may be advised to reach out to non-members to make their voices stronger, forming alliances beyond the confines of their traditional membership.

8.8 UNIONS REACTIONS TO AUTOMATION RISKS

A recent report commissioned by the International Trade Union Confederation finds that unions across the globe explore how to respond to, and to protect workers from the risks associated with the increasing use of algorithms in the automation and surveillance of workplaces. However, the report also calls for trade unions to "move more beyond discussion and analysis of the problem to concrete advocacy relating to [automated decision-making] systems in the workplace" (AlgorithmWatch 2023, p. 6). A few country case studies shed light on the activities and achievements of trades unions in their campaigns to help to promote a human-centric application of advanced digitalisation.

Krzywdzinski et al.'s (2022a) study of German works councils points to local- and federal-level initiatives, above all, the German metal workers' union, IG Metall, and its "Transformation Atlas". The Atlas surveyed close to 2,000 works councils across Germany in 2019 to determine their experiences and preferences about consultation in digitalisation processes in their business (IG Metall, 2019). At about the same time, the country's services union, ver.di, engaged with IBM Germany in a collaborative sociological multiple-case study of AI tools introduction in workplaces, also involving Siemens AG (HR chatbot) and Telekom Service GmbH (Personal Inactive Assistant) (Fregin et al., 2020). The study finds that AI tools in workplaces can lead to greater job satisfaction, whilst acceptance of this technology requires transparency of use, purpose and method, and training across an organisation.

In a further study, this time funded by trades unions and the European Social Fund, Bosch and Schmitz-Kießler (2020) undertook case studies of 28 plants (within the metal union's scope) to observe and understand the change process associated with digital transformation at the plant level, beginning in 2015. By the end of 2019, 13 of the 28 plants had reached agreements with the work councils on the management of digital transformation processes, covering skills development, working time flexibility, data protection, matters concerning the monitoring of employee performance, health and safety, including workload reductions.

In a notable development in Spain, forthcoming legislation provides works council with the right to be "informed by the company of the parameters, rules, and instructions on which algorithms or artificial intelligence systems that affect any decision-making that may have an impact on working conditions, access to and maintenance of employment are based, including profiling" (Villarroel Luque, 2021).

Further afield, in the US, the American Federation of Labor and Congress of Industrial Organizations' Commission on the Future of Work and Unions set into motion an US union initiative to ensure that "technology improves lives and raises standards and wages across the board" (AFL-CIO 2019, foreword). In 2021, it culminated in the launch of the Technology Institute as originally recommended by the AFL-CIO Commission.

These initiatives and outcomes not only aim for a human-centric adoption of advanced technology, but also to engage and retain businesses that may consider outsourcing or offshoring as their preferred strategy of managing growing wage pressures resulting from the drive for more technology in the workplace.

8.9 DISCUSSION

This chapter has explored how advanced technology, like AI, is changing workplaces. We gave examples of where it can help but also where it can be dangerous to workers' health and safety. Studies, including our own in Australia (Cebulla et al., 2021, 2022), have shown that it is essential to talk to workers about the risks of new technology. A meaningful consultation may help them accept it and use it well.

As we write this, a new type of technology called generative AI is developing quickly, resulting in unprecedented AI-powered productivity tools such as ChatGPT AI chatbot transforming how people search, write and edit text, and even program computers. These developments are accompanied by amazement and concerns, hype and hysteria that this new technology might take over the jobs that humans used to do (e.g., Goldman Sachs, 2023; Felten et al., 2023). There are also worries about ChatGPT mistakes because it uses information from all over the internet and can make up false stories and references (Europol, 2023).

Businesses will soon transition older, less-advanced chatbots to ChatGPT. The increased proliferation of chatbots means that people may talk to machines more often than humans. At first, this will happen for customer service, but businesses might also use it to manage their workers. Eventually, generative AI could be used to write important legal documents, like agreements between employers and employees.

More automated document writing will likely lead to a higher pace of information sharing and increased worker task switching and cognitive load. As chatbots become more talkative and seem as intelligent as humans, companies may use them to evaluate human performance. For instance, imagine a 360-degree performance review done by an AI bot that gathers information from people's conversations and actions at work. The data collection could include monitoring how people type on their computers and analysing their emotions based on what they say.

As machines replace people in doing specific jobs, who should be held responsible if something goes wrong? Some people suggest giving machines legal status, but others disagree (De Stefano 2019). If machines were given equal legal status as humans, people might have to change their behaviour to accommodate the machines instead of the other way around. It is unclear what the punishment would be for a machine doing something wrong. Would it be taken apart? Ultimately, if something goes wrong with a machine, humans are affected because they would lose the help of the machine and might not know how to do the work themselves.

Each new application of an AI tool offers additional opportunities for data collection. Some companies might not be interested or able to do this, but others will want to use this information to improve their business and stay ahead of competitors. If a company does not collect data, they might fall behind other companies that are using the data to make their operations more efficient and profitable. This incentive can lead to companies finding ways to make money from their employee's data.

AI technology is slowly making its way into workplaces, and its implementation may only happen in stages. While some people believe that AI will eventually become all-encompassing, businesses will take a while to adopt it fully due to cost and lack of understanding. Making a good case for using these technologies may take time, especially when there is slow wage and economic growth, and declining job security. For workplaces, this means more incremental, rather than radical, change. Of course, gradual change may not be as readily observed as fundamental shifts, posing a new risk of intrusion by stealth.

8.10 CONCLUSION

The digital transformation of production processes is rapidly advancing, with AI playing a pivotal role in improving work processes through workforce planning, product enhancement and service operation optimisation. However, the impact of workplace AI adoption is complex, potentially leading to the displacement of workers or harm through anonymous and autonomous performance monitoring. The introduction of AI tools can lead workers to adopt active strategies of re-appropriating agency in how they perform their job. Workplace operations that AI is most likely to change are job control and workload, supervisor/peer and more general organisational relations. The collaborative transformation envisaged in Industry 5.0 may be challenging without revamping business strategies and commercial philosophy. Legal frameworks for worker representation are necessary to facilitate human-centricity in the workplace. A systematic, continuous AI risk and hazard review is needed, with a strategic approach to assessing the workplace risk of AI, ensuring effective communication of the purpose and functioning of AI, and identifying ethical, moral and social principles that the use of AI may affect. The development of AI must consider the risks associated with later stages, including interconnectivity, differential effects on worker status, discontinuity of service or business, and physical workplace impacts. Finally, countries with the highest levels of AI skills penetration in the workforce have a mixed track record in employment protection and collective bargaining, making it imperative to balance technological progress with ethical considerations and workers' rights.

REFERENCES

Aboubichr, B., & Conway, N. (2023). The gaming of performance management systems in British universities. Human Relations, 76(4), 602–628. https://doi.org/10.1177/00187267211052827

Acemoglu, D., & Restrepo, P. (2022). Tasks, automation, and the rise in U.S. wage inequality. Econometrica, 90(5), 1973–2016. https://doi.org/10.3982/ECTA19815

AFL-CIO (2019). AFL-CIO commission on the future of work and unions. Report to the AFL-CIO general board. Aflcio.org. https://aflcio.org/reports/afl-cio-commission-future-work-and-unions

AlgorithmWatch. (2023). Algorithmic transparency and accountability in the world of work A mapping study into the activities of trade unions. Conducted on behalf of the International Trade Union Confederation (ITUC). https://algorithmwatch.org/en/study-trade-unions-algorithmic-transparency/

Ammanath, B., & Blackman, R. (2021). Everyone in your organization needs to understand AI ethics. Harvard Business Review, Leadership and Managing People Digital Article, 26 July. https://hbr.org/2021/07/everyone-in-your-organization-needs-to-understand-ai-ethics

Arnold, Z., & Toner, H. (2021). AI Accidents: An Emerging Threat. Center for Security and Emerging Technology, Georgetown University, Washington, DC, United States. https://cset.georgetown.edu/publication/ai-accidents-an-emerging-threat/

Atwell, C. (2017). Yes, Industry 5.0 is already on the horizon. Machine Design. https://www.machinedesign.com/industrial-automation/yes-industry-50-already-horizon

Ayers, G. (2018). Worker engagement in OHS decision making: A literature review with an Australian focus. Journal of Health & Safety Research & Practice, 10(1), 3–10. https://issuu.com/safetyinstitute/docs/jhsrpvol102020

Baethge-Kinsky, V. (2020). Digitized industrial work: Requirements, opportunities, and problems of competence development. Frontiers in Sociology, 5, 33. https://doi.org/10.3389/fsoc.2020.00033

Barley, S.R. (1986). Technology as an occasion for structuring: Evidence from observation of CT scanners and the social order of radiology departments. Administrative Science Quarterly 31, 78–108. https://www.jstor.org/stable/2392767

Barth, E., Roed, M., Schone, P., & Umblijs, J. (2020). How robots change within-firm wage inequality. IZA Discussion Paper No. 13605. http://dx.doi.org/10.2139/ssrn.3679011

Bartley, T., Soener, M., & Gershenson, C. (2019). Power at a distance: Organizational power across boundaries. Sociology Compass, 13, e12737. https://doi.org/10.1111/soc4.12737

Belloc, F., Burdin, G., & Landini, F. (2020) Robots and Worker Voice: An Empirical Exploration. IZA Discussion Paper No. 13799. http://dx.doi.org/10.2139/ssrn.3718179

Bosch, G., & Schmitz-Kießler, J. (2020). Shaping Industry 4.0 – An experimental approach developed by German trade unions. Transfer: European Review of Labour and Research, 26(2), 189–206. https://doi.org/10.1177/1024258920918480

Braganza, A., Chen, W., Canhoto, A., & Sap, S. (2021). Productive employment and decent work: The impact of AI adoption on psychological contracts, job engagement and employee trust. Journal of Business Research, 131, 485–494. https://doi.org/10.1016/j.jbusres.2020.08.018

Breque, M., De Nul, L., & Petridis, A. (2021). Industry 5.0. Towards a sustainable, human-centric and resilient European industry. Brussels, Belgium: European Commission, Directorate-General for Research and Innovation. https://op.europa.eu/en/publication-detail/-/publication/468a892a-5097-11eb-b59f-01aa75ed71a1/

Brynjolfsson, E., Mitchell, T., & Rock, D. (2018). What can machines learn and what does it mean for occupations and the economy? MIT Initiative on the Digital Economy Research Brief, Vol. 4. MIT Sloan School of Management https://ide.mit.edu/wp-content/uploads/2018/12/2018-08-MITIDE-researchbrief-Erikb.final_.pdf

Bughin, J., & van Zeebroeck, N. (2018). Artificial intelligence: Why a digital base is critical. McKinsey Quarterly. McKinsey Insights. https://www.mckinsey.com/business-functions/quantumblack/our-insights/artificial-intelligence-why-a-digital-base-is-critical

Burri, R.V. (2008). Doing distinctions: Boundary work and symbolic capital in radiology. Social Studies of Science, 38(1), 35–62. https://doi.org/10.1177/0306312707082021

Cebulla, A., Szpak, Z., Howell, C., Knight, G., & Hussain, S (2022). Applying ethics to AI in the workplace: The design of a scorecard for Australian workplace health and safety. AI & Society https://doi.org/10.1007/s00146-022-01460-9

Cebulla, A., Szpak, Z., & Knight, G. (2023). Preparing to work with artificial intelligence: Assessing WHS when using AI in the workplace. International Journal of Workplace Health Management, ahead-of-print. https://doi.org/10.1108/IJWHM-09-2022-0141

Cebulla, A., Szpak, Z., Knight, G., Howell, C., & Hussain, S. (2021). Ethical use of artificial intelligence in the workplace. Final report. Centre for Work Health and Safety, NSW Department of Customer Service, Sydney, Australia. https://www.centreforwhs.nsw.gov.au/Projects/ethical-use-of-artifical-intelligence-in-the-workplace

Chhillar, D., & Aguilera, R. V. (2022). An Eye for Artificial Intelligence: Insights into the Governance of Artificial Intelligence and Vision for Future Research. Business & Society, 61(5), 1197–1241. https://doi.org/10.1177/00076503221080959

Chui, M., Roberts, R., & Yee, L. (2022). Generative AI is here: How tools like ChatGPT could change your business. McKinsey Insights. https://www.mckinsey.com/capabilities/quantumblack/our-insights/generative-ai-is-here-how-tools-like-chatgpt-could-change-your-business#/

Cyphers, B. (2021). Google Is Testing Its Controversial New Ad Targeting Tech in Millions of Browsers. Here's What We Know. Electronic Frontier Foundation, 30 March. https://www.eff.org/deeplinks/2021/03/google-testing-its-controversial-new-ad-targeting-tech-millions-browsers-heres

De Cremer, D. (2022). With AI entering organizations, responsible leadership may slip!. AI Ethics, 2, 49–51. https://doi.org/10.1007/s43681-021-00094-9

De Stefano, V. (2019). 'Negotiating the algorithm': Automation, artificial intelligence and labour protection. Comparative Labor Law & Policy Journal, 41(1). http://dx.doi.org/10.2139/ssrn.3178233

De Stefano, V., & Taes, S. (2022). Algorithmic management and collective bargaining. Transfer: European Review of Labour and Research. https://doi.org/10.1177/10242589221141055

Deloitte Insights. (2019). Automation with intelligence. Reimagining the organisation in the 'Age of With'. https://www2.deloitte.com/us/en/insights/focus/technology-and-the-future-of-work/intelligent-automation-technologies-strategies.html

Demir, K.A., Döven, G., & Sezen, B. (2019). Industry 5.0 and human-robot co-working. Procedia Computer Science, 158, 688–695. https://doi.org/10.1016/j.procs.2019.09.104

Dery, K., Sebastian, I.M., & van der Meulen, N. (2017). The digital workplace is key to digital innovation. MIS Quarterly Executive, 16(2), Article 4. https://aisel.aisnet.org/misqe/vol16/iss2/4

Diessner, S., Durazzi, N., & Hope, D. (2022). Skill-biased liberalization: Germany's transition to the knowledge economy. Politics & Society, 50(1), 117–155. 1 https://doi.org/10.1177/00323292211006563

Dignam, A. (2020). Artificial intelligence, tech corporate governance and the public interest regulatory response. Cambridge Journal of Regions, Economy and Society, 13(1), 37–54. https://doi.org/10.1093/cjres/rsaa002

Dignum, V. (2019). Responsible Artificial Intelligence. How to Develop and Use AI in a Responsible Way. Cham, Switzerland: Springer Nature Switzerland AG.

Doellgast, V., & Wagner, I. (2022). Collective regulation and the future of work in the digital economy: Insights from comparative employment relations. Journal of Industrial Relations, 64(3), 438–460. https://doi.org/10.1177/00221856221101165

Domini, G., Grazzi, M., Moschella, D., & Treibich, T. (2022). For whom the bell tolls: The firm-level effects of automation on wage and gender inequality. Research Policy, 51(7). https://doi.org/10.1016/j.respol.2022.104533

Downs, J.S., Holbrook, M.B., Sheng, S., & Cranor, L.F. (2010). Are your participants gaming the system? screening mechanical Turk workers. In Proceedings of the SIGCHI Conference on Human Factors in Computing Systems (CHI '10). Association for Computing Machinery, New York, NY, USA, 2399–2402. https://doi.org/10.1145/1753326.1753688

Etzioni, A., & Etzioni, O. (2016). Keeping AI legal. Vanderbilt Journal of Entertainment & Technology Law, 19(1). https://scholarship.law.vanderbilt.edu/jetlaw/vol19/iss1/5

Europol (2023). ChatGPT The impact of Large Language Models on Law Enforcement. European Union Agency for Law Enforcement Cooperation. https://www.europol.europa.eu/publications-events/publications/chatgpt-impact-of-large-language-models-law-enforcement

Faraj, S., Pachidi, S., & Sayegh, K. (2018). Working and organizing in the age of the learning algorithm. Information and Organization, 28, 62–70. https://doi.org/10.1016/j.infoandorg.2018.02.005

Felten, E., Raj, M., & Seamans, R. (2023). How will language modelers like ChatGPT affect occupations and industries?. https://arxiv.org/pdf/2303.01157.pdf

Fountaine, T., McCarthy, B., & Saleh, T. (2019). Building the AI-powered organization. Harvard Business Review, July–August. https://hbr.org/2019/07/building-the-ai-powered-organization

Fregin, M.-C., Levels, M., de Grip, A., Montizaan, R., & Kensbock, J. (2020). Künstliche Intelligenz: Ein sozialpartnerschaftliches Forschungsprojekt untersucht die neue Arbeitswelt. IBM Deutschland GmbH und Vereinte Dienstleistungsgewerkschaft ver.di. ROA External Reports. https://www.verdi.de/themen/digitalisierung/++co++36946346-3578-11eb-8c4b-001a4a160129

Frey, C.B., & Osborne, M.A. (2017). The future of employment: How susceptible are jobs to computerisation? Technological Forecasting and Social Change, 114, 254–280. https://doi.org/10.1016/j.techfore.2016.08.019

Global Deal. (2021). The impact of Artificial Intelligence on the labour market and the workplace: What role for social dialogue? Global Deal Thematic Brief. https://www.theglobaldeal.com/news-and-events/the-impact-of-ai-on-the-labour-market-and-the-workplace.html

Goldman Sachs (2023). The potentially large effects of artificial intelligence on economic growth (Briggs/Kodnani). 26 March 2023. https://www.key4biz.it/wp-content/uploads/2023/03/Global-Economics-Analyst_-The-Potentially-Large-Effects-of-Artificial-Intelligence-on-Economic-Growth-Briggs_Kodnani.pdf

Grassegger, H., & Krogerus, M. (2017). The data that turned the world upside down. Public Policy Program, Stanford University. https://www.vice.com/en/article/mg9vvn/how-our-likes-helped-trump-win

Graveling, R. (2020). The mental health of workers in the digital era: How recent technical innovation and its pace affects the mental well-being of workers. Brussels, Belgium: European Parliament, Directorate-General for Internal Policies of the Union. https://www.europarl.europa.eu/thinktank/en/document/IPOL_BRI(2020)642368

Hanelt, A., Bohnsack, R., Marz, D., & Antunes Marante, C. (2021). A systematic review of the literature on digital transformation: Insights and implications for strategy and organizational change. Journal of Management Studies, 58, 1159–1197. https://doi.org/10.1111/joms.12639

Helper, S., Martins, R., & Seamans, R. (2019). Who profits from Industry 4.0? Theory and evidence from the automotive industry. NYU Stern School of Business. 31 January. http://dx.doi.org/10.2139/ssrn.3377771

Holmström, J., & Hällgren, M. (2021). AI management beyond the hype: exploring the co-constitution of AI and organizational context. AI and Society, 37, 1575–1585. https://doi.org/10.1007/s00146-021-01249-2

Huang, F., Kwak, H., & An, J. (2023). Is ChatGPT better than human annotators? Potential and limitations of ChatGPT in explaining implicit hate speech. arXiv:2302.07736. https://doi.org/10.48550/arXiv.2302.07736

IG Metall. (2019). Transformationsatlas IG Metall Vorstand. Transformationsatlas. Wesentliche Ergebnisse. Pressekonferenz der IG Metall. 5 June. IG Metall Vorstand. https://www.igmetall.de/download/20190605_20190605_Transformationsatlas_Pressekonferenz_f2c85bcec886a59301dbe-bab85f136f36061cced.pdf

Jarrahi, M.H., Newlands, G., Lee, M.K., Wolf, C.T., Kinder, E., & Sutherland, W. (2021). Algorithmic management in a work context. Big Data and Society, 8(2). https://doi.org/10.1177/20539517211020332

Jarrahi, M.H., & Sutherland, W. (2019). Algorithmic management and algorithmic competencies: Understanding and appropriating algorithms in gig work. In N. Greene Taylor, C. Christian-Lamb, M. H. Martin, & B. Nardi (Eds.), Information in contemporary society. iConference 2019. Lecture Notes in Computer Science, Information in Contemporary Society, 14th International

Conference, iConference 2019, Washington, DC, USA, March 31–April 3, 2019, Proceedings (LNCS 11420, pp. 578–589). Springer, Cham. https://doi.org/10.1007/978-3-030-15742-5_55

Jeffries, A., & Yin, L. (2021). Amazon puts its own "brands" first. The Markup. https://themarkup.org/amazons-advantage/2021/10/14/amazon-puts-its-own-brands-first-above-better-rated-products

Kellogg, K. C., Valentine, M. A., & Christin, A. (2019). Algorithms at work: The new contested terrain of control. Academy of Management Annals, 14(1), 366–410. https://doi.org/10.5465/annals.2018.0174

Klengel, E., & Wenckebach, J. (2021). Artificial intelligence, work, power imbalance and democracy – Why co-determination is essential. Italian Labour Law e-Journal, 14(2). https://doi.org/10.6092/issn.1561-8048/14099

KPMG. (2019). AI transforming the enterprise. 8 key AI adoption trends. https://advisory.kpmg.us/articles/2019/ai-transforming-enterprise.html

Krzywdzinski, M., Gerst, D., & Butollo, F. (2022a). Promoting human-centred AI in the workplace. Trade unions and their strategies for regulating the use of AI in Germany. Transfer: European Review of Labour and Research. https://doi.org/10.1177/10242589221142273

Krzywdzinski, M., Pfeiffer, S., Evers, M., & Gerber, C. (2022b). Measuring work and workers. Wearables and digital assistance systems in manufacturing and logistics. Discussion Paper SP III 2022–301. Berlin, Germany: WZB Berlin Social Science Center. https://EconPapers.repec.org/RePEc:zbw:wzbgwp:spiii2022301

Lloyd, C., & Payne, J. (2023). Food for thought: Robots, jobs and skills in food and drink processing in Norway and the UK. New Technology, Work and Employment. https://doi.org/10.1111/ntwe.12194

Longo, F., Padovano, A., & Umbrello, S. (2020). Value-oriented and ethical technology engineering in Industry 5.0: A human-centric perspective for the design of the factory of the future. Applied Sciences, 10(12), 4182. https://doi.org/10.3390/app10124182

Marmo, M., Sinopoli, E.A., & Guo, S. (2022). Worker exploitation in the Australian gig economy: Emerging mechanisms of social control. Griffith Law Review, 31(2), 171–192. https://doi.org/10.1080/10383441.2022.2076036

Mayer, A-S., Strich, F., & Fiedler, M. (2020). Unintended consequences of introducing AI systems for decision making. MIS Quarterly Executive 19(4), Article 6. https://aisel.aisnet.org/misqe/vol19/iss4/6

McKinsey Analytics. (2021). The state of AI in 2021. https://www.mckinsey.com/business-functions/quantumblack/our-insights/global-survey-the-state-of-ai-in-2021

Moore, P.V. (2018). The threat of physical and psychosocial violence and harassment in digitalized work. Geneva, Switzerland: International Labour Office. https://www.ilo.org/actrav/pubs/WCMS_617062/lang--en/index.htm

Morley, J., Floridi, L., Kinsey, L., & Elhalal, A. (2020). From what to how: An initial review of publicly available AI ethics tools, methods and research to translate principles into practices. Science and Engineering Ethics, 26, 2141–2168. https://doi.org/10.1007/s11948-019-00165-5

Nissim, G., & Simon, T. (2021). The future of labor unions in the age of automation and at the dawn of AI, Technology in Society, 67(101732). https://doi.
org/10.1016/j.techsoc.2021.101732

Nurski, L., & Hoffman, M. (2022). The impact of artificial intelligence on the
nature and quality of jobs. Working Paper 14/2022, Bruegel.

Oosthuizen, R.M. (2022). The fourth industrial revolution – Smart technology, artificial intelligence, robotics and algorithms: Industrial psychologists in future workplaces. Frontiers in Artificial Intelligence, 5. https://doi.
org/10.3389/frai.2022.913168

Patel, V., Chesmore, A., Legner, C.M., & Pandey, S. (2022). Trends in workplace
wearable technologies and connected-worker solutions for next-generation
occupational safety, health, and productivity. Advanced Intelligent Systems, 4.
https://doi.org/10.1002/aisy.202100099

Pepito, J.A., & Locsin, R. (2018). Can nurses remain relevant in a technologically
advanced future?. International Journal of Nursing Sciences, 6(1), 106–110.
https://doi.org/10.1016/j.ijnss.2018.09.013

Perez, F., Conway, N.; & Roques, O. (2022). The autonomy tussle: AI technology and employee job crafting responses. Industrial Relations/Relations
Industrielles, 77(3), 1–19. https://doi.org/10.7202/1094209ar

PWC. (2021). AI predictions 2021. https://www.pwc.com/us/en/tech-effect/ai-
analytics/ai-predictions.html

Ranganathan, A. (2021). Identification and worker responses to workplace change:
Evidence from four cases in India. ILR Review, 74(3), 663–688. https://doi.
org/10.1177/0019793921989683

Rutherford, T.D. & Frangi, L. (2020). Is Industry 4.0 a good fit for high performance work systems? Trade unions and workplace change in the south-
ern Ontario automotive assembly sector. Relations industrielles/Industrial
Relations, 75(4), 751–773. https://doi.org/10.7202/1074563ar

Sanderson, C., Douglas, D., Lu, Q., Schleiger, E., Whittle, J., Lacey, J., Newnham,
G., Hajkowicz, S., Robinson, C., & Hansen, D. (2021). AI ethics principles in
practice: Perspectives of designers and developers. arXiv:2112.07467v1 [cs.
CY]. https://doi.org/10.48550/arXiv.2112.07467

Simao, D. Da Conceicao, Karanikas, N., Cortes-Ramirez, J., & Sav, A. (2021).
Workplace health and safety consultation in Australia: A scoping review.
Journal of Health, Safety and Environment, 37(2), 97–116. https://eprints.
qut.edu.au/213681/

Smids, J., Nyholm, S., & Berkers, H (2020). Robots in the workplace: A threat
to—Or opportunity. Philosophy and Technology, 33, 503–522. https://doi.
org/10.1007/s13347-019-00377-4

Sniderman, B., Mahto, M., & Cotteleer, M.J. (2016). Industry 4.0 and manufacturing ecosystems. New York, USA: Deloitte. https://www2.deloitte.com/us/en/
insights/focus/industry-4-0/manufacturing-ecosystems-exploring-world-
connected-enterprises.html

Stelmaszak, M., & Aaltonen, A. (2018). Closing the Loop of Big Data Analytics:
The Case of Learning Analytics. Research Papers, 82. https://aisel.aisnet.org/
ecis2018_rp/82

Tarafdar, M., Pullins, E. B., & Ragu-Nathan, T. S. (2015). Technostress: negative effect on performance and possible mitigations. Information Systems Jourbal, 25, 103–132. https://doi.org/10.1111/isj.12042

Trenerry, B., Chng, S., Wang, Y., Suhaila, Z.S., Lim, S.S., Lu, H.Y., & Oh, P.H. (2021). Preparing workplaces for digital transformation: An integrative review and framework of multi-level factors. Frontiers in Psychology, 12, 620766. https://doi.org/10.3389/fpsyg.2021.620766

van den Broek, E., Sergeeva, A., & Huysman Vrije, M. (2021). When the machine meets the expert: An ethnography of developing AI for hiring. MIS Quarterly, 45(3), 1557–1580. https://doi.org/10.25300/MISQ/2021/16559

Villarroel Luque, C. (2021) Workers vs Algorithms: What can the new Spanish provision on artificial intelligence and employment achieve?. Verfassungsblog, 2021/5/27. https://verfassungsblog.de/workers-vs-ai/

Walsh, M. (2019). When Algorithms Make Managers Worse. Harvard Business Review, 8 May. https://hbr.org/2019/05/when-algorithms-make-managers-worse

Ward, M. (2021). Google blocks Australian news in 'experiment'. Australian Financial Review, 13 January. https://www.afr.com/companies/media-and-marketing/google-blocks-australian-news-in-experiment-20210113-p56tqd

Waring, P., Bali, A., & Vas, C. (2020). The fourth industrial revolution and labour market regulation in Singapore. The Economic and Labour Relations Review, 31(3), 347–363. https://doi.org/10.1177/1035304620941272

Wilson, H.J. (2013). Wearables in the workplace. Harvard Business Review, 91(11), 23–25.

Xu, X., Lu, Y., Vogel-Heuser, B., & Wang, L. (2021). Industry 4.0 and Industry 5.0—Inception, conception and perception. Journal of Manufacturing Systems, 61, 530–535.

CHAPTER 9

More than Programming?

The Impact of AI on Work and Skills

Toby Walsh

> In my opinion, ignoring AI is like ignoring blogging in the late 1990s, or social media circa 2004, or mobile in 2007. Very quickly, some degree of facility with these tools will be increasingly essential for all professionals, a primary driver for new opportunities and new jobs. Developing skills and competencies in it now will yield benefits for years to come.
>
> It's also true that the changes AI will bring will have negative impacts as well as positive ones. Previous technology revolutions disrupted specific subgroups, like craftsmen whose production was replace by factories – or, more recently, factory workers who lost their jobs to increased automation.
>
> Now, knowledge workers are also facing these challenges. While I strongly believe that these new AI tools will create new jobs and new industries, along with great economic benefits and other quality-of-life gains, they will also eliminate some jobs, both blue- and white-collar.
>
> (Hoffman & GPT4, 2023, pp. 110–111)

It seems certain that artificial intelligence (AI) will have a large impact on economy and society. For instance, one study estimates that it will grow the world's economy by around 15 percent or so, contributing over $15 trillion annually in inflation-adjusted terms (Rao & Verweij, 2017). Such

DOI: 10.1201/9781003393757-9

disruption will not be without pain. One of the greatest fears about AI is the impact it will have on work. Will it eliminate many jobs? Will workers who embrace AI be more productive and replace those workers who do not? For jobs that are not replaced by AI, how will the skills that workers need evolve? For the new jobs that AI creates, what skills will be needed? And will AI be a net positive, creating more jobs than it destroys? Or will it be a net negative?

It is clear already that the impacts will not be even. Some countries will be impacted greater than others. Even within a country, impacts will not be even. Some sectors of the economy will be more severely disrupted than others. Predicting where those impacts will fall and what they will be is not easy. It isn't as simple as the blue-collar workers doing manual work who will be replaced by robots and white-collar workers doing cognitive work who will be saved. There are, unfortunately, blue-collar workers doing jobs too poorly paid for it to be economically viable to replace. There are also blue-collar workers doing jobs that robots cannot do. Plumbers and electricians are, for example, likely safe from automation for a long time. And some blue-collar jobs may be invulnerable to technological disruption even when AI could, in theory, do them. We will likely always value the artisan over the mass produced: so, in opposition to what Reid Hoffman argued in the opening quotation, jobs such as cabinet maker may remain even when machines could in theory do the work. On the other hand, there are white-collar workers who are perhaps less confident today that their jobs are safe from automation than they were a decade ago. For instance, graphic designers were perhaps not too concerned about their jobs until image-to-text tools like Stable Diffusion and DALL-e arrived hinting at a future where a lot of graphic design might be automated.

Computer programmers, especially those writing (AI) software, might be more confident than graphic designers that their skills will remain in high demand. But even they cannot be certain. The irony is that machine learning is getting computers to program themselves. The largest bits of software constructed today are large neural networks, with billions of parameters that are set by gradient descent and not by any human. In addition, even when limiting our attention to more conventional software, AI is changing the nature of computer programming. Large language models can easily be trained not to produce natural language but computer code. This should not be surprising as computer languages are more regular than natural language. Large language models trained on computer code can greatly improve the productivity of a competent programmer.

One able programmer with such a tool might therefore be able to do the work of several human programmers. Will this mean we need fewer computer programmers in the future?

9.1 TECHNOLOGICAL UNEMPLOYMENT

The fear that technology would disrupt employment is an old one. In 1930, John Maynard Keynes warned:

> a new disease of which some readers may not have heard the name, but of which they will hear a great deal in the years to come: namely, technological unemployment. This means unemployment due to our discovery of means of economising the use of labour outrunning the pace at which we can find new uses for labour.
>
> (Keynes, 1930, p. 325)

Economists can often be wrong, so perhaps it should not be surprising that this prediction has not, at least yet, come true. Unemployment did shortly become a major problem, but the reason was not technological but financial. The Great Depression led to a rapid rise in unemployment that lasted a decade. Today, however, unemployment has fallen and is at historic low levels in most countries. This is despite the world's population being at historic high levels. Work hasn't ended, though many of us are working fewer hours.

Nevertheless, fears about technological unemployment have continued to grow since then. In 1949, Alan Turing put it in very plain terms[1] in an interview with *The Times* newspaper:

> This is only a foretaste of what is to come, and only the shadow of what is going to be. We have to have some experience with the machine [the Manchester Mark 1 computer] before we really know its capabilities. It may take years before we settle down to the new possibilities, but I do not see why it should not enter any one of the fields normally covered by the human intellect, and eventually compete on equal terms.
>
> (Turing, 1947)

If machines can compete with humans, then what chance is there for humans? It is hard to understand how Turing can suggest machines would compete on equal terms with humans. Machines don't need to rest, or be paid. These are surely unfair advantages and unequal terms?

Three years after Turing's comment, the famous economist Wassily Leontief wrote, somewhat optimistically, about how the working week and income distribution would permit the economy to adapt to technological advances (Leontief, 1952). He used horse labour as an example of the threat posed to human labour by technological change. Following the invention of the railroads and the telegraph, the role of horse labour in the US economy actually increased. The equine population grew sixfold between 1840 and 1900 to more than 21 million horses and mules as the United States grew and prospered. In 1900, horses might therefore have felt safe from technological change. While their job transporting people and messages between towns and cities had started to disappear, other jobs had arrived to replace this.

Horse weren't to know that this good fortune was to be short-lived. The invention of the internal combustion engine rapidly reversed this trend. The US population grew larger, and the nation became richer. But horses began to disappear from the labour market. By 1960, there were just three million horses in the United States, a decline of nearly 90 percent. Economists debating the future role of horse labour in the economy in the early 1900s might have predicted that, just as in the past, new jobs for horses would emerge in areas enabled by the new technologies. They would have been very wrong.

These early worries about technology unemployment came to a head in March 1964. President Lyndon Johnson received a short, but alarming, memorandum from the Ad Hoc Committee on the Triple Revolution (Agger et al., 1964). The memo was signed by luminaries including Nobel Prize–winning chemist Linus Pauling, *Scientific American* publisher Gerard Piel, and Gunnar Myrdal who was to go on to win the Nobel Prize in Economics. The memo warned that technology would soon create mass unemployment. It predicted that automation and computers were set to change the economy in as fundamental a way as the industrial revolution changed the agricultural era before it, and that this revolution would occur at a speed never witnessed before.

In absolute terms, the memorandum (like Keynes before it) was wrong. There has not been mass unemployment. In fact, since 1964, the US economy has added over 70 million new jobs. But computers and automation have radically changed the jobs that are available, the skills those jobs require, and the wages paid for those jobs. And it is very unlikely that we have got to the end point yet. Like the example of horses at the start of the industrial revolution, we should be cautious about extrapolating forwards from today. There are early warnings of more troubling times ahead.

In 2015, for example, 22 percent of men in the United States without a college degree aged between 21 and 30 had not worked at all during the prior 12 months. Twenty-something male high-school graduates used to be the most reliable cohort of workers in America. They would leave school, get a blue-collar job, and work at it till their retirement some 40 or more years down the road. Today over one in five are out of work. The employment rate of this group has fallen 10 percentage points. And this appears to have triggered cultural, economic, and social decline. Without jobs, this group is less likely to marry, to leave home, or to engage politically (Wilson, 1987). The future for them looks rather bleak. If they cannot get on the employment ladder, are they going to be forever without a decent job?

9.2 MACHINE LEARNING PREDICTIONS

A number of studies have tried to quantify the impact more precisely. One of the most widely reported was a study out of the University of Oxford (Frey & Osborne, 2013). This report famously predicts that 47 percent of jobs in the United States are under threat of automation in the next two decades or so. Studies for other countries like Australia have reached broadly similar conclusions. Most recently, similar studies are starting to appear about the impact of generative AI on jobs despite concerns about the methodology of the original Oxford study (e.g., Hatzius et al., 2023).

Ironically, the writing of the 2013 Oxford report was itself partially automated. The authors used machine learning to predict precisely which of 702 different job types could be automated. They used machine learning to train a classifier, a program to predict which jobs would be automated. They first fed the program with a training set, 70 jobs that they had labelled by hand as automatable or not. The program then predicted whether the remaining 632 jobs could be automated. Even the job of predicting which jobs will be automated in the future has already been partially automated.

As with any machine learning problem, the predictions of the classifier depend critically on the training data. The training set of 70 out of the 702 different jobs was classified by hand. The classification was binary: at risk of automation, not at risk of automation. Some of the jobs classified likely fell in-between. For instance, one job which they classified as at risk of automation was accountant and auditor. They are certainly parts of being an accountant and auditor that will be automated in the next few decades. But it is very doubtful that all parts of the job of being an accountant or auditor will disappear.

In total, the hand classified training set had 37 of the 70 jobs at risk of automation. That is, over half of their training data – provided as input to the classifier – were jobs said to be risk of automation. Not surprisingly, then, the output of the classifier was a prediction that around half the full set of 702 jobs were at risk of automation. One might expect if their training set had been more cautious, say labelling only one in four jobs in the training set at risk of automation, then their overall prediction on the full set of jobs would have been equally cautious.

To explore this, I ran a survey of my own (Walsh, 2018). I asked 300 experts in AI and robotics to classify which of the jobs in the training set were at risk of automation in the next two decades. I also asked the same questions of nearly 500 non-experts, members of the public who read an article I wrote about advances in poker bots. The non-experts agreed almost exactly with the classifications in the training set. But the experts in AI and robotics were significantly more cautious. They predicted around 20 percent fewer jobs were at risk of automation. This would translate into a significant reduction in the predicted number of jobs at risk of automation.

Even if you agree with all the assumptions and predictions of the Frey and Osborne report, you cannot conclude that half of us will be unemployed in a couple of decades. The report merely estimates the number of jobs that are potentially automatable over the next few decades. There are many reasons why this will not translate into 47 percent unemployment.

First, the report merely estimated the number of jobs that are susceptible to automation. Some of these jobs won't be automated in practice for economical, societal, technical, and other reasons. For example, we can pretty much automate the job of an airline pilot today. Indeed, most of the time, a computer is flying your plane. But society is likely to continue to demand the reassurance of having a pilot on board for some time to come even if they are just reading their iPad most of the time.

Second, we also need to consider all the new jobs that technology will create. For example, we don't employ many people setting type anymore. But we do employ many more people in the digital equivalent, making web pages. Of course, if you are a printer and your job is destroyed, it helps if you're suitably educated so you can reposition yourself in one of these new industries. There is sadly no fundamental law of economics that requires as many new jobs to be created by new technologies as destroyed. It happens to have been the case in the past. But as horses have discovered over the last century, it is not necessarily the case with all new technologies.

Third, some of these jobs will only be partially automated, and automation may in fact enhance our ability to do the job. For example, there are many new tools to automate scientific experiments: gene sequencers that can automatically read our genes, mass spectrometers that can automatically infer chemical structure, and telescopes that can automatically scan the skies. But this hasn't put scientists out of a job. In fact, more scientists are alive and doing science today than have ever lived in the history of civilisation. Automation has lifted their productivity. Scientific knowledge is simply discovered faster.

Fourth, we also need to consider how the working week will change over the next few decades. Most countries in the developed world have seen the number of hours worked per week decrease significantly since the start of the industrial revolution. In the United States, the average working week has declined from around 60 hours to just 33 (Whaples, 2001). Other developed countries are even lower. German workers effectively only work 26 hours per week once we take into account annual leave entitlements and public holidays.[2] If these trends continue, we will need to create more jobs to replace these lost hours.

Fifth, we also need to factor in changes in demographics. The number of people seeking employment will surely change. In many developed economies, populations are ageing. If we can fix pension systems, then many more of us may be enjoying retirement, unbothered by the need to work. Indeed, in countries like Japan, there are already significant concerns that there will be too few workers left below retirement age (Hong & Schneider, 2020).

Sixth, we also need to consider how automation will grow the economy. Some of the extra wealth generated by automation will "trickle down" into the economy, creating new job opportunities elsewhere. This argument depends on redistribution mechanisms like taxes which may require adjusting for the new shape of the economy. On the other side, automation may lower costs, making the cost of the basic essentials for living cheaper. If it costs less to live, we may work less.

9.3 THE PRESENT

AI is constantly in the news today. It is impossible to open a newspaper without reading multiple stories about some new application of AI. Many, including those working in the field, are concerned about the impacts it is going to have, especially on jobs. My colleague, Moshe Vardi, put it starkly at the 2016 Annual Meeting of the Association for Advancement of Science:

> We are approaching a time when machines will be able to outperform humans at almost any task … I believe that society needs to confront this question before it is upon us: If machines are capable of doing almost any work humans can do, what will humans do? … We need to rise to the occasion and meet this challenge before human labor becomes obsolete.
>
> (Rice University, 2016)

There is some evidence that some jobs are starting to be automated, and that some of these jobs are not being replaced by jobs elsewhere. An MIT study from 2017 analysed the impact of automation in the United States from 1993 to 2007 (Acemoglu & Restrepo, 2017). It found that industrial robots reduced overall jobs. Every new robot replaced around 5.6 workers on average. And offsetting gains were not observed in other occupations. In fact, the study estimated that every additional robot per 1,000 workers reduced the total population in employment in the U.S. by 0.34 percentage points. Automation also put pressure on the jobs that remained. Every additional robot per 1,000 workers also reduced wages by 0.5 percent. During that 17-year period of the study, the number of industrial robots in the United States quadrupled, eliminating what they estimated was around half a million jobs.

The oil industry provides an informative case study of the scale of the challenge. The price of oil collapsed from $115 per barrel in August 2014 to below $30 at the start of 2016.[3] This drove the industry to decrease headcount[4] and introduce more automation. Nearly half a million jobs disappeared from the oil industry worldwide. But now, as the price of oil is rebounding, and the industry is again growing, less than half of those jobs have returned. Automation has reduced the 20 people typically needed to work a well down to just five.[5]

9.4 OPEN JOBS

One reason automation won't eliminate some jobs is that, in some cases, automation will just let us do more of that particular job. It's useful in this respect to distinguish between "open" and "closed" jobs. Automation will tend to augment open jobs but replace closed jobs. What do I mean by open and closed jobs?

Closed jobs are those where there is a fixed amount of work. For example, window cleaner is a closed job. There are only a fixed number of windows to be cleaned on the planet, and there's no point cleaning a window that hasn't got dirty again. Window cleaning robots are now starting to appear. Once robots can clean windows cheaper than a human, which I suspect is not far away, the job of human window cleaner will disappear. At least, the job of window cleaner will disappear from developed countries where human window cleaners are expensive and prone to fall off ladders. As a second example, the job of processing insurance claims is a closed job. Customers of an insurance firm only file a certain number of insurance claims. When we automate the processing of insurance claims, we don't generate demand to process more claims. We simply reduce this cost from the insurance industry.

Open jobs by comparison expand as you automate them. For instance, chemistry is an open job. If you are a chemist, AI tools that help automate your job will merely help you do more chemistry. You can push back the frontiers of our understanding of chemistry that much faster. You are unlikely to run out of new chemistry to understand. As a second example, the job of a police detective is an open job. AI tools that help a detective investigate crime will speed up their work, permitting them to consider many of the crimes that are currently ignored.

Of course, most jobs are neither completely open nor completely closed. Take the legal profession. As computers take over more and more routine legal work, the cost of accessing the law will fall. This will expand the market for lawyers, generating more demand and giving all of us better access to legal advice. This will likely create more work for experienced lawyers. But it is hard to imagine that lots of entry-level legal jobs will remain. It may be hard for young graduates to compete with robo-lawyers that have read all the legal literature, never need to sleep, never make mistakes, and don't need any salary.

9.5 PARTIAL AUTOMATION

One argument put forwards why the automation of 47 percent of jobs won't translate into mass unemployment is that only some parts of these 47 percent of job will be automated. This argument is problematic. If you automate parts of a job, then you can usually do the same work with fewer people. Consider again a job like being a lawyer. Closer analysis of the time spent by a lawyer on different aspects of their work suggests that only around one quarter of their time is spent doing tasks that could be automated in the near future (Manyika et al., 2017). Unless we create more legal work (and see the discussion earlier about open and closed jobs for discussion around this topic), averaged over all lawyers, we could therefore do current legal work with three quarters of the current lawyers we have today. Lawyers might lift their game and use the time freed up to do better quality work. But some law firms will simply lower their prices by three quarters, and cut one quarter of their staff to pay for their reduced income.

This argument that only parts of jobs will be automated has even been used to argue that one of the jobs most at risk of automation is, in fact, safe from replacement. Truck drivers need not worry, they say, as there will always be edge cases that defeat the machines. The truck arrives at some engineering works where a road worker signals to the truck by hand. The truck needs to drive around a factory that is not on any GPS maps. Autonomous trucks will simply not be able to cope with such situations. The bad news for truck drivers is that this neglects remote driving. Companies like Starksy Robotics are already testing autonomous trucks in which remote drivers take over when the machine cannot cope. One such remote driver will be able to take care of multiple autonomous trucks. So we might have human driving trucks remotely for some time still, but there will be many fewer of them than now.

9.6 NEW JOBS

All technologies create new jobs as well as destroy them. That has been the case in the past, and it might seem reasonable to suppose that it will also be the case in the future. There is, however, no fundamental law of economics that requires the same number of jobs to be created as destroyed. In the past, more jobs were created than destroyed, but it doesn't have to be so in the future. This time could be different. In the Industrial Revolution, machines took over many of the physical tasks we used to do. But we humans were still left with all the cognitive tasks. This time, as machines start to take on many of the cognitive tasks too, there's the worrying question: what is left for us humans?

One of my colleagues has suggested there will be plenty of new jobs like robot repair person. I am entirely unconvinced by such claims. The thousands of people who used to paint and weld in most of our car factories got replaced by only a couple of robot repair people. There's also no reason why robots won't be able to repair robots. We already have factories where robots make robots. There are dark factories, factories where there are no people and so no need for lights, in which robots work night and day making other robots. FANUC, one of the largest manufacturers of industrial robots, has operated such a dark factory near Mount Fuji since 2001. This has helped FANUC post annual sales of around $6 billion, selling robots into booming markets like China. Another of my colleagues has suggested we'll have robot psychologists. As though we'll need one robot psychologist per robot. Robot psychology will be conducted at best by a few people on the planet. So there won't be many jobs looking after the robots.

The new jobs will have to be doing jobs where either humans excel or where we choose not to have machines. Machines might be physically and cognitively better than us at certain jobs, but we nevertheless choose to have humans do them. We might decide that we prefer human judges, hairdressers, influencers, or CEOs.

9.7 THE IMPORTANT SKILLS

Finally, let me address the question of what are the important jobs skills in this race against the machines. The Oxford report identifies three job skills which it is claimed will be difficult to automate in the next few decades: our creativity, our social intelligence, and our ability at perception and manipulation. I would agree with the first two but am uncertain about the third. Computers already perceive the world better than us, on more wavelengths, and at higher precision. What is true is that manipulation is difficult for robots, especially away from the factory floor in uncontrolled environments. This is likely to remain so for some time to come. And even when robots have better manipulation skills than humans, a human may do these manipulation tasks cheaper than an expensive robot.

My best advice here is to head towards one or more of the corners of what I call "the triangle of opportunity". On one corner, we have the geeks, the technically literate. There is a future in inventing the future. It is still very challenging to get computers to program themselves. Computers are also challenged at created a novel future. Be someone then that does that.

Of course, not all of us are technically minded. If you are not, I recommend you head towards one of the other two corners. On one of these corners are those with emotional and social intelligence. Computers are still very poor at understanding emotions. And they don't have emotions of their own. As we will spend more and more of our lives interacting with machines, they will eventually have to understand our emotions better. We may even give them "emotions" of their own so that we can relate to them better. But for some time, computers are likely to have a low emotional intelligence.

On the third and final corner of the triangle of opportunity, we have the creatives and artisans. One reaction to increasing automation in our lives is likely to be an increasing appreciation for that made by the human hand. Indeed, hipster fashion already seems to be embracing this trend. I find it rather ironic then a job like a carpenter, one of the older jobs on the planet, might become one of the safest. So another opportunity is to develop your creativity or learn some artisan skills. Make traditional cheeses. Write novels. Play in a band.

Could computers take on some of these creative tasks? This is a question that has haunted the field of artificial intelligence from the very start. Ada Lovelace famously wrote,

> The Analytical Engine has no pretensions to originate anything. It can do whatever we know how to order it to perform. It can follow analysis; but it has no power of anticipating any analytical relations or truths. Its province is to assist us to making available what we are already acquainted with.
>
> (Lovelace, 1843, p. 722)

Alan Turing attempted to refute Ada Lovelace's objection.

> Who can be certain that "original work" that he has done was not simply the growth of the seed planted in him by teaching, or the effect of following well-known general principles. A better variant of the objection says that a machine can never "take us by surprise". This statement is a more direct challenge and can be met directly. Machines take me by surprise with great frequency.
>
> (Turing, 1950, p. 450)

The multidisciplinary field of "computational creativity" has emerged since Turing's original paper explored this issue. Like AI explores whether computers can model, simulate, or replicate human intelligence, computational creativity explores whether computers can model, simulate, or replicate human creativity. There is still no consensus on whether machines are creative in the same ways as humans. However, we have seen computers make paintings that have sold for hundreds of thousands of dollars at auction, discover new drugs, and invent devices that have been patented. But even if computers can replace some creative jobs, society may simply choose to value more those things that carry the label "made by hand". Economists would have us believe that the market will respond in this way.

9.8 CONCLUSIONS

The irony is that our technological future will not be about technology but all about our humanity. The jobs of the future are the very human jobs. AI could help us build a much gentler society. Jobs looking after the young, the sick, the elderly, and the handicapped are not, and perhaps never will be, jobs for robots. We need therefore to start valuing them more. By valuing those that look after the young, the sick, the elderly, and the handicapped as much or perhaps even more than those in traditional employment, it will be a more caring society. We might also see a flowering of creativity. This could be the Second Renaissance. Even if robots can create arts or crafts, we will value more objects made by humans. Artificial intelligence could provide the productivity gains that pay for more of us to be artists and artisans.

It is worth remembering past technological changes and learning from history. If we look at the industrial revolution, we made some significant changes to society to deal with the disruption that technological change brought to our lives. We introduced institutions like unions, labour laws, universal education, and the welfare state so that all of us shared the prosperity brought by technological change. We should remember this as we enter another period of profound technological change. Artificial intelligence will change our world dramatically, especially work. We need therefore to think big about the changes to make to society today to ensure it is the world that we want it to be. I shall, however, leave the last word appropriately to AI.

> GPT-4: AI will likely disrupt some professions more than others, but the potential for positive change is immense. In some cases, such as with sales, AI will likely lead to a reduction in the overall number of jobs, but will also enable the remaining professionals to become more productive and effective. In other cases, such as with law, AI may lead to an overall improvement in the happiness and satisfaction of the profession.
>
> While it is important to be aware of the ways in which AI may disrupt traditional career paths, it is also important to remember that AI can create new opportunities for growth and advancement. As we move into a future where AI tools are a core part of normal work processes, it is essential for professionals to take advantage of the opportunities that AI presents in order to achieve greater productivity and more meaningful work.
>
> (Hoffman & GPT4, 2023, p. 131)

NOTES

1 Britain's 50-pound bank note includes Alan Turing's portrait along with the first part of this quotation: "This is only a foretaste of what is to come, and only the shadow of what is going to be".
2 https://www.destatis.de/EN/Themes/Labour/Labour-Market/Quality-Employment/Dimension3/3_1_WeeklyHoursWorked.html
3 https://en.wikipedia.org/wiki/2014%E2%80%932016_world_oil_market_chronology; https://www.statista.com/statistics/262860/uk-brent-crude-oil-price-changes-since-1976/
4 https://www.statista.com/statistics/465871/global-oil-and-gas-industry-employment-cuts/#statisticContainer
5 https://www.bloomberg.com/news/articles/2017-01-24/robots-are-taking-over-oil-rigs-as-roughnecks-become-expendable#xj4y7vzkg

REFERENCES

Acemoglu, D., & Restrepo, P. (2017). Robots and Jobs: Evidence from US Labor Markets. MIT Department of Economics Working Paper No. 17-04. https://ssrn.com/abstract=2940245 or http://dx.doi.org/10.2139/ssrn.2940245

Agger, D.G., Armstrong, D., Boggs, J., Ferry, W., Gitlin, T., Hagan, R., & Harrington, M., et al. (1964). The Triple Revolution. https://scarc.library.oregonstate.edu/coll/pauling/peace/papers/1964p.7-01.html

Frey, C., & Osborne, M. (2013). The Future of Employment: How Susceptible are Jobs to Computerisation? Technical Report. Oxford Martin School. https://www.oxfordmartin.ox.ac.uk/publications/the-future-of-employment/

Hatzius, J., Briggs, J., Kodnani, D., & Pierdomenico, G. (2023). The Potentially Large Effects of Artificial Intelligence on Economic Growth. Technical Report. Goldman Sachs. Global Economics Analyst. https://www.ansa.it/documents/1680080409454_ert.pdf

Hoffman, R., & GPT4. 2023. Impromptu: Amplifying Our Humanity Through AI. Dallepedia LLC. https://www.impromptubook.com/

Hong, G.H., & Schneider, T. (2020). Shrinkonomics. Lessons from Japan. International Monetary Fund. https://www.imf.org/en/Publications/fandd/issues/2020/03/shrinkanomics-policy-lessons-from-japan-on-population-aging-schneider

Keynes, J. (1930). Economic Possibilities for Our Grandchildren. The Nation and Athenaeum (London) 48(2–3), pp. 36–37, 96–98.

Leontief, W. (1952). Machines and Man. Scientific American, 187(3), pp. 150–160.

Lovelace, A. (1843). Notes by the Translator. In R. Taylor (Ed.), Scientific Memoirs, Selected from the Transaction of Foreign Academies of Science and Learned Societies and from Foreign Journals, 3, pp. 691–751.

Manyika, J., Chui, M., Miremadi, M., Bughim, J., George, K., Willmott, P., et al. (2017). A Future that Works: Automation, Employment and Productivity. Technical Report. McKinsey Global Institute. https://www.mckinsey.com/featured-insights/digital-disruption/harnessing-automation-for-a-future-that-works/de-DE

Rao, A. S., & Verweij, G. (2017). Sizing the Prize: What's the Real Value of AI for Your Business and How Can You Capitalise?. Technical Report. PwC. https://www.pwc.com/gx/en/issues/analytics/assets/pwc-ai-analysis-sizing-the-prize-report.pdf

Rice University. (2016). When Machines Can Do Any Job, What Will Humans Do? https://phys.org/news/2016-02-machines-job-humans.html

Turing, A. (1947). The Mechanical Brain: Answer Found To 300 Year-Old Sum. The Times, 11 June.

Turing, A. (1950). Computing Machinery and Intelligence. MIND: A Quarterly Review of Pyschology and Philosophy, 59(236), 433–460.

Walsh, T. (2018). Expert and Non-expert Opinion About Technological Unemployment. International Journal of Automation and Computing, 155, 637–642. https://doi.org/10.1007/s11633-018-1127-x

Whaples, R. (2001). Hours of Work in U.S. History. In R. Whaples (Ed.), EH.Net Encyclopedia. http://eh.net/encyclopedia/hours-of-work-in-u-s-history/

Wilson, J.W. (1987). The Truly Disadvantaged: The Inner City, the Underclass, and Public Policy. University of Chicago Press.

CHAPTER 10

Reaching for Utopia

Opportunities for Redistributing Work and Leisure, Strengthening Dignity and Social Justice

John Quiggin

UTOPIAN THINKING HAS BEEN out of fashion for a long time. Unsurprisingly, conservatives have rejected any kind of thinking about a better world than the one we have now. As Mannheim (1960, p. 176) observed:

> The representatives of a given order will label as Utopian all conceptions of existence which from their point of view can in principle never be realized.

Even on the left, there has, until recently, been little interest in utopian thinking. The social democratic left has been in retreat for decades and has mostly been concerned with moderating the demands of neoliberalism, in its various forms. The intellectual left has been dominated by postmodernist critiques of 'grand narratives', critiques that sound radical but lead to political paralysis.

But with the collapse of neoliberalism and the emergence of dystopian 'polycrisis' (Tooze, 2022) as the new world reality, neither cautious centrism nor ironic detachment is an adequate response. Rather, we need a vision of a radically better future. Recognition of this need has led to a revival of utopian thinking (Bregman, 2016; Wright, 2010).

The economic, political and environmental disasters of this century have confronted us all with the fact that nothing in our lives is truly secure. Just because we have become used to peace, to the normal turn of the

---

                    DOI: 10.1201/9781003393757-10

seasons and to the ability to move freely from one place to another does not mean that these things will continue indefinitely. But equally, we have learned that, just because a particular pattern of work and life has prevailed for a hundred years or more does not mean that there is no alternative. The time is right to consider fundamental changes to the way we work and live.

10.1 THE SOCIAL DEMOCRATIC MOMENT 1945–75

In most societies, there is a myth of a 'Golden Age', a time when men and women lived simply and happily, free from the cares and troubles that afflict them today. This myth usually includes an account of how, through foolishness or malice, the Golden Age was lost. In Western versions, the blame has been placed upon women – Pandora opening the box and Eve taking the apple.

In the economic history of the developed world, there is one historical episode which might reasonably be regarded as a Golden Age. Between 1945 and 1973, developed countries in Western Europe, North America and Oceania experienced strong economic growth, combined with minimal levels of unemployment and a sharp decline in inequality (Marglin & Schor, 1991).

In the decades after 1945, social democratic ideas were dominant throughout the developed world. Whether or not social democratic parties held office, they drove the policy debate, to the extent that terms like 'progressive' inherently incorporated the notion of 'progress in the direction of more social democracy' (Quiggin, 2007).

The starting point of 20th-century social democracy was the combination of the welfare state, macroeconomic stabilisation and the mixed economy. In policy terms, the dominant features of this period were the use of Keynesian macroeconomics to stabilise the economy and the development of a fairly comprehensive welfare state, protecting citizens from falling into poverty due to old age, incapacity or unemployment.

Their combined effect was to transform the lived experience of capitalist society. The risks of falling into destitution as a result of unemployment, illness or old age, previously an ever-present reality for the great majority of workers, were eliminated almost completely by social security systems and, except in the United States, publicly provided healthcare.

10.2 THE FUTURE WE DIDN'T HAVE

Projections of the future made during the Golden Age were generally rosy. While there were plenty of radical critics of the existing social order, most expected that the problems they pointed out would be resolved, whether through radical change or gradual progress.

Compared to our disappointing actual experience, the future we didn't have looks positively utopian. One aspect of this disappointment is technological ('where are all the flying cars'), but even more is social, economic and environmental.

10.2.1 Poverty

The mass poverty of the Depression and earlier history had disappeared by the 1960s. But studies like those of Harrington (1962/1997) in the United States and the Henderson Review into Poverty (Henderson, 1975) in Australia revealed that significant pockets of poverty existed. The successes of the Golden Age supported an expectation that poverty could be eliminated.

In the United States, this belief formed the basis of the War on Poverty launched by the Johnson administration, which produced rapid reductions in poverty. However, the simultaneous expansion of military spending for the Vietnam War illustrated the difficulty of fighting two wars at once.

Going beyond these immediate measures, the idea of a Guaranteed Minimum Income (GMI) emerged as the hope for the future. It was supported by political figures as diverse as Martin Luther King and Richard Nixon, and by intellectuals including Daniel Moynihan and (in the form of a negative income tax) Milton Friedman. The US House of Representatives twice passed bills that would have created a GMI, but the bills failed to pass the Senate. With the onset of economic crisis in the early 1970s, the idea was forgotten.

10.2.2 Working Life

The century that culminated in the Golden Age saw steady reductions in working hours across many dimensions: the hours in the standard working week, the expansion of various kinds of leave and the availability of early retirement. This trend was seen as the natural consequence of technological progress, which enabled workers to produce as much or more in fewer hours.

The big question of the day was, 'What will we do with all that free time?' explored both in fiction (Vonnegut, 1952) and in non-fiction (Jones, 1982). Linder (1970) argued that the big problem was the fact that the goods we consume require ever more time for their enjoyment.

As it turned out, these concerns were beside the point. The long decline in working hours came to a halt in the 1970s. It was replaced by relentless pressure for intensification of work, backed up by the increasingly present threat of unemployment. By 2001 Australia's Prime Minister John Howard was describing the (newly named) problem of work–life balance as a 'barbecue stopper' (Hewitt, 2001; quoted at https://wordhistories.net/2021/12/15/barbecue-stopper/).

Time at work also seemed to be changing for the better in the Golden Age. Unions, of which the great majority of workers were members, had pushed back against the arbitrary power of employers and managers, demanding and achieving better working conditions (later derided as 'restrictive work practices'). Looking ahead, initiatives like co-management in Germany and the Meidner plan for worker ownership in Sweden seemed to herald the dawn of a new era of industrial democracy.

None of this came to pass. Instead, there was a reassertion of managers' 'right to manage'. The cult of the CEO, epitomised by job-cutters like 'Chainsaw Al' Dunlap (and more recently by Elon Musk), reached absurd heights. The fact that these heroes frequently destroyed the companies they ran was passed over in silence.

10.2.3 Environmental Sustainability

The Golden Age saw the emergence of environmental sustainability as a major political concern. The passage of the Clean Air Acts in the United States and the UK (and similar measures) signalled an end to the uncontrolled growth of pollution that had turned the skies of California brown and produced the catastrophic Great Smog of London in 1952. In the optimistic atmosphere of the 1960s, it seemed possible that we would see a fundamental resetting of humanity's relationship with the natural environment. The first Earth Day in 1970, which attracted the support of widely disparate groups, was an expression of this optimism.

Unlike in other areas, the era of neoliberalism has seen some progress on environmental sustainability. Local air and water pollution has been reduced, at least in developed countries. National parks have expanded, and many species threatened with extinction have been saved, at least for the moment. World governments acted decisively to control the threat to the ozone layer posed by emissions of chlorofluorocarbons.

There has been no such success with the far more serious problem of global heating. Mainstream economic theory provides a straightforward policy response to the problem. Greenhouse gas emissions represent an externality which should be remedied by imposing a price on emitters. Paradoxically, this orthodox solution has been rejected by most neoliberals. On the other hand, it has been embraced by environmentalists more concerned with effectiveness than ideology. The result has been a policy stalemate which has, so far, prevented sustained reductions in emissions and rendered almost unattainable the goal of stabilising the global climate.

10.3 THE RISE OF NEOLIBERALISM

The economic crisis of 1973–75 brought an end to the social democratic moment. Unlike previous recessions, which had always been accompanied by deflation, or at least by a slowdown in inflation, the 1973–75 crisis paired levels of unemployment not seen since 1945 with double-digit inflation. This 'stagflation' created obvious management problems for Keynesian economists, who prescribed a stimulatory policy of budget deficits and monetary relaxation to deal with unemployment, and a contractionary policy of budget surpluses and tight money to deal with inflation. Most countries initially adopted policies of fiscal stimulus. However, poor results and balance-of-payments pressure led to a general swing away from Keynesian stabilisation policy towards a monetarist policy framework based on medium-term control of inflation.

Although macroeconomic performance under monetarist policies was not particularly satisfactory in the 1970s and 1980s, the indirect effect on microeconomic policy was profound. By undermining Keynesian arguments in favour of public spending, monetarist theories set the stage for a return to the microeconomic orthodoxy of the period before World War II, based on the desirability of a small public sector and limited government intervention in the economy.

Over time, the combination of monetarist macroeconomic policy and free-market microeconomic solidified into a dominant ideology. This ideology has been variously referred to as Thatcherism, the Washington Consensus and, in Australia, economic rationalism. But the name that has been widely used is 'neoliberalism'.[1]

For a brief period in the 1990s, neoliberalism seemed to have triumphed. This was a period of economic boom and rising stock markets particularly in the United States. The collapse of the Soviet Union removed the clearest alternative to capitalism and supported the idea of a tight link between capitalism and democracy.

The stock market bubble of the 1990s ended with a spectacular bust, as the price of 'dotcom' stocks collapsed. But it was not until the Global

Financial Crisis (GFC) that the failure of neoliberalism became broadly evident. The GFC exposed the falsity of crucial ideas underlying neoliberalism. In my book *Zombie Economics* (Quiggin, 2010), I discussed six such ideas:

The Great Moderation: the idea that the period beginning in 1985 was one of unparalleled macroeconomic stability that could be expected to endure indefinitely.

The Efficient Markets Hypothesis: the idea that the prices generated by financial markets represent the best possible estimate of the value of any investment. (In the version most relevant to public policy, the efficient markets hypothesis states that it is impossible to outperform market valuations on the basis of any public information.)

Dynamic Stochastic General Equilibrium (DSGE): the idea that macroeconomic analysis should not be concerned with observable realities like booms and slumps, but with the theoretical consequences of optimising behaviour by perfectly rational (or almost perfectly rational) consumers, firms and workers.

The Trickle-Down Hypothesis: the idea that policies that benefit the wealthy will ultimately help everybody.

Privatisation: the idea that nearly any function now undertaken by government could be done better by private firms.

Austerity: The claim that, in conditions of recession, cuts in government spending will promote economic growth.

As the title 'Zombie Economics' implied, these ideas were discredited by the GFC and should have been killed by it. Instead, they returned in zombie form and promoted the economic and social disasters of the subsequent decade.

Thanks to the pursuit of zombie neoliberal policies, particularly the austerity regime imposed in Europe, recovery from the GFC was slow and painful in most countries. Even where austerity was avoided and economic growth returned, as in Australia, the combination of trickle-down economics and privatisation meant that the benefits were distributed unevenly. The failure of the neoliberal program is now evident. While there has been some resurgence of left-wing critiques, the biggest beneficiaries in the short run were right-wing populists, most notably Donald Trump. The rise of Trumpism is emblematic of the dystopian possibilities we now face.

10.4 DYSTOPIA

Thinking about utopia has mostly been confined to speculative fiction. Until recently, the same was true of dystopia. While dystopian futures were a staple of speculative fiction, the present was comfortably prosaic, at least for those in developed countries. But recent years have loosed upon us the Four Horsemen of the apocalypse: War, Pestilence, Famine and Death.

10.4.1 War

The world has never been free of war, but until Vladimir Putin's invasion of Ukraine in 2022, wars of conquest seemed to be a thing of the past. Putin's invasion has clearly failed, but that has not prevented him from continued aggression. With hundreds of thousands already killed or wounded, the war looks like grinding on for some time to come.

Meanwhile, despite the absence of any evidence that aggressive Chinese actions amount to more than nationalist sabre-rattling, Australia is being rushed into preparations for a hypothetical invasion of Taiwan. The failure of the Russian invasion of Ukraine provides clear evidence that such an invasion would fail even in the absence of military involvement by the United States and alliance such as AUKUS. Even less plausible threats such as that of a naval blockade of Australia have been advanced as a reason for massive spending on naval power, including a hugely expensive fleet of submarines.

10.4.2 Pestilence

The COVID-19 pandemic was, in retrospect, an inevitable consequence of the expansion of global travel that was part of the process of globalisation. It was exacerbated by the increase in global population since the last great influenza pandemic, in 1919. These factors determined both ease with which the virus spread and the rapidity with which it mutated.

The weakness of the policy response was due, in large measure, to the failure of neoliberal policy structures and, in particular, to the set of reforms known as 'New Public Management'. As I observed in Quiggin (2021, online),

Suppose that a Commonwealth government like the one we had 50 years ago was in place when the pandemic began. It's highly unlikely that management would have been left to the states. In the 1970s, the Commonwealth still operated quarantine facilities, and had its own Department of Works, capable of building new facilities or expanding old ones. In the previous decades it had managed both the repatriation of hundreds of thousands of troops from World War II and the provision of housing to deal an immigration program on an unparalleled scale.

The farcical situation where stranded Australians have to pay horrendous amounts for a handful of available seats on commercial flights would scarcely have occurred if, as in the 1970s, the Commonwealth owned its own airline (and, for that matter, rail and shipping businesses).

On the medical front, the Commonwealth ran its own network of repatriation hospitals, and owned Commonwealth Serum Laboratories, now privatised as CSL. The question of vaccine passports would certainly not have been controversial, since the government required a range of vaccinations for travellers (indeed, the scar from smallpox inoculation, required before overseas travel, served as kind of permanent passport).

Above all, the Commonwealth government had confidence in its own capacity.

The hollowing out of state capacity was on full display during the first two years of the pandemic. Vital tasks were contracted out or handed over to state governments. This was the inevitable consequence of neoliberalism.

10.4.3 Famine

Until relatively recently, the world was making progress in reducing hunger. Between 1990 and 2015, due largely to a set of sweeping initiatives by the global community, the proportion of undernourished people in the world was cut in half. But the upsurge in war has interacted with the increasingly severe consequences of global heating to reverse this progress. Samberg (2017, online) observed:

Since 2010, state-based conflict has increased by 60 percent and armed conflict within countries has increased by 125 percent. More than half of the food-insecure people identified in the U.N.

report (489 million out of 815 million) live in countries with ongoing violence. More than three-quarters of the world's chronically malnourished children (122 million of 155 million) live in conflict-affected regions.

At the same time, these regions are experiencing increasingly powerful storms, more frequent and persistent drought and more variable rainfall associated with global climate change. These trends are not unrelated. Conflict-torn communities are more vulnerable to climate-related disasters, and crop or livestock failure due to climate can contribute to social unrest.

The COVID pandemic, the Ukraine War and the continued rise in mean global temperatures have made these trends even worse. The number of people affected by hunger globally rose to as many as 828 million in 2021, an increase of about 46 million since 2020 and 150 million since the outbreak of the COVID-19 pandemic (WHO, 2022) and exacerbated by the loss of food production caused by the Russian war in Ukraine.

10.4.4 Death

Neoliberalism has produced a resurgence of inequality wherever it has prevailed. And when inequality is bad enough, it is deadly. The most extreme case is that of the United States, where inequality, poverty and despair have outweighed decades of medical progress.

Unlike most countries, the United States uses absolute measures of poverty, rather than using a poverty line expressed as a proportion of mean or median income. The standard poverty measure was developed in 1963 by economist Mollie Orshansky (Fisher, 1992; Orshansky, 1969), who looked at the cost of buying a minimally acceptable food supply as one-third of a poverty-line income.

As shown in Figure 10.1, official poverty rates have increased since 2000. And, since the US population is growing, the number of poor people is increasing even faster. In the wake of the GFC, the number of poor people in the United States is the highest level since measures began, and possibly at the highest level in US history.[2]

This decline is reflected in 'deaths of despair' (Case & Deaton, 2020; Sterling & Platt, 2022). Although the effects are largest for those on low incomes, the social pathologies created by gross inequality affect nearly everyone: the United States has lower life expectancy than other developed countries, at all income levels except those at the very top of the income distribution (cp. Burn-Murdoch, 2023).

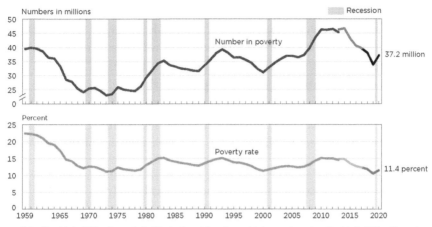

FIGURE 10.1   Poverty in the United States.

Source: USCB, 2021.

This may seem like an opportunity for self-congratulation for Australians, who, until recently, have seen only modest increases in inequality (ACOSS & UNSW Sydney, 2022) and have enjoyed rising life expectancy (AIHW, 2022). But experience suggests that where the United States leads, others are likely to follow.

10.5 UTOPIAN ALTERNATIVES

The disasters of the 21st century have discredited neoliberalism. But the most prominent alternative to emerge has been 'populist' right-wing eth-nonationalism and religious nationalism, represented by political figures like Narendra Modi in India, Viktor Orban in Hungary, Vladimir Putin in Russia and, most prominently, Donald Trump in the United States. Resistance to the far-right based on cautious centrism has had, at most, moderate success.

To defeat right-wing populism, it is necessary to offer something more than a softened version of neoliberalism. What is needed is a radically different view of the future, what Labor leader Ben Chifley, Australia's 16th Prime Minister, in 1949, called 'the light on the hill' (Chifley Research Centre, 2020).

Among many other effects, the COVID-19 pandemic has provided a radical and unexpected shake-up of all kinds of living and working arrangements. In the process it has shown up weaknesses in the existing social order and given us experience of new possibilities.

Crucial lessons from the lockdown phase of the pandemic include:

- The importance of maintaining a strong state, willing to act as necessary to protect the health and economic security of the people it serves;

- The power of expansionary Keynesian fiscal policy;

- The ease with which poverty and homelessness can be eliminated, or greatly reduced, given political will; and

- The fact that radical changes in the organisation of work are possible.

These lessons suggest a range of more or less utopian possibilities. Having lived through the failure of neoliberalism, we can return to the trajectory implied by the progress of the social democratic Golden Age. Some of these possibilities are close at hand, others more distant.

10.5.1 The Four-Day Week

Proposals to reduce the standard working week to four days are a clear example of a return to the trajectory of the Golden Age. Working hours had been on a downward trend for more than a century when the process was halted by the rise of neoliberalism. It was taken for granted that continued reductions in standard working hours were a natural consequence of steadily increasing productivity.

Output per hour worked has increased by around 60 percent since the last change in standard working hours, from 40 to 38 in the late 1980s (ABS, 2023). If only a third of that increase in productivity had translated into reduced working hours, we would already be working one day (20 percent) less per week.

After decades of stasis, the idea of a four-day week is back on the agenda, largely through initiatives from the private sector. New Zealand firm Perpetual Trustee adopted a four-day week in 2018 and experienced no loss of productivity as a result (Perpetual Guardian, 2019). The experiment was so successful that the CEO of the firm founded an organisation (4Day Week Global) to encourage others to undertake similar trials.

The nature of the recovery from COVID-19 lockdowns provides partial explanation for the success of remote work and moves towards a four-day working week. While restrictions limited spending on travel, entertainment and other services, households built up wealth. Once restrictions were lifted there was a surge in demand, while supply was initially slow to adjust. In these circumstances, as shown by Menezes and Quiggin (2022), firms with market power can increase their profit margins, amplifying an initial inflationary shock.

The labour market is very tight, and inflation is eroding real wages. But nominal wages aren't rising fast, partly because of stickiness in bargaining processes and partly because employers suffer from money illusion and reject the idea of 5–10 percent wage increases (which would compensate, at least in part, for rising prices). So, to attract and retain workers, they have to give ground on conditions.

More generally, the failure of neoliberalism has led to more and more disillusionment with the status quo. The radical, if temporary, changes triggered by the pandemic and the subsequent lockdowns have opened our minds to the idea that a much better future is possible. The most substantial change has been the shift to working from home for substantial groups of workers, including around two-thirds of managers and professionals (ABS, 2021). Australia's peak employer organisation AI Group (n.d., online) concludes that '[t]here also appears to be a work-from-home 'ratchet' at play. While initially adopted as a temporary measure, it has now shifted to become a normal and expected workplace practice'.

The shift to remote work is large and measurable. Harder to measure, but at least as important, is a shift in attitudes, away from the idea that paid work is, and should be, central to life. This shift was reflected in discussion of 'work-life balance' in the early 2000s, a reaction against the work intensification of the 1990s. Since the pandemic, more overtly anti-work attitudes have come to the form, epitomised by terms such as 'quiet quitting' and the 'Great Resignation'.

10.5.2 Livable Income Guarantee

The idea of a universal basic income (UBI), which emerged towards the end of the Golden Age, has received increasing attention in recent years (Arthur, 2016; Bregman, 2016; Widerquist et al., 2013). As with the four-day week, attention has focused on the failure of technological change to deliver transformative changes in our lives.

The simplest version of UBI and therefore the one with the most immediate appeal would be a payment to every member of the community, regardless of their existing income and wealth, or of family status, sufficient to sustain a decent life. At least in the Australian context, such a proposal seems utopian in the pejorative sense. A payment of $25,000 per person to each of 26 million people would cost $650 billion a year or around 30 percent of national income. At most $100 billion a year would be saved from benefits replaced by the UBI. Allowing for around $400 billion a year in other public expenditure would imply a ratio of public expenditure to GDP of more than 50 percent. This could not be financed without radical changes to our taxation system. The difficulties are explored further by Kay (2017).

A more plausible, but still radical, approach is based on Atkinson's (2015) idea of a participation income, providing a basic standard of living to everyone willing to contribute according to their abilities. In the Australian context, Quiggin, Klein and Henderson (2020) propose a version of the participation income, called a Liveable Income Guarantee (LIG) (see also Quiggin, 2019). The proposal starts with one of the most successful institutions of the social democratic welfare state: the age pension. Before the age pension was introduced in 1908, retired Australians were highly likely to be poor. But now retired Australians are less likely to be in poverty than Australians of less than pension age (Coates & Chen, 2019).

The idea of the LIG is to replicate this success for the entire population. The LIG would be a payment equal to the pension, and subject to the same asset and income tests, that would be provided to everyone who is willing to make a contribution to society consistent with their ability to do so. 'Contribution' would be defined broadly to maximise eligibility. Examples would include full-time study, volunteering, caring for children, ecological care and starting a small business.

Unlike some proposals for a universal payment to all citizens, the increased expenditure required for the LIG would be relatively modest, perhaps $50 billion a year, depending on eligibility and take-up rates. This is a significant amount, but comparable to major policy initiatives such as large-scale tax cuts and military expenditures. It could be achieved with a return to the income tax scales that prevailed in the 1980s, with a top marginal tax rate between 65 and 70 percent. This rate may appear high after decades of neoliberal cost cutting. But it is actually lower than the effective marginal tax rate (EMTR) faced by many in our existing system, once the effects of means testing 'clawbacks' are taken into account.

Under current policy, effective marginal tax rates for low- to middle-income households receiving means-tested benefits have typically been around 60 percent. Complex tax-welfare systems are prone to 'poverty traps' where EMTRs are close to or even above 100 percent. By contrast, the top marginal rate of taxation is 47 percent, and this rate only applies at very high incomes. The proposed EMTR schedule for the LIG would essentially reverse this pattern, lowering the EMTR for LIG recipients and raising it for those above the relevant threshold (Limerick & Quiggin, 2022).

The Livable Income Guarantee differs from most proposals for a universal payment in that it is directed at households rather than individuals. This reflects the fact that it takes the social welfare system, rather than the income tax system, as its starting point. Since most measures of poverty are based on household incomes, the LIG is more cost-effective at reducing poverty than a universal payment (Limerick & Quiggin, 2022).

Experiments with various forms of Basic Income have been undertaken around the world (e.g., Samuel, 2020). Most, though not all, are targeted at poor and disadvantaged people. This brings them closer to the LIG model than to that of a universal payment. Results have generally been positive, including improvements in physical and mental health and other measures of well-being.

A central theme underlying Basic Income proposals is that the best way to help poor people is to give them money. This point is relevant in relation both to poverty alleviation within a country and to international development aid (Banerjee & Duflo, 2012; Davala et al., 2015).

10.5.3 Jobs Guarantee

Full employment was the central achievement of the social democratic Golden Age. Employment was listed as a fundamental human right by the United Nations (UN), with the goal of full employment universally understood as a necessary condition for stability and well-being within and between countries. This went beyond the right to income through government transfers; instead, work was seen as a foundational right from which other rights flowed.

In Australia, the foundational document of the postwar era was the White Paper on Full Employment on the instructions of the Curtin–Chifley Labor government of the 1940s (Commonwealth of Australia, 1945). The present Federal Labor government was elected, in 2022, on a commitment to produce a policy for sustained full employment based on the 1945 White Paper.

Thanks to the successful use of expansionary fiscal policy in response to the COVID-19 pandemic, we have finally returned to unemployment levels comparable to those of the Golden Age. This, then, would be an ideal time to restate a commitment to full employment (Dawson & Quiggin, 2022). Yet nothing of the kind is happening. Despite its legal obligation to pursue a goal of full employment, the Reserve Bank of Australia (RBA) is remorselessly focused on returning inflation to an arbitrarily chosen target range of 2–3 percent, for which the bank was recently criticised (Commonwealth of Australia, 2023). Worse still, the present Federal government has chosen to drop the crucial word 'Full' from the title of the Employment White Paper now being prepared by the Commonwealth Treasury (a body that has been notably unenthusiastic about full employment).

Such a commitment could be sustained by a Jobs Guarantee, ensuring that properly paid work is available to all who are willing to undertake. To allow appropriate interaction with a Livable Income Guarantee, this would require a minimum wage significantly in excess of the LIG.

The utopian outcome would be one where paid work was a genuine choice: available to everyone, but not necessary to receive a livable income. With such choices, workers would be genuinely free to choose their way of life, in a way that has never been true under capitalism, or under any preceding economic system.

10.6 CONCLUDING COMMENTS

This chapter has focused on utopian policy ideas for developed countries, including Australia. A more comprehensive utopian vision must address the need to end global poverty and restore the natural environment.

The ideas discussed here, including shorter working hours, an LIG and a commitment to full employment are radical but feasible changes to an increasingly dystopian global system. It makes sense to reach for utopia.

NOTES

1 Adherents of neoliberalism typically reject labelling of their views, which they regard as common sense. But ideology always looks like common sense from the inside. Although (like all political labels) the term 'neoliberalism' has many shades of meaning, and is often used loosely, most of us can recognise neoliberalism when we see it.

2 The standard measure does not take account of the value of cash benefits provided to the poor, which expanded greatly during the War on Poverty and, to a more limited extent, with the expansion of the Earned Income Tax Credit in the 1990s. A variety of supplemental measures incorporating these

benefits have been developed. But even on these measures, many households remained poor by the standards of 1960. Moreover, there has been little, if any, improvement since the beginning of the 21st century.

REFERENCES

ABS. (2021). More than 40 percent of Australians worked from home. Australian Bureau of Statistics. Media Release. Released 14/12/2021. https://www.abs.gov.au/media-centre/media-releases/more-40-cent-australians-worked-home

ABS. (2023). Australian national accounts: National income, expenditure and product. Australian Bureau of Statistics. https://www.abs.gov.au/statistics/economy/national-accounts/australian-national-accounts-national-income-expenditure-and-product/latest-release

ACOSS & UNSW Sydney. (2022). The wealth inequality pandemic: COVID and wealth inequality. Australian Council of Social Service, in partnership with UNSW Sydney. https://povertyandinequality.acoss.org.au/covid-inequality-and-poverty-in-2020-and-2021-2/

AI Group (n.d. undated). Deep dive – Working from where, and why?. https://www.aigroup.com.au/resourcecentre/research-economics/economics-intelligence/2022/work-from-where/

AIHW. (2022). Deaths in Australia. Web report. https://www.aihw.gov.au/reports/life-expectancy-death/deaths-in-australia/contents/life-expectancy

Arthur, D. (2016). Basic income: a radical idea enters the mainstream. Parliamentary Library Research Paper Series 2016–17. https://www.aph.gov.au/About_Parliament/Parliamentary_Departments/Parliamentary_Library/pubs/rp/rp1617/BasicIncome

Atkinson, A.B. (2015). Inequality: What can be done. Harvard University Press.

Banerjee, A.V., & Duflo, E. (2012). Poor economics: A radical rethinking of the way to fight global poverty. Hachette UK,

Bregman, R. (2016) Utopia for realists: The case for a universal basic income, open borders, and a 15-hour workweek. The Correspondent.

Burn-Murdoch, J. (2023). Why are Americans dying so young?, Financial Times, 31 March, https://www.ft.com/content/653bbb26-8a22-4db3-b43d-c34a0b774303

Case, A., & Deaton, A. (2020). Deaths of despair and the future of capitalism. Princeton University Press.

Chifley Research Centre. (2020). The light on the hill: Celebrating the 75th anniversary of Ben Chifley's prime ministership. https://www.chifley.org.au/publications/the-light-on-the-hill-celebrating-75-years/

Coates, B., & Chen, T. (2019). Why Australia's old-age poverty rates are far lower than you might think. https://grattan.edu.au/news/why-australias-old-age-poverty-rates-are-far-lower-than-you-might-think/

Commonwealth of Australia (1945). Full Employment in Australia. Commonwealth Government Printer.

Commonwealth of Australia (2023). An RBA fit for the future. The Australian Government Review of the Reserve Bank of Australia Report. https://rbareview.gov.au/final-report

Davala, S., Jhabvala, R., Standing, G., Mehta, S. K. (2015). Basic Income: A Transformative Policy for India. Bloomsbury Publishing.

Dawson, L.-C., & Quiggin, J. (2022). Full employment in 21st century Australia: a lode star policy in an age of uncertainty. Per Capita Institute, Submission to Employment White Paper.

Fisher, G.M. (1992). The development and history of the poverty thresholds, Social Security Bulletin, 55(4), 3–14.

Harrington, M. (1962/1997). The other America. Poverty in the United States. Scribner.

Henderson, R.F. (1975). Poverty in Australia: First main report. April 1975, Commission of Inquiry into Poverty, AGPS, Canberra.

Hewitt, J. (2001). Man on a mission. The Sydney Morning Herald, 27 October.

Jones, B. (1982). Sleepers, Wake!: Technology and the future of work. Oxford University Press.

Kay, J. (2017). The basics of basic income. Intereconomics, 52(2), 69–74. https://www.intereconomics.eu/pdf-download/year/2017/number/2/article/the-basics-of-basic-income.html

Limerick, P. & Quiggin, J. (2022). Household structure and basic incomes policy, paper presented at Basic Income Earth Network (BIEN) Conference.

Linder, S.B. (1970). The harried leisure class. Columbia University Press.

Mannheim, K. (1960). Ideology and utopia. Routledge and Kegan Paul.

Marglin, S., & Schor, J.B. (1991). The golden age of capitalism. Clarendon Press.

Menezes, F., & Quiggin, J. (2022). Market power amplifies the price effects of demand shocks. Economics Letters, 221, 110908.

Orshansky, M. (1969). How poverty is measured. Monthly Labor Review, 92(2), 37–41. http://www.jstor.org/stable/41837556

Perpetual Guardian. (2019). White Paper: the four-day week: guidelines for an outcome-based trial: Raising productivity and engagement. https://www.voced.edu.au/content/ngv:82553

Quiggin, J. (2007). Blog post: Word for wednesday repost: Progressive. https://johnquiggin.com/2007/07/25/word-for-wednesday-repost-progressive/

Quiggin, J. (2010). Zombie economics: How dead ideas still walk among us. Princeton University Press.

Quiggin, J. (2019). Basic or universal? Pathways for a universal basic income. In E. Klein, Mays, J., & Dunlop, T. (Eds.) Implementing a basic income in Australia: Pathways forward (pp. 147–161). Melbourne University Press.

Quiggin, J. (2021). Dismembering government: New public management and why the Commonwealth government can't do anything anymore. The Monthly September, https://www.themonthly.com.au/issue/2021/september/1630418400/john-quiggin/dismembering-government

Quiggin, J., Klein, E., & Henderson, T. (2020). Forget JobSeeker. In our post-COVID economy, Australia needs a 'liveable income guarantee' instead. The Conversation. https://theconversation.com/forget-jobseeker-in-our-post-covid-economy-australia-needs-a-liveable-income-guarantee-instead-141535

Samberg, L. (2017). World hunger is increasing thanks to wars and climate change. The Conversation, October 18, https://theconversation.com/world-hunger-is-increasing-thanks-to-wars-and-climate-change-84506

Sterling, P., & Platt, M.L. (2022). Why deaths of despair are increasing in the US and not other industrial nations—Insights from neuroscience and anthropology. JAMA Psychiatry, 79, 368–374. https://jamanetwork.com/journals/jamapsychiatry/article-abstract/2788767

Tooze, A. (2022). Welcome to the world of the polycrisis. Financial Times October 22, https://www.ft.com/content/498398e7-11b1-494b-9cd3-6d669dc3de33

USCB. (2021). Number in poverty and poverty rate, 1959 to 2020. https://www.census.gov/content/dam/Census/library/visualizations/2021/demo/p60-273/Figure8.pdf

Vonnegut, K. (1952). Player piano. Charles Scribner's Sons.

WHO. (2022). UN Report: Global hunger numbers rose to as many as 828 million in 2021. https://www.who.int/news/item/06-07-2022-un-report--global-hunger-numbers-rose-to-as-many-as-828-million-in-2021

Widerquist, K., Noguera, J.A., Vanderborght, Y., & De Wispelaere, J. (2013). Basic income: An anthology of contemporary research. Wiley Blackwell.

Wright, E.O. (2010). Envisioning real utopias. Verso.

CHAPTER 11

The Mission Ahead

*How to Prepare for the Right Type of Change**

Andreas Cebulla

T HE PRECEDING CHAPTERS IN this volume have explored the challenges
and opportunities for technology and future work in Australia from a
variety of perspectives. In an interesting balancing act, those authors with
their core expertise in technology and computing noted the economic or
employment risks that "their" technologies may entail, just as contributors especially concerned with the future of labour markets or workplaces
noted the versatility and the economic and social opportunities associated
with advanced technology.

If one were to distil the contributors' key messages, there would be
three core themes:

- Making and using new, innovate, safe, technologically advanced
  products and tools, and "greening" the economy are opportunities
  in Australia – but realising those opportunities require purposeful
  policy direction and would benefit from an open, radical (utopia-
  friendly) mind. Thinking and policy aren't quite right yet.

---

* In the spirit of this book, this chapter began as a work composed with the aid of ChatGPT/GPT-4.
  Alas, after discovering that about half of the references the tool proposed either could not be found
  (and must be assumed not to exist) and/or whose URL or DOI led to very different, typically unrelated publications (if not to '404 error' messages), and realising the paucity of the material offered,
  this project was abandoned and only occasional remnants of the original ChatGPT text remain.

                                                            DOI: 10.1201/9781003393757-11

- Using smart(er) machines will not mean the end-of-work – in fact, there's no precedent to suggest that might be the case, but socially and economically equitable use and impact remain challenges.

- The risks that using smart(er) machines entails in practice are reasonably well understood (whilst arguably evolving and monitored by research) and democratic strategies for their risk management are available.

Industrial policy, amongst which we subsume innovation policy, lost its appeal and was sidelined in the latter decades on the last century as neoliberal economics took over ideological hegemony (Chang et al., 2013; Tucker, 2019; Chang and Andreoni, 2020). This began to change with the Global Financial Crisis (GFC) which demonstrated to many nations the need for a re-balancing of their economy and a better set of regulatory tools to prevent, or at least lessen the impact of, future economic crises.

The COVID-19 pandemic added further impetus to a policy rethink in the US (Gerstel & Goodman 2020) and Australia (Dean & Rainnie, 2021), which saw a plethora of new policy initiatives and policy papers released. Especially in the last five or so years, digital technology steadily took centre stage as a potential instrument for economic development and growth, supply chain or financial management tool. In Australia, a change in Government in 2022 added to a process of policy reviews and public consultations and public enquiries initiating new policy formulation exercises. A policy reset may be expected – following a tradition.

11.1 CURRENT FOCUS OF INDUSTRY POLICY IN AUSTRALIA

Industrial policy in Australia features a mix of policies and initiatives aimed at supporting innovation and research through grants to industry, tax incentives and promotion of education/academy-industry collaboration (for industry impact); export promotion; business support, especially small and medium-sized enterprises (SME). The country also has a track record of using infrastructure projects for strategic economic and development purposes, such as in response to the GFC in 2008/9 (Kennedy, 2009), occasional misuse for political pork-barrelling notwithstanding (Griffiths et al., 2022).

Pro-active, interventionist policy has, however, not been the norm, as policy switched with political parties in charge. This is reflected in the narrow terrain of innovation policy, which has had a chequered history in Australia. As Lewis and Mikolajczak (2023) demonstrated in a recent examination of official documents published between 1979 and 2019, public policy defined innovation either as a technological matter or as one of organisational culture. Translating conceptualisation into policy practice, the former favoured market-oriented interventions and the latter took a system-thinking, interventionist line (George & Tarr, 2021). In both instances, concepts and policy preferences closely aligned with political allegiances: conservative–liberal parties preferred the former; progressive, labour-oriented parties favoured the latter. With each change in government, policy changed in line with the dominant party ideology, disrupting policy-making or resulting in stop-go processes. As George and Tarr (2021) argue, these changes may have cut short opportunities and time for promising initiatives to bed down and intended actions to emerge in sufficient magnitude.

11.2 OPTIONS FOR AND PATHWAYS TO INNOVATION

Looking ahead, economies globally, and Australia specifically, have several options and pathways for innovation in what may become an increasingly automated economy. Two have been specifically addressed in this volume, namely:

- Digital transformation – using digital technologies such as artificial intelligence (AI), big data and the Internet of Things (IoT) to automate processes, improve efficiency and create new products and services (Manyika et al., 2017; Brynjolfsson & McAfee, 2017);

- Developing a green/circular economy – creating closed-loop systems where waste is minimised, resources are conserved, and materials are reused and recycled. Advanced technology can play a role in enabling the circular economy where it improves efficiency and reduces waste (Kirchherr et al., 2017; Stahel, 2016).

Two contributions in this volume (by Dean and Gamble, respectively) have pointed to mission-oriented innovation as a strategic implementation option, using innovation to achieve set societal as well as industry goals. Typical examples of mission-oriented innovation include using new technologies to reduce carbon emissions or improve public health (Mazzucato,

2016; Schot & Steinmueller, 2018). In a similar vein, mission-oriented innovation may be the tool for achieving digital transformation whilst developing a green/circular economy. Yet both ambitions face the automation replacement-versus-augmentation challenge, that is, whether to use technology to augment human capabilities or to replace them. AI and robotics (as described by Kottege, and Cebulla and Szpak, in this volume) can be used to facilitate the safe undertaking of new tasks (see O'Keeffe and Howard, in this volume), enhance workers' skills and enable them to do their jobs more effectively (Davenport & Kirby, 2015; Autor 2015) – thus freeing time (as noted by Quiggin and Walsh, in this volume).

An important variant of digital innovation is platform-based innovation, that is, creating computer systems that allow multiple stakeholders to collaborate and create value together. Examples are crowdfunding platforms, sharing economy platforms and open innovation platforms (Parker et al., 2016; Chesbrough, 2011). Whilst these are potentially beneficial, platforms economies have their dark side as they undermine ("disrupt") existing working practices with, too often, little concern for the vulnerabilities that are created (Marmo et al., 2022). As Beale argues in this volume with respect to "green" innovation, to address newly emerging as well as inherited social and environmental challenges such as poverty, inequality and climate change, innovation needs to be "social" (Mulgan et al., 2007) and to transcend one-dimensional economic thinking and the boundaries within which it resides.

11.3 MISSION-ORIENTATION INTERNATIONALLY

The challenge ahead thus is to integrate technological solutions with social, well-being objectives to extract their individual benefits whilst avoiding their potential harms. One of the conceptual advantages of mission-orientation is that it can help to drive innovation in areas that might otherwise be neglected, addressing social benefit, overcoming social need and avoiding becoming "socially useless", as banking with all its financial innovations was described in the shadow of the GFC (Turner, 2009).

In a market-driven economy, companies will focus on areas where there is a clear financial incentive to innovate. This means that some important social and environmental challenges may be overlooked – the essence of market failure. By setting specific goals or missions, however, it is believed possible to encourage innovation in areas that are not traditionally seen as profitable.

11.3.1 Mission Examples

The idea that "missions" may guide policymaking has seen its strongest recent advocate in Mariana Mazzucato (2011) whose 2011 publication on "The Entrepreneurial State" popularised the insight that the state has – and many states have had – an active role in promoting industrial innovation and funding the design and development of new technologies. Mission orientation articulates this role and shifts the purpose of public policy from merely managing the risk of market failure to becoming a tool for market-shaping (Mazzucato, 2023).

The US *Apollo* programme is prominently cited – also in this volume – as a successful mission-oriented approach to innovation (European Commission, 2017). In fact, taking its cue from the *Apollo* programme, "moonshot" has become the term widely used to describe "an ambitious, exploratory and ground-breaking project undertaken without the assurance of near-term profitability or benefit and, perhaps, without a full investigation of potential risks and benefits".[1] Today, it is the title given to Japan's ambitious Research 7 development programme, which includes visions and missions for 2040 and 2050 (Larrue, 2021).

Recent years have seen several initiatives aimed at addressing social and environmental challenges appropriating the label "mission-oriented". Notable amongst them, international initiatives, such as the United Nations' Sustainable Development Goals (SDGs) or the European Union's Horizon 2020 (research) programme.

Adopted in 2015, the UN 2030 Agenda for Sustainable Development aims to end poverty, protect the planet and promote prosperity for all (United Nations, 2022), specifying 17 SDGs, ranging from "no poverty "and "zero hunger" (SDGs 1 and 2) to "peace, justice and strong institutions" (SDG 16) and "partnership for the goals" (SDG 17 – describing international support to developing countries). Progress towards achieving these goals is monitored annually in ministerial-level meetings of UN member states and every four years in meetings of Heads of State and Government. The SDGs have been critiqued for being too many to be strategically useful (Hausmann, 2023) – highlighting perhaps one of the weaknesses of mission orientation that takes a systemic view and hence is inherently complex, generating multiple goals (as in the case of Japan's Moonshot R&D programme, which started off with 25 goals, eventually reduced to 7; see OECD, 2021, p. 62).

The European Union's Horizon Europe Program has funded intra-EU research and innovation collaborations since 2014 and since 2021 has added an explicit emphasis on supporting mission-oriented projects that address societal challenges, involve a multitude of sectors and stakeholders, and include developing new technologies. For this purpose, five EU Missions[2] to be achieved by 2030 were identified, namely: addressing climate adaptation and resilience; improving cancer prevention, cure and management; restoring oceans and waters; making 100 cities climate-neutral and smart; and transition towards healthy soil.

Mission-oriented policy initiatives do not all take an inter- or multi-national form. As already noted with respect to Japan, several countries have announced and funded their own national missions. The OECD's case study review of some of these initiatives provides a generic overview of current live initiatives (OECD, 2021). Table 11.1 provides a synopsis of national mission frameworks identified on the OECD's database of "mission-oriented innovation policies". The database is work-in-progress and does not claim to be comprehensive and, therefore, is not necessarily up-to-date. It nonetheless identifies some prominent national initiatives with their timelines. In it, Australia appears to be a latecomer in mission-oriented policy formulation and also a comparatively small spender in terms

TABLE 11.1   Case Studies – The National Mission Overarching Frameworks

Country	Title	Period	Societal Challenges	Budget
Germany	Hightech Strategy 2025	2006, current period 2020–2025 – Ongoing	Ageing populations; Health; Climate change; Environmental sustainability; Food security and Energy security	€14.7bn (2020) [AUD23.8bn]
Germany	Energiewende	2010–ongoing	Climate change; Environmental sustainability; Energy security	Estimated €5.8bn in (2016) [AUD9.4bn]
Netherlands	Mission Driven Top-Sector Policy	2011 (revised in 2018 as a Mission-oriented policy)–2024	Ageing populations; Health; Climate change; Environmental sustainability; Food security and Energy security	€4.9bn p.a. (2020, 2021), incl. €2.85bn from public funds. [AUD7.9bn/4.6bn]

(Continued)

TABLE 11.1 (*Continued*)

Country	Title	Period	Societal Challenges	Budget
Japan	Impulsing Paradigm Change through Disruptive Technologies (ImPACT) Program	2014–2019	Ageing populations; Health and Climate change; Environmental sustainability and Energy security	Total budget 2014–2019: Yen 55bn [AUD0.6bn]
Japan	Cross-ministerial Strategic Innovation Promotion Program (SIP)	2014–2022	Ageing populations; Health; Climate change; Environmental sustainability; Food security and Energy security	32.5bn Yen per year from 2014 to 2017; 28bn Yen in 2018 [AUD0.35bn/0.30bn]
Belgium	The Vision for a Sustainable and Competitive Bioeconomy in 2030 (incomplete)	2014–ongoing	Climate change; Environmental sustainability	n/a
Norway	Long-term plan for Research and Higher Education	2014–Ongoing	Ageing populations; Health; Climate change; Environmental sustainability; Food security and Energy security	2019: NOK 136m. 2019–2028: NOK 1500m. [AUD18.6m/205m]
Belgium	Vision 2050 – Flanders (incomplete)	2016–ongoing	Ageing populations; Health; Climate change; Environmental sustainability; Food security and Energy security	n/a

(*Continued*)

TABLE 11.1 (*Continued*)

Country	Title	Period	Societal Challenges	Budget
Canada	Pan-Canadian Framework on Clean Growth and Climate Change (incomplete)	2016–ongoing	Climate change; Environmental sustainability	n/a
United Kingdom	UK Industrial Strategy	2017–	Ageing populations; Health and Climate change; Environmental sustainability	GBP4.7bn for 2017–2024 [AUD8.8bn]
Australia	The Genomics Health Future's Mission[a] (incomplete)	2019–2028	Ageing populations; Health	2019–2020 to 2027–2028: AUS$106m
Japan	Moonshot Research and Development Program	2020–Support is available for up to 10 years from the start of the research	Ageing populations; Health; Climate change; Environmental sustainability; Food security and Energy security	5-year (from 2018): Yen 100bn [AUD1bn]
European Union	Horizon Europe's missions	2021–2027	Ageing populations; Health; Climate change; Environmental sustainability; Food security and Energy security	Capped at 10 percent of annual budget of Pillar II during first three years (2021–2027: €53.516bn). [AUD86.7bn]

Note: Budget data from OECD website. AUD = author's conversion (on 6 June 2023).
    a https://www.health.gov.au/our-work/genomics-health-futures-mission
Source: https://stip-pp.oecd.org/moip/types-of-moip/overframe (as of 15 May 2023).

of allocated budget. This is true even when Australia is compared with similarly sized countries (e.g., the Netherlands), which may have a broader, more ambitious, but possibly for this reason also riskier, mission agenda.

That said, the Commonwealth Scientific and Industrial Research Organisation (CSIRO), the Australian Government agency responsible for scientific research, has adopted the terminology of "missions" to describe its newest innovation research and development initiatives. CSIRO is itself the third largest Australian Government science and research budget item, accounting from 8 percent of total S&R allocation in 2021/22 (Brennan et al., n.d.) and, as indicated in Table 11.2, invests on eight additional mission projects, as far as could be established, funds three-times the value of the genomics projects listed by the OECD (Table 11.1).

It is not clear whether CSIRO's missions fully qualify for this title, as missions are more than programmatic calls for industry collaboration (as seen on the CSIRO website), but established networks of joint working. In the words of a team of CSIRO researchers, mission-oriented innovation remains a "nascent development" (Fielke et al., 2023, abstract). Fielke et al. (2023) touch upon opportunities for linking missions to "responsible innovation", that is, channelling missions explicitly towards (awareness of the) socio-environmental challenges that they are expected to address. That is recognition that ultimately missions are not technology- but human-centred and about social objectives as much as technological innovation.

TABLE 11.2   CSIRO Missions and Their Goals

Mission	Goal	Budget
Drought resilience	Reducing the impacts of drought in Australia by 30 percent by 2030.	AUD150m[a]
Trusted agrifood exports	We aim to boost the global export earnings of Australian grown food by $10 billion by 2030 through tools and technologies that verify our food quality, safety and sustainability credentials.	
Future Protein	To leverage increasing global demand for high-quality protein and create new Australian protein products and ingredients that earn an additional $10 billion in revenue by 2030.	
Ending plastic waste	Our goal is an 80 percent reduction in plastic waste entering the Australian environment by 2030.	AUD50m[b]
Hydrogen Industry	The hydrogen industry mission will support global decarbonisation through a commercially viable Australian hydrogen industry comprising both domestic and export value chains by 2030.	AUD68m[c]

(Continued)

TABLE 11.2 (*Continued*)

Mission	Goal	Budget
Towards net zero	Bringing together research, industry, government and communities to help Australia's hardest to abate sectors – including steel, sustainable aviation fuel and agriculture – halve their emissions by 2035.	AUD22m[d]
Minimising antimicrobial resistance	To halt the rising death rate and economic burden of antimicrobial resistance (AMR) in Australia by 2030 … by enabling and accelerating R&D and providing pathways to market for new and emerging solutions to prevent, manage and respond to AMR in humans, animal and the environment.	n/a
AquaWatch Australia	Establish an integrated ground-to-space national water quality monitoring system, to help safeguard our freshwater and coastal resources in Australia and around the world	AUD83m[e]

Notes:

[a] https://www.csiro.au/en/news/All/News/2021/September/$150-million-missions-to-boost-Australian-agriculture-and-food-sectors

[b] https://www.nationaltribune.com.au/csiro-on-mission-to-end-plastic-waste/

[c] https://www.csiro.au/en/news/All/News/2021/May/CSIRO-launches-$68-million-Australian-Hydrogen-Industry-Mission

[d] https://www.afr.com/technology/csiro-launches-90m-research-mission-targeting-agriculture-steel-20221010-p5boim

[e] https://www.innovationaus.com/locally-made-satellite-sensors-and-ai-in-csiros-water-mission/

Source: after: https://www.csiro.au/en/about/challenges-missions

11.4 INGREDIENTS TO WORKING MISSIONS

Drawing liberally but loosely on Mazzucato (2016, 2018, 2021), Mazzucato and Semieniuk (2017), Larrue (2021) and Lindner et al. (2021), for missions to "work", they require:

- Sound problem diagnosis: Understanding a mission's challenge requires knowing the strengths and weaknesses of (here: innovation) systems upon which missions can be anchored or which missions seek to "fix". It is also critical for knowing actors (including institutions) and their linkages that can progress or slow mission building.

- Clear and specific goals: Genuine mission-oriented initiatives are focused on and driven by specific and measurable goals that align with broader societal priorities, tied to concrete outcomes, which in turn are consistent with the mission's broader societal priorities.

- Wide-ranging stakeholder engagement: Mission-oriented innovation requires engagement, consensus and collaboration across a wide range of stakeholders, including government, industry, academia and civil society, at diagnosis, goal setting and implementation.

- Clear standards and guidelines: Goals need to be aligned with or translated into standards and guidelines that drive positive change and which maintain collaborative implementation amongst partners that is also complementary.

- Transparency and accountability: Stakeholders need to be transparent about their goals, progress, challenges and setbacks experienced in pursuing mission-oriented innovation, and report regularly on progress towards specific goals.

- Independent evaluation and validation: Third-party evaluation and validation can help to ensure that mission-oriented initiatives are genuine and are making meaningful progress towards their goals.

11.5 WHAT COULD BE MISSING FROM MISSIONS?

Coordination and cooperation between mission partners to meet all those "working conditions" can be challenging. Risk aversion, short-termism and siloed thinking can be their barriers (Mazzucato, 2018). Mission partners may not be used to collaborative working, especially across organisations, – and their organisational and commercial principles and pre-occupations may conflict with those that make for good collaboration. As Fielke et al. (2023) note with respect to science and innovation in agriculture – a small but politically and ecologically important sector contributing about 2 percent of Australia's Gross Domestic Product and 10 percent of its exports – there is little tradition of such collaboration there. This view is echoed by Webster (2019, online), who notes in relation to earlier science and innovation policy in Australia, "businesses do not always voice strong support for public strategies to improve their long-term performance. Instead, on the whole they tend to preference tax cuts – although some prefer programs to build capabilities".

Webster touches upon the capitalist coordination problem, that is, the contradiction between what an individual business may believe is good for them and what is good for their collective of businesses, and for society as a whole. The prevailing neoliberal market ideologies have defended that former view, rooted in a doctrine of entrepreneurial individualism with a supply-side supremacy at the expense of a more complete understanding of the complexity of economic interactions and development.

The neoliberal position has been consistently advocated by the Australian Productivity Commission, the agency advising Government on economic, social and environmental policy matters. The Commission has proven a stalwart of a hands-off, non-interventionist approach to industry policy, preferring regulation, data use and standards as tools "to lift digital 'laggards' [rather than]…to build national digital niches or champions … [creating] the enabling environment … [in which] firms can make their own choices about which technologies will benefit them and which ones will not" (Australian Productivity Commission and New Zealand Productivity Commission, 2019, p. 2).

Despite evidence of Australia's internationally lagging productivity and slowing growth rates (Eslake, 2011; Quiggin, 2018), and despite criticism of its economic doctrine (Green & Toner, 2023), the Commission's message nonetheless carried: the drive towards business growth and, specifically, innovation has to – and can only – come from business, even if that business, as years of statistics demonstrate, is typically a reluctant innovator. This point of view, however, fails to realise – or at least fails to acknowledge – that innovation economics requires "cash and control" (Janeway, 2013): resources to invest and command over outcomes, that is, a promise, if not certainty, of returns on investment. The precursor to innovation – research and development – cannot guarantee the latter, and the means to the former may frequently be lacking too. R&D investment is not only in the moment, but it must also hold the promise of compensation (mainly of transaction costs) in the long run. Where it cannot, business has historically sought insurance against the risk of loss – typically from the state (Rodrik, 2011).

Australia has been sardonically described as the "lucky country" (Horne 1964/2005, p. 233) able to rely on resource extraction as its primary source of export income, often aided by and undertaken with foreign capital, and saved from the consequences of being "run mainly by second-rate people who share its luck". But, as argued elsewhere in this volume (see Gamble, Dean), in doing so, it has failed to capture income from trade to build a diversified, complex economy. Innovative (innovation) policy requires a greater role of the public sector to help us "move away from market fundamentalism in designing innovation policy" (Acemoglu, 2023, online).

It is not, though, that this has been for a lack of ideas or intention. Industrial policy in Australia has seen a diversity of proposals, concepts and initiatives. In its then landmark document on promoting innovation in Australia, Innovation and Science Australia (ISA, 2017, p. 105) (since then renamed Industry Innovation and Science Australia, IISA, highlighting the lead role of the private sector and the secondary role of the public sector) made 30 recommendations, including to "[e]nhance the national culture of innovation by launching ambitious National Missions" specifically identifying genomics and personalised medicine (which is happening) as well as (albeit only in an Appendix) "Restore the [Barrier] Reef" and "Hydrogen City" (also now being implemented). Realisation and implementation of such recommendations has, however, come about only slowly.

Besides prevailing non-interventionist economic thinking, progressive industry and innovation policy in Australia face practical hurdles it would need to overcome to have any chance of seeing the light of day. Namely, first, a lack of (and reluctance to engage in) policy experimentation and, consequently, evaluation. Without experiment and evaluation, policy cannot develop, cannot mature (Berggruen Institute, 2022). The argument is not new to Australia, quite the opposite. It was a point made a decade ago in a report on the "The role of science, research and technology in lifting Australian productivity" published by the Australian Council of Learned Academies (ACOLA) (Bell et al., 2014). A little later, in its above noted report, the ISA (2017, p. 105) also recommended Government "[i]nvest in developing a more effective framework to evaluate the performance of Australia in the innovation race in an effective and timely manner" and "[s]upport the development of a suite of innovation metrics and methodologies to fully capture innovation and link it to economic, social and environmental benefits". Work on the latter began to bear fruit with the publication of a new composite indicator of innovation five years later (Australian Bureau of Statistics, 2022).

Second, Australian governance suffers the side effects of an under-resourced public service. Decades of efficiency thriving through means such as the outsourcing of policy advice and design have undermined "experimental learning" (Lindner et al., 2021, p. 9). Concurrent claims that the public sector has an inherent "knowledge problem" (Kiesling, 2015; Farrell, 2023) rendering it incapable of taking sound economic policy decisions as they may imply "picking winners" further justified depriving the Australian Public Service of resources once deemed quintessential to its effective operation (The Senate, 2021; GAP, 2021), including an ability to conduct or guide evaluations of its public policies (Graves, 2020; Gray & Bray, 2019; Tofts-Len, 2023).

Whilst the expectation now may be for research to be outsourced to industry (as is indeed happening; see Cebulla in Chapter 1 of this volume), this still leaves a role for the public sector, be it as active agent and researcher (such as CSIRO) or procurer of research services (Edler & Georghiou, 2007) – and as is also acknowledged by both ISA (2017) and PMC (2019), this requires a competent, capable and enabled public sector. This is not denying the capabilities and competencies of public sector employees but pointing to structural deficits in the utilisation of these skills – and the challenging tasks of public sector reform.[3]

Third, Australia's governance structures are not conducive to decisive, perhaps mission-oriented, action. Division of responsibilities between Federal Government and the country's eight States and Territories results in the former controlling much of revenue-raising, whereas the latter bearing considerable expenditures (Tilley, 2022). In this competitive setting that also affected relations between States and Territories, policymaking across government levels relies on consensus building, which can prove – and has been proven to be – difficult to achieve. Federal government has limited direct influence on policy at sub-federal levels, where States and Territories defend their own relative political autonomy. Lacking strong, reliable independent resources, though, States and Territories struggle to finance and shape innovation policy – and policy innovation. Innovation policy then takes the shape of sector-specific initiatives promoted at the Federal Government level (as demonstrated by the current innovation missions' foci), without necessarily aligning with States and Territories priorities (Gill, 2023).

Fourth, like other countries, Australian politics remains prone to corporate capture. Whilst Australia has made progress towards better regulating political lobbying at Parliament House (Ng, 2020), the strategic influence of business over the body politic persists (Denniss & Richardson, 2013; Edwards, 2020), not halting at using membership of, and donations to, political parties as their tools.[4] Lucas (2021) vividly illustrates the interweaving of corporate and political leadership and how this has delayed Australia's energy transition. Such influence undermines the collaborative principles of missions that aspire to socially and societally benefit, instead trapping policymaking in "market fundamentalism" (Acemoglu, 2023).

To conclude with the words of Nobel Prize Laureate and economist Michael Spence (2023, online): the "goals [of industrial policy] should be precise, limited, and clear, and guardrails must be erected to protect against private-sector capture. Industrial policy is not corporate welfare".

11.6 CONCLUSION

In their contributions to this volume, the authors have noted the opportunities and challenges that automation presents for and to the Australian economy. While there is potential for increased productivity, economic growth, a turn towards a "greener" economy and perhaps even away from the fetish of labour, there are also concerns around job displacement and social inequality. Mission-oriented approaches to innovation and strategic industry policy have been proposed as aids in addressing these challenges, bringing together government, industry, academia and civil society to create a sense of urgency and focus on innovation. But the sources of resistance to these approaches, from practical barriers to risks of misappropriation, are hard to ignore.

Policy-makers, the adopters and operators of new technologies, and, more broadly, civic society are well advised to carefully consider the implications of automation and take proactive steps to ensure that the benefits are shared equitably, and any negative consequences are minimised. By international comparison, there appears still to be significant scope for raising the profile of mission-oriented approaches and further integrating them into Australian industrial and innovation policy. There is also scope, if not need, for increasing investment in advanced technology. Both require a new set of shared standards and guidelines, and new ways of thinking about innovation outside the box of orthodox economics.

NOTES

1 https://www.techtarget.com/whatis/definition/moonshot
2 https://research-and-innovation.ec.europa.eu/funding/funding-opportunities/funding-programmes-and-open-calls/horizon-europe/eu-missions-horizon-europe_en
3 As PMC (2019, p. 16) pointed out in its review of the Australian Public Service: "There have been at least 18 significant reviews of different aspects of APS operations over the past ten years. Although these have resulted in some change, this review diagnoses similar problems to those identified in previous assessments".
4 https://michaelwest.com.au/two-party-state-top-corporations-lobbyists-revealed-members-of-liberal-and-labor-parties/

REFERENCES

Acemoglu, D. (2023). In search of a new political economy. Project Syndicate, 7 April. https://www.project-syndicate.org/onpoint/shift-from-market-fundamentalism-to-economy-for-social-benefit-by-daron-acemoglu-2023-04?barrier=accesspaylog

Australian Bureau of Statistics. (2022). Development of a composite indicator for business innovation activity in Australia (innovation index). 8 July. https://www.abs.gov.au/articles/development-composite-indicator-business-innovation-activity-australia-innovation-index

Australian Productivity Commission and New Zealand Productivity Commission (2019). Growing the digital economy in Australia and New Zealand. Maximising opportunities for SMEs. https://www.pc.gov.au/research/completed/growing-digital-economy

Autor, D. (2015). Why are there still so many jobs? The history and future of workplace automation. Journal of Economic Perspectives, 29(3), 3–30.

Bell, J., Frater, B., Butterfield, L., Cunningham, S., Dodgson, M., Fox, K., Spurling, T., & Webster, E. (2014). The role of science, research and technology in lifting Australian productivity. Report for the Australian Council of Learned Academies. https://acola.org/role-science-research-tech-lifting-aust-saf04/

Berggruen Institute. (2022). Re-opening the coordination problem: Beyond neoliberal organization. Workshop Report. https://www.berggruen.org/ideas/articles/re-opening-the-coordination-problem-beyond-neoliberal-organization-workshop-report/

Brynjolfsson, E., & McAfee, A. (2017). The business of artificial intelligence. Harvard Business Review, 95(1), 57–66.

Chang, H.-J., & Andreoni, A. (2020). Industrial policy in the 21st century. Development and Change, 51, 324–351. https://doi.org/10.1111/dech.12570

Chang, H-J., Andreoni, A., & Kuan, M. L. (2013). International industrial policy experiences and the lessons for the UK. Future of Manufacturing Project: Evidence Paper 4. UK Government Office for Science.

Chesbrough, H.W. (2011). Open services innovation: Rethinking your business to grow and compete in a new era. John Wiley & Sons.

Davenport, T.H., & Kirby, J. (2015). Beyond automation: Strategies for remaining gainfully employed in an era of very smart machines. Harvard Business Review, 93(6), 58–65.

Dean, M., & Rainnie, A. (2021). Industrial policy-making after COVID-19: Manufacturing, innovation and sustainability. The Economic and Labour Relations Review, 32(2), 283–303. https://doi.org/10.1177/10353046211014755

Denniss, R., & Richardson, D. (2013). Corporate power in Australia. Policy Brief No. 45. The Australia Institute.

Edler, J., & Georghiou, L. (2007). Public procurement and innovation—Resurrecting the demand side. Research Policy, 36(7), 949–963. https://doi.org/10.1016/j.respol.2007.03.003

Edwards, L. (2020). Corporate power in Australia, do the 1% rule? Monash University Publishing.

Eslake, S. (2011). Productivity: The lost decade. Reserve bank of Australia. https://www.rba.gov.au/publications/confs/2011/eslake.html

European Commission. (2017). Mission-oriented research & innovation in the European Union - A problem-solving approach to fuel innovation-led growth. https://research-and-innovation.ec.europa.eu/knowledge-publications-tools-and-data/publications/all-publications/mission-oriented-research-innovation-eu-problem-solving-approach-fuel-innovation-led-growth_en

Farrell, H. (2023). Industrial policy and the new knowledge problem. https://crookedtimber.org/2023/04/13/industrial-policy-and-the-new-knowledge-problem/

Fielke, S.J., Lacey, J., Jakku, E., Allison, J., Stitzlein, C., Ricketts, K., Hall, A., & Cooke, A. (2023). From a land 'down under': The potential role of responsible innovation as practice during the bottom-up development of mission arenas in Australia. Journal of Responsible Innovation. https://doi.org/10.1080/23299460.2022.2142393

GAP. (2021). Enhancing public sector policy capability for a COVID world. Global Access Partners Pty Ltd, Institute for Integrated Economic Research Australia Ltd.

George, A.-J., & Tarr, J.-A. (2021). Addressing Australia's collaboration 'problem': Is there a brave new world of innovation policy post COVID-19?. Australian Journal of Public Administration, 80, 179–200. https://doi.org/10.1111/1467-8500.12470

Gerstel, D., & Goodman, M.P. (2020). From industrial policy to innovation strategy lessons from Japan, Europe, and the United States. Center for Strategic and International Studies.

Gill, J. (2023). Sectoral, systemic and spatial: Rethinking Australia's approach to national industry policy. SGS Economics and Planning Pty Ltd. https://sgsep.com.au/publications/insights/australia-needs-a-new-spatial-industry-strategy

Graves, P. (2020). Evaluation in the Australian Public Service: Formerly practised – Not yet embedded. Evaluation Journal of Australasia, 20(4), 229–243. https://doi.org/10.1177/1035719X20971853

Gray, M., & Bray, J. R. (2019). Evaluation in the Australian public service: Current state of play, some issues and future directions. An ANZSOG research paper for the Australian Public Service Review Panel. Australia & New Zealand School of Government. https://www.apsreview.gov.au/sites/default/files/resources/appendix-b-evaluation-aps.pdf

Green, R., & Toner, P. (2023). Reforming the productivity commission. https://johnmenadue.com/reforming-the-productivity-commission/

Griffiths, K., Stobart, A., & Wood, D. (2022). Pork-barrelling is a waste of taxpayer money. Here's how to stop it. The Conversation. 22 August. https://theconversation.com/pork-barrelling-is-unfair-and-wasteful-heres-a-plan-to-end-it-188898

Hausmann, R. (2023). ChatGPT's lessons for economic development. Project Syndicate. May 8, 2023. https://www.project-syndicate.org/commentary/applying-the-lessons-of-chatgpt-to-economic-development-by-ricardo-hausmann-2023-05?barrier=accesspaylog

Horne, D. (1964/2005). The lucky country. Penguin Books.

ISA. (2017). Australia 2030: Prosperity through innovation. Innovation and Science Australia, Australian Government, Canberra.

Janeway, W.H. (2013). Doing capitalism in the innovation economy: Markets, speculation and the state. Cambridge University Press.

Kennedy, S. (2009). Australia's response to the global financial crisis. https://treasury.gov.au/speech/australias-response-to-the-global-financial-crisis

Kiesling, L. (2015). The Knowledge Problem. In C.J. Coyne, & P. Boettke (Eds.), The Oxford handbook of Austrian economics (2015; online edn). https://doi.org/10.1093/oxfordhb/9780199811762.013.3

Kirchherr, J., Reike, D., & Hekkert, M. (2017). Conceptualizing the circular economy: An analysis of 114 definitions. Resources, Conservation and Recycling, 127, 221–232.

Larrue, P. (2021). The design and implementation of mission-oriented innovation policies: A new systemic policy approach to address societal challenges. OECD Policy Papers No. 100. Organisation for Economic Cooperation and Development.

Lewis, J. M., & Mikolajczak, G. (2023). Policy on innovation in Australia: Divergence in definitions, problems, and solutions. Australian Journal of Public Administration, 1–20. https://doi.org/10.1111/1467-8500.12575

Lindner, R., Edler, J., Hufnagl, M., Kimpeler, S., Kroll, H., Roth, F., Wittmann, F., & Yorulmaz, M. (2021). Mission-oriented innovation policy. From ambition to successful implementation. Policy Brief 02-2021. Fraunhofer Institute for Systems and Innovation Research ISI Karlsruhe.

Lucas, A. (2021). Investigating networks of corporate influence on government decision-making: The case of Australia's climate change and energy policies. Energy Research & Social Science, 81(November). https://doi.org/10.1016/j.erss.2021.102271

Manyika, J., Lund, S., Chui, M., Bughin, J., Woetzel, J., Batra, P., Ko, R., & Sanghvi, S (2017). What the future of work will mean for jobs, skills, and wages. McKinsey Global Institute https://www.mckinsey.com/featured-insights/future-of-work/jobs-lost-jobs-gained-what-the-future-of-work-will-mean-for-jobs-skills-and-wages

Marmo, M., Sinopoli, E.A., & Sanzhuan, G. (2022). Worker exploitation in the Australian gig economy: Emerging mechanisms of social control. Griffith Law Review. https://doi.org/10.1080/10383441.2022.2076036

Mazzucato, M. (2011). The entrepreneurial state. Demos.

Mazzucato, M. (2016). From market fixing to market-creating: A new framework for innovation policy. Industry and Innovation, 23(2), 140–156. https://doi.org/10.1080/13662716.2016.1146127

Mazzucato, M. (2018). Mission-oriented innovation policies: Challenges and opportunities. Industrial and Corporate Change, 27(5), 803–815, https://doi.org/10.1093/icc/dty034

Mazzucato, M. (2021). Mission economy: A moonshot guide to changing capitalism. Allen Lane.

Mazzucato, M. (2023). A collective response to our global challenges: A common good and 'market-shaping' approach. UCL Institute for Innovation and Public Purpose, Working Paper Series (IIPP WP 2023-01). https://www.ucl.ac.uk/bartlett/public-purpose/wp2023-01

Mazzucato, M., & Semieniuk, G. (2017). Public financing of innovation: New questions. Oxford Review of Economic Policy, 33(1), 24–48.

Mulgan, G., Tucker, S., Ali, R., & Sanders, B. (2007). Social innovation: What it is, why it matters, how it can be accelerated. University of Oxford, Young Foundation. https://youngfoundation.org/wp-content/uploads/2012/10/Social-Innovation-what-it-is-why-it-matters-how-it-can-be-accelerated-March-2007.pdf

Ng, Y-F. (2020). Regulating the influencers: The evolution of lobbying regulation in Australia. Adelaide Law Review. 41(2), 507–543.

Parker, G. G., Van Alstyne, M. W., & Choudary, S. P. (2016). Platform revolution: How networked markets are transforming the economy and how to make them work for you. WW Norton & Company.

PMC. (2019). Our public service, our future. Independent Review of the Australian Public Service. Department of the Prime Minister and Cabinet. https://www.pmc.gov.au/publications/independent-review-australian-public-service

Quiggin, J. (2018). The not-so-strange death of multifactor productivity growth. Australian Economic Review, 51, 269–275. https://doi.org/10.1111/1467-8462.12275

Rodrik, D. (2011). The globalization paradox. Why global markets, states and democracy can't coexist. Oxford University Press.

Schot, J., & Steinmueller, W. E. (2018). Three frames for innovation policy: R&D, systems of innovation and transformative change. Research Policy, 47(9), 1554–1567.

Spence, M. (2023). In defense of industrial policy. Project Syndicate, May 5, 2023. https://www.project-syndicate.org/commentary/industrial-policy-us-chips-and-science-act-debate-by-michael-spence-2023-05?barrier=accesspaylog

Stahel, W.R. (2016). The circular economy. Nature News, 531(7595), 435–438.

The Senate (2021). APS Inc: Undermining public sector capability and performance. The current capability of the Australian Public Service. Finance and Public Administration References Committee, Commonwealth of Australia. https://www.aph.gov.au/Parliamentary_Business/Committees/Senate/Finance_and_Public_Administration/CurrentAPSCapabilities/Report

Tilley, P. (2022). State and territory tax reform. TTPI- Working Paper 2/2022. Tax and Transfer Policy Institute, Crawford School of Public Policy, The Australian National University.

Tofts-Len, S. (2023). We need more randomised trials to evaluate public policy. https://www.ceda.com.au/NewsAndResources/Opinion/Economy/We-need-more-randomised-trials-to-evaluate-public

Tucker, T. (2019). Industrial Policy and Planning: What It Is and How to Do It Better. Roosevelt Institute, 2019, Available at SSRN: https://ssrn.com/abstract=3456981

Turner, A. (2009). How to tame global finance. Prospect, 162, 27 August 2009, https://www.prospectmagazine.co.uk/magazine/how-to-tameglobal-finance

United Nations (2022). The sustainable development goals report 2022. https://unstats.un.org/sdgs/report/2022/

Webster, B. (2019). Enough with the pilot programs: We need to kickstart innovation in Australia. The Conversation, May 29. https://theconversation.com/enough-with-the-pilot-programs-we-need-to-kickstart-innovation-in-australia-117826

Index

Pages in *italics* refer to figures, pages in **bold** refer to tables, and pages followed by "n" refer to notes.

For Product Safety Concerns and Information please contact our
EU representative GPSR@taylorandfrancis.com Taylor & Francis
Verlag GmbH, Kaufingerstraße 24, 80331 München, Germany